Latin & Caribbean
Grocery Stores Demystified

Latin
& Caribbean
Grocery Stores
Demystified

Linda Bladholm

RENAISSANCE BOOKS
Los Angeles

This book is for my parents,

John and Ann Bladholm, who always

encouraged my love of other cultures

Library of Congress Control Number: 2001095676
ISBN: 1-58063-212-2

10 9 8 7 6 5 4 3 2 1

Design by Lisa-Theresa Lenthall
Illustrations by Linda Bladholm
Typesetting by Michele Lanci-Altomare

Published by Renaissance Books
Distributed by St. Martin's Press
Manufactured in the United States of America
First Edition

Contents

Acknowledgments

Living in Miami helped immensely in the making of this book, as it is a microcosm of Latin and Caribbean cultures. Many people who helped me are named, yet there are many more unnamed folks who helped in some small way or another—muchas gracias! Certain people who helped make this book possible deserve special mention. Most of all, my friend and husband, Joel Weltman, who was my constant companion on adventures to Latin and Caribbean markets, and who always encouraged me and helped sample my recipes. Much thanks to my friend and mentor, Kathy Martin at the *Miami Herald,* who not only believed in this book but also induced me to start a column called "The Ethnic Explorer" to share my extensive knowledge of south Florida's multiethnic grocery stores. Special thanks to Eva Lewitus in Lima, Peru, and to Trudi Langendorf for introducing me to her. Extra thanks to my dear friend Roberto Requeña in Chicago, my sister Sharon Bladholm, my brother Eric Bladholm, and my wonderful mother-in-law, Freda Weltman.

Many thanks to all the patient and helpful Miami and Broward Latin and Caribbean market and restaurant owners and employees, including Ravi and Seeta Bedessee of East West Indian Foods; Jame Avando, Carmen, and Marybelle of El Chalan; Dariel Carvallo of Mexico Market; Angela Malbran of Pamela's Chilean Deli; Claudia Niera of Sabores Chilenos, Maria Tassi of Venezuelan European Corner; Joaquim Bras of Moises Bakery; Alex Petkovitch of Los Guachitos; Nachir Gil of Colombian Los Balkanes; Teresa San Martin and Sara Trimino of Panderia los Guaduales; Ricardo and Yolanda Rivera of Souveniles de Puerto Rico, George Bloomfield of Island Restaurant; Samuel and Fabia Jack and Sister Providentia Gboelusi of Sam's Place, Segundo; Felicita and Jessica Lee of Chifa Chinese Restaurant; Reinaldo Bermudez and his niece Elietter Bermudez of Palacido de los Jugos; Fabrice Rivèra of La Autentica Foods; Cesar Macedo of Las Americas News; Mario Graziano of Carniceria Argentina; Hebert Rocha of Brazilian Food Market, Joao Pietrowicz of Brasil Original; Joe Menezes of Via Brazil; Eduardo Lopera of Arco Iris, Lidia and Carlos Martinez of Las Vasca; Hassan, Mike, and Richard of Latin American Supermarket, and the Art Deco Market in Miami Beach. More thanks to Don and Katie Chafin, the Miami Beach Library, Professor Dario Moerno, Luis De Rosa, Jeanette Clark, Alan Kaufman, Steve O'Hair, Victor Silvas, Vivian Carballo, Lydia Martin, Patty Shillington, Pedro and Theresa Maia, Andrew Miller, Reneé Howell-Miller, Diane Spivey, Susana Bellido, Chris Rollins of the Fruit and Spice Park in Homestead, Kristen Davis of Echo agricultural resources, and Lisa Kloak for bringing Fred into my life.

In Chicago, I would like to thank Jorge and Cindy Sanchez for the help, the music, and the wine; the Wallner family—Joe, Liz, Sarah, and Carolyn; Adam and Denise Volpendesta of the Old World Market, the biggest Afro-Caribbean market in the country, and the store's manager, Andreas Hernandez; Tony Macias, Noe Garcia, and Leo Delgado of La Fruteria; Antonio of La Unica Foods; Edmund Okoli; Beata Siemazko; Peter Kardaras; Alex Castro of La Guadalupana of "La Casa de la Masa" supermercado; and Evelyn Thompson. Special thanks to Jayson Harrison and David Lintzenich, now in the Canary Islands.

In New York, much thanks to Victor Gonzalez; Nach Waxman; Marc, Eve, Ruby, and Red Zimmetbaum; Amanda Hesser; Patricio Osses, "the Chilean fish guy"; Paul Wenzel; Susan and Allen Gonzalez; Francois Anate of the West African Grocery; Abdoulaye Da from the Senegal Commission; Astrid Gallego of Ecuatoriana; and Raymond Hadley, Tracey, and Elliot.

In California, many thanks to Marc Novak, Karen Maish, Jennifer and Amanda Quinn, Joan Quinn, Lisa Heidel and John Culpepper, Bill Cheal and Jackie Walker, Tomita, Mark, and Tae Li Shimamoto, Debbie Puente, Cindy Mushet, and Willy Guillermo Veliz of Amazonas Natural Foods.

This book would not have come into being without Richard F. X. O'Connor or the staff at Renaissance Media, including publisher Bill Hartley, my editor Amanda Pisani, Michael Dougherty, Lisa Lenthall, Arthur Morey, Michele Lanci-Altomare, Jens Hussey, Jesus Arellano, and Kimbria Hays. Thanks also to Maluvi Martin Kaesbeck, William Anderson, Gabriel Bolaffi, Barbara Ezell, Tom James, Chris Ho, Father David Caron, Nick Malgieri, Janice Finney, Mary Myslis, Joe Windley, Robin Kennedy, Barbara Gillman, Dan Jaffe, Joan Chrissos, Diana de la Torriente, the turtles, bears, mouse king, and Fred, the best cat in the world.

Part 1

LATIN BASICS

· 1 ·

Latin Culture
& Cooking

Latin and Caribbean cuisines are a sensational melding of tropical tastes with multicultural influences. A sizzling fiesta of hot, sweet, tangy, and spicy flavors dancing to a samba of salsas, citrus mojos, and aromatic herb-infused sauces tempered with creamy coconut, tart tamarind, and cooling fruits. The purpose of this book is to give anyone who wants to try cooking Latin food a blueprint to navigating the more than 60,000 Latin markets in America. With this guide in hand, you will be able to identify and use a variety of exciting ingredients. To locate your nearest Latin market, scan the Yellow Pages of your local phone book. Retailers may be listed under Grocers or Food, but smaller mom-and-pop places may not be listed at all. Customers find them by word of mouth. In large metropolitan areas, Latin markets may be listed in city guides. If you're interested in a particular country's cuisine, staff at that country's consulate may give you some leads as to where locals shop. When you visit a Latin restaurant, ask where you can find the food, or who supplies it—some may be right next to or very near a market. Many Latin basics are available by mail order and on the Web, but you miss the atmosphere, home-cooked snacks, and the experience of meeting people who will be glad to help you, and share their culture and recipe tips.

Should you be traveling to Mexico, South America, or the Caribbean, pack this book and use it to demystify the markets and menus you will encounter. The Latin groceries in the United States carry just about everything you will encounter abroad (although a market in Mexico City, Rio de Janeiro, or San Juan will have fresher tropical produce). You'll find the same baked goods, snacks, and sweets described in the ensuing pages. Let this book be your passport to culinary culture.

Two-thirds of all the foods we eat have their origin in pre-Columbian America. The Mayas, Aztecs, and Incas had highly developed agricultural systems long before Columbus arrived on the scene with the conquistadors hot on his heels.

It is hard to imagine European cooking without potatoes, tomatoes, corn, beans, peppers, chocolate, or vanilla—all gifts brought from the New World. On the other hand, it's hard to conceive of Latin American cuisine without the wheat, rice, beef, pork, cheese, citrus, grapes, olives, and almonds brought from the Old World. This cross-cultural exchange of foodstuffs and cooking methods created the present day larder found throughout Latin America and forever changed how and what we eat.

Creole, criollo, and mestizo all refer to cuisines that arose from the mingling of Indian and European ingredients in the cooking pot (in addition to those born of both cultures). African slaves brought by the Europeans further stirred up the pot and influenced Latin culture. The 19th century brought an influx of Chinese and Japanese immigrants along with their culinary traditions, expanding the pantry of South America and forming hybrid dishes blending Asian and Latin flavors.

While there is a shared Spanish or Portuguese heritage, each Latin country developed its own distinct dishes based on the evolution of Old and New World ingredients and cooking styles. Naturally, there is much overlapping and borrowing of foods and popular preparations, creating a rich and diverse unity. What binds this culinary tapestry together is the use of similar ingredients. These staples—from rice and beans to chilies and tomatoes—are all found in an enormous region stretching from the Mexican border to northern Patagonia and the far-flung islands of Cuba and Puerto Rico.

The staples in part 1 of this book, Latin Basics, form the foundation of Latin American cooking. The ingredients important to a specific Latin cuisine are

The so-called Columbian exchange and intermixing of the foods from the New World and the Old was ongoing for several centuries. In fact, many New World foods were not received very enthusiastically in Europe—especially potatoes and tomatoes—both members of the nightshade family and believed to be toxic. It was only when famine struck that the potato caught on. And it is interesting to note that an attempt to poison George Washington was made by slipping tomatoes into his dinner. The would-be assassin was amazed when the next morning Washington was still alive.

discussed in later chapters. In these sections the contents of Mexican, Central American, Colombian, and Venezuelan markets will be investigated as well as what is stocked in Peruvian, Chilean, Argentine, and Brazilian grocery stores. Cuban and Puerto Rican culinary traditions are also mentioned, although they are geographically part of the Caribbean. Because these islands were once Spanish colonies, they retain more of an Iberian influence than their neighbors colonized by the French, British, Dutch, and Danish. Cuba had particularly close ties with Spain, and Spanish immigration to the island continued up until the late fifties, stopping only with the revolution. Caribbean cultural and culinary currents are also found in the second part of this book, along with Afro-Caribbean foods and traditions.

Latin staples can be found in the Hispanic goods aisle of your nearest supermarket. Most carry flour and corn tortillas, Latin cheeses, spices, chilies, chorizo sausages, bacalao (salt cod), beans and rice, root vegetables, plantains, and tropical fruits. Caribbean markets are another resource for many Latin basics and tropical produce. If you live in a city with a large Latino community, such as Los Angeles, Chicago, New York, Boston, Houston, or Miami, there are whole neighborhoods with Latin American markets. You'll find butchers, bakeries, fish markets, and botanicas—small shops selling herbs, scented oils, and other paraphernalia used in the Santeria religion. Every corner bodega is stocked with everyday essentials like milk and bread, as well as Latin basics from rice and beans to spicy sauces and sausages, with Goya as the reigning brand.

Stocking Up
on Latin Basics

To start your Latin pantry, you'll want rice, both long grain for everyday use and short grain for soups and paella, and several types of beans, dried or in cans. Get some yuca and other starchy roots, plantains, and cornmeal for tamales and arepas—and, if you are ambitious, to make corn tortillas. Select several types of chilies, both mild and hot, and fresh, dried, canned, pickled, and powdered. Choose a variety of fresh vegetables, including avocados, bell peppers, calabaza pumpkin-squash, corn, onions, and tomatoes. Pick whatever tropical fruits are in season and round out the selection with some frozen exotic fruit pulps—these are handy for shakes, juices, and sauces. Essential seasonings would be fresh cilantro, black pepper, garlic, cinnamon, cumin, and fresh or dried oregano. Add some dried corn husks if you plan to make tamales, queso blanco for an all-purpose fresh cheese, and both soft chorizo for cooking and hard, cured sausages for slicing as an appetizer or in sandwiches. Chocolate, caramel, and preserved fruit pastes come in handy as sweet endings to a Latin meal.

The essential ingredients needed to cook Latin cuisine follow. Rather than repeat staples such as beans and corn in each country-specific market, they are discussed here. Stock your pantry with a selection from the following chapters and you will have the means to whip up any number of dishes, from a Mexican sopa seca (dry soup) and Brazilian black-eyed pea fritters to Venezuelan arepas and Argentine beef stew cooked in a pumpkin.

Buen provecho!

2

Starches

Although many different starches are used in Latin American food, rice and beans are undoubtedly the foundation of the cuisine. Beans have always been an important part of the Latin diet, and many, such as the Lima, pinto, kidney, and black bean are native to the region. Beans are nourishing, packed with essential proteins, and economical. Partnered with rice, beans make a healthy, filling, and delicious meal. Rice has been a Latin American staple only since the 17th century, introduced by the Spanish colonists. Mounds of plain rice became the perfect foil for richly spiced beans, a perfect marriage of Old and New World foods.

Rice

Rice is deeply ingrained in Latin culture, and cooks pride themselves on their ability to turn out a perfect pot of rice. To do so is considered a measure of one's culinary skills—the end result should be tender rice with every grain separate.

While all rice comes from a common Asian species, *Oryza sativa,* it is divided into two main groups, indica and japonica. There is green, red, and yellow rice, tinted and flavored with freshly chopped herbs, tomato sauce, or saffron.

In Latin kitchens, rice is usually cooked in a caldera, a heavy cast iron or aluminum pot with a round bottom and straight sides. After years of loving use, it darkens, like a well-seasoned wok. Rice is mainly cooked by the absorption method with a little salt and oil added. Rice is added to chicken soup or served as sopa seca (dry soup), usually right after a wet soup. Plain rice is dished up with picadillo (ground beef sauce), stews, fried fish, grilled or roasted meats, shredded beef, shrimp in creole sauce, boiled crabs, and of course, beans. In Cuba, rice is also cooked in lots of boiling water until al dente; drained; tossed with butter, melted lard, or oil; then put back in the pot and steamed over very low heat for 15 to 20 minutes. This ensures that the coveted thick, slightly crisped, chewy crust, called a raspa, will form on the bottom. In Puerto Rico this rice crust is called a pegao and is equally relished. If steamed rice (with or without a crust) is not being served right away, cover it with a clean cotton dishcloth and then put the lid on. This will prevent condensed moisture from turning the rice mushy. The rice will stay hot for about 20 minutes.

After buying rice, transfer it from the bag into clean jars or airtight containers. Store in a cool, dry place and it will keep for a long time. Add a dried chili pepper to prevent weevil infestation. Refrigerate leftover cooked rice in a well-sealed container as it will harden if exposed to cold. Reheat cold rice with a few spoonfuls of water in a microwave or covered pot over low heat. The following are the types of rice found in Latin markets, listed from most popular to lesser used.

LONG-GRAIN RICE

Long-grain rice is the rice of choice in Latin America. Long-grain rices are of the indica type and grow well in hot, dry climates. Kernels are about five times as long as they are wide. Long-grain rice is the least starchy of all rice and cooks up dry and fluffy with separate grains. It is the best type for steamed rice, pilafs, and fried rice dishes.

There are many brands and varieties to choose from, including Thai jasmine, Texas jasmati (less fragrant), basmati, Calmati, Texmati, and Carolina gold types. Some brands to look for are Goya Baby Elephant Thai jasmine in 20-pound bags and Molinera, Canilla, Iberia, Mahatama, Conchita, and Riceland in smaller packages.

BASMATI RICE

Basmati is an aromatic long-grain rice of the indica variety with very slender, pointy-shaped grains. It has translucent, milky-white grains, a silky texture, and buttery, nutlike taste. It expands greatly, especially

basmati rice

lengthwise, as it cooks, creating distinct, dry, fluffy grains. Calmati is a basmati-type of rice grown in the Sacramento valley of California. The grains are not as long or aromatic as the Indian-grown type. It is a cross between brown rice and basmati and is sold polished (white) or unmilled (brown). Texmati and Kasmati are Texas-grown varieties of basmati, also not as fragrant.

Basmati rice complements any Latin dish and is excellent for rice-based salads. The brands from India have to be rinsed several times and checked for grit and small particles of stone. It is best to soak basmati in cold

Brazil is the largest rice producer in Latin America. Rice is also grown in Colombia, Costa Rica, Venezuela, Peru, and Argentina. Most rice in these countries is grown "dry," called upland rice, meaning on the slopes of hills, often using slash-and-burn cultivation. Some rice is also grown "wet" in flooded paddies, mostly in the Dominican Republic and Cuba.

water about half an hour before cooking. This helps the long, fragile grains absorb a little water and relax slightly for even cooking. Basmati grown in the United States is sold in plastic bags or screw-cap containers while Indian brands are usually in burlap, jute, or stiff plastic bags. A few brands are packaged in small boxes. Some to look for are Rice Select, Goya (grown in India), Lundburg, Creole Rose (grown in Louisiana, this brand has a popcorn aroma), and Cache River from Arkansas. A recipe for basmati and coconut rice is on page 245.

MEDIUM-GRAIN RICE

Medium-grain is another all-purpose rice. Kernels are shorter and wider than long-grain varieties and can be of either indica or japonica origin. Medium-grain indica is the favorite rice of Mexico. Some Spanish paella rices are medium-grain, others are pearl-shaped. If the rice is not long or very stubby and almost round, then it is medium-grain. Medium-grain rice is good as an everyday table rice, cooking up soft with a slightly sticky texture (especially those of japonica strain). It is good in soups or sopa seca. All supermarkets, Latin or otherwise, carry medium-grain rice.

SHORT-GRAIN RICE

The plump, little kernels of short-grain rice are less than twice as long as they are wide and are often called pearl or pudding rice. Short-grain rice is of the japonica strain (think sushi rice)—the type grown throughout Latin America.

The best-known variety and most popular in Latin cuisine is the Valencia type, originally from the Valencia region of Spain. Most Latin markets (and regular supermarkets) stock California-grown Valencia pearl rice. This rice is stubby, almost round, and very absorbent. Pearl rice is usually cooked in broth or a flavor base called sofrito. It is used to make paella and many Spanish-influenced dishes such as arroz con pollo (rice with chicken), clam and green rice soup, and sweet puddings with caramel toppings. Plain steamed Valencia pearl rice is slightly sticky and forms clumps of tender grains that cling together and have a shiny texture. It makes very creamy risotto and rice pudding. Italian Arborio is also ideal for these types of dishes. Some brands are Sello Rojo pearl rice, Calusa, Molinera, Diana, Goya Valencia, Dacsa, and Conchita. See page 251 for a recipe for arroz con pollo.

pearl rice

PARBOILED RICE

Also called converted or instant rice, parboiled rice is long- or medium-grain rice that has been soaked and steamed in its husk before being milled. The steaming process forces the water-soluble vitamins and minerals in the germ and outer layers back into the heart of the rice kernel, so that they are not removed during polishing. Parboiled rice looks glassy and pale yellowish-tan, but turns white when cooked. It rarely sticks and is lighter and more delicately flavored than brown rice. This is the most nutritious white rice, but because the bran layer has been removed, it is not as nutritious as brown rice.

Parboiled rice cooks more quickly than regular rice. To retain the nutrients, do not rinse or drain parboiled rice. Just add water and steam. Avoid "minute" rice that is pre-cooked and dried—it is totally devoid of flavor. Some brands of parboiled rice are Vitarroz extra fancy long-grain rice, Riceland, and Iberia. Also Mahatama extra long-grain gold, and of course, good old Uncle Ben's.

B e a n s

Beans are an essential part of the Latin diet, and big pots of beans simmer on kitchen stovetops or over charcoal fires everywhere in Latin America. The earthy, almost meaty aroma permeates the air, emanating from homes, restaurants, cafés, and the cauldrons of street vendors.

Beans and legumes such as chickpeas and split peas come in many shapes, sizes, and colors and are, of course, dried versions of the tender seeds from various pole beans and pods. There are black beans, splotched pintos, white beans, red kidney beans, canary beans, Limas, pink beans, habas (fava beans), black-eyed peas, pigeon peas, chickpeas, and lentils. Each one has a unique flavor and texture. Beans are sold by bulk, scooped out of bins in some Latin markets as well as in bags and pre-cooked in cans. When buying dried beans, look for smooth, unshriveled specimens, as old ones will take longer to cook. For the best flavor, start with dried beans. Canned are okay if you doctor them with seasonings.

Beans are an indispensable part of meals—with rice, in stews and soups, or baked with pork. It's not surprising that the national dishes of many Latin countries include beans. Brazil's is feijoãda completa, black beans cooked with mixed meats. In Colombia, it is the bandeja paisa platter, a plate of rice, red beans, sweet plantains, steak, pork rind, an egg, and avocado slices. In Venezuela, black beans are called "caviar criollo" and are served mashed with arepas (corn cakes). In Mexico, refried beans are rolled up in burritos, tucked into tacos, and smeared on tostados and piled with shredded meat, lettuce, and grated cheese. It should be noted that refried beans are not actually fried twice. In Spanish the prefix "re" emphasizes the meaning of something, such as a food will be really good (retebien), so refrito means well-fried, rather than re-fried. Of course leftover refried beans can be re-fried! Beans begin the day, paired with eggs; are eaten with the main course of the mid-day meal, and end the day as a light supper.

Cooks throughout the Latin world debate the proper way to cook beans. Traditionalists soak the beans overnight (8 to 10 hours), then cook them. This is the most effective method for reducing the notorious flatulence caused by eating beans. Others insist on starting off with unsoaked beans in cold water and add an hour to the total cooking time. Yet others bring the beans to a boil, boil 5 minutes, turn off the heat, cover the pot and let the beans soak for one hour, then proceed.

When cooking beans, the important thing to remember is to start with cold water. If using beans soaked overnight or quick-soaked, drain them and place in a heavy pan with 8 cups of water for each pound of beans and bring to a boil. (If using unsoaked beans, add them to the pot, then pour in the water.) Cover and boil over moderate heat until the beans are tender, about one hour for overnight-soaked beans and two hours for quick-soaked. Do not add salt or acidic ingredients such as tomatoes or vinegar, or the beans will never become tender. Once the beans are cooked, the salt is added and they are seasoned with sofrito, cooking wine, tomato sauce, chopped bell peppers, garlic, onion, or boullion. To do this, fry the seasonings in a little oil, add some liquid then add the beans and simmer over low heat about 30 minutes or until the beans are very tender and the sauce has thickened. Another method is to bake the beans with chopped onion and seasonings with water to cover by one inch, checking to make sure it doesn't evaporate during the time in the oven—about 45 minutes to an hour. Whether they're called frijoles, habichuelas, or granos, most Latin meals are not considered complete without a serving of beans.

BLACK BEANS

Frijoles negros, feijão (Brazil), caraotas negras (Venezuela), or black turtle beans. These are fairly large, somewhat kidney-shaped beans with shiny black skins and dark, slightly grainy meat. They are less starchy than many beans and have a strong, full flavor with just a tinge of bittersweetness and a meaty, mushroom essence. Black beans cook into the richest of all bean soups and are often served with wedges of lemon on the side or slices floating on top to cut the richness.

Black bean soup is the quintessential Cuban dish (see the recipe on page 241), followed in popularity by morros y cristianos, or black beans and rice. The name derives from the dark-skinned Moors who made Spain the center of European culture from the eighth to the sixteenth century and the white-skinned Christians who eventually drove them out. The dish is often shortened to moros and is also called congrí.

Black beans are equally popular in Brazil, cooked with every part of the pig but the squeal (snouts, ears, feet, tails, etc.). In Oaxaca, Mexico, pureed black beans and boiled green bananas mashed with butter, beaten egg, and grated Parmesan cheese are layered in a casserole and baked—the bean layer on top—to make torta de plátano. The Guatémalan take on this combo is deep-fried green banana fritters stuffed with black bean paste and cream cheese.

For salads, the cooked beans are marinated in olive oil and vinegar (balsamic adds a gourmet touch) with chopped onion and tomatoes or chunks of pineapple and seasoned with salt and pepper just before serving. A little Dijon mustard is also good in the marinade. Mix together cooked black beans, kidney beans, and blanched, chopped green beans, and toss in a dressing of oil, vinegar, honey, powdered cumin, and crumbled bacon for a tri-color bean salad. Drained and rinsed canned beans can be used for salads, but dried black beans are best for flavorful soups, stews, and mashes. Some specialty stores and international markets have calypso beans, which are large, kidney-shaped beans with black and white splotches. They're good in any recipe calling for black beans. Ready-made black bean soup is found on the shelves of Latin and major supermarkets.

BLACK-EYED PEAS

Cow peas. Thought to have originated in Africa, black-eyed peas were brought to the New World by Spanish colonists and African slaves. The name for these buff-colored, kidney-shaped beans comes from their dark spot, or "eye." This is the hilum, or scar from where the seed was attached inside the pod. It disappears when the legume is cooked. They have fairly thick skins; a subtle nutty aroma; a rich, earthy, almost buttery taste; and a creamy texture. Look for plump, smooth, unbroken beans. Old ones have a brownish cast and are wrinkled.

Cooked black-eyed peas are added to rice dishes and soups, stewed with vegetables and sausage, or made into fritters. In Chile, poroto pelado is a pot of creamy black-eyed peas and other beans simmered in chicken stock with rice and seasonings. Before serving, garlic-laced paprika oil is stirred in. Black-eyed peas taste deliciously rich without much seasoning and are doubly good with extra spices and liberal amounts of hot sauce or chilies. A pale flour, harina para, is made from cooked, dried, and ground black-eyed peas. This is used to make hush puppy–like fritters, called bollitos, which are served as snacks with hot sauce.

black-eyed peas

CANARY BEANS

Frijol canario and frijoles peruano. Canary beans are pale yellow, medium-sized, oval-shaped, smooth-skinned beans native to Peru. They're stocked in most large Latin supermarkets, both in dried form and refried in cans. They have a rich, hearty flavor and look like pinto beans when cooked, turning pinkish-tan. A typical Peruvian dish is sopa de frijol, a bean and meat soup in which the beans are simmered with chunks of beef, pork, squash, potatoes, and pasta, seasoned with fried garlic, onions, and chilies. Canary beans are good cooked and mashed with olive oil or butter and parsley, pureed with cream for smooth soups, refried, stewed with spicy sausage and pumpkin, or added to vegetable and root vegetable soups.

CHICKPEAS

Garbanzos. Chickpeas were brought to the New World by the Spanish and Portuguese colonists. They are rather large, creamy-tan legumes with a peak at one end and an indent in the other. The thick, wrinkled skins slip off during soaking and cooking. After soaking, they nearly double in size. Some markets offer smooth, skinless chickpeas that cook tender in less than an hour. Chickpeas have a pasty texture and earthy, nutty flavor. Their addition to any dish gives it a thick, creamy consistency, thus they are used in hearty soups and stews, rice dishes, and creamy dips.

chickpeas

They can be partially cooked, then roasted and sprinkled with salt and chili powder as a snack. Chickpeas absorb the flavorings they are cooked with and are delicious teamed with garlic, onions, chorizo, and chilies. Sancocho criollo is a hearty tomato-based Latin stew with chickpeas, chunks of squash, starchy tubers, plantain, bell peppers, and cabbage. Pigs' feet (patas de cerdo) are also stewed with chickpeas and chorizo in a spicy sauce. Many Spanish-style soups popular in Latin countries—such as cocido and garbanzo soups—feature chickpeas cooked with side pork, chorizo, and ground, smoked pork. Nacatamales are Nicaraguan tamales made of white cornmeal dough stuffed with a meat (naca), chickpea, and vegetable mixture flavored with crumbled bacon, pimentos, capers, raisins, and olives. The tamales are wrapped in banana leaf packets and steamed.

Cooked (or canned) chickpeas are good tossed with minced garlic, olive oil, and fresh herbs and added to salads.

CRANBERRY & ROMAN BEANS

Cranberry beans are called Barlotti, saluggia, shell beans, and, in Chile, porotos. Roman beans are known as cargamanto in Spanish and fagiolo romano in Italian. Cranberry beans are smallish, kidney-shaped, creamy-pink beans with streaks and specks of maroon. They have a low starch content, hearty taste, and smooth texture. The beans lose their beautiful mottling when cooked. They are used in soups, stews, and cassoulet dishes (baked bean and meat casseroles), as they absorb the flavors they are cooked with. Porotos granados (grand stew) is one of Chile's national dishes—cooked cranberry beans simmered with fresh corn kernels, fresh or frozen Lima beans, and chunks of pumpkin, seasoned with olive oil, paprika, basil, and black pepper. Cranberry beans are not as common in Latin markets as other beans and it may be a challenge to find them. Fresh cranberry beans are in season from July to October and can be used in place of the dried type. The shelled beans have a delicate flavor and buttery texture.

roman beans

Dried and canned Roman beans are almost identical to cranberry beans, are widely available, and can be used interchangeably. They are slightly larger with pinkish-beige skins and dark red streaks and splotches. They are popular cooked and seasoned with ham, spices, and tomato sauce and served with rice.

HABAS

Fabas, fava beans, broad beans, ful. Dried habas vary in size, but most resemble a large Lima bean with smooth, almost silky skins ranging in color from olive green to buff and purplish-brown. The skins have a bitter taste and should be removed by soaking 48 hours, then firmly squeezing to pop each bean out of its skin. If that fails, split the skin with the point of a sharp knife, then squeeze. They are also sold skinned, skinless, and split. Skinned beans have a light yellowish color and are much easier to cook. Habas' full flavor and creamy, rather starchy texture make them good for simmered dishes, used whole or cooked and pureed.

Whole, soaked habas take about 2½ hours to cook. Skinned or split ones only need to be soaked 8 to 12 hours and cook in about 1½ hours. Fresh habas are sometimes available in the produce section. You will find large, firm, dark green pods about 6 to 12 inches long with a pointed tip at one end. Open the thick pods and inside a whitish, downy lining encases 6 to 10 flattish, rounded seeds about 1 to 2 inches wide. The seeds can vary from green to brownish or purplish. To remove the skins, plunge the beans in boiling water for a few minutes, drain, and rinse under cold water, and they should slide off. If not, peel off any tough skins. Fresh habas take about 20 minutes to cook and are good seasoned with melted butter, salt, pepper, and a splash of vinegar; or added to soup, stews, and salads. Eating undercooked habas or even getting a whiff of the pollen is toxic to a very few people of Mediterranean descent, causing severe anemia and allergic reactions.

In Ecuador, a Lenten chowder called fanesca is made with salt cod, cheese, corn, and a variety of grains—but no meat. It is served only during Holy Week. It must also include twelve types of beans to represent the twelve apostles. The salt cod is cooked in milk thickened with toasted, ground peanuts, and the dish is served with fried plantains, dough fritters, and hot sauce.

LENTILS

Lentejas. Lentils are the seeds of oblong pods that grow on small, bushy plants. The type most commonly found in markets are the round, unskinned, greenish-brown lentils shaped like bi-convex discs, a little larger than a split pea. This legume originated from a variety native to Chile. They do not need soaking and cook in about an hour—but they'll turn to mush if overcooked. The most popular use is in soups, where the tendency to fall apart lends a thick texture. Lentils have a rich, earthy flavor and give off a meaty aroma when cooking. They team well with pork, chorizo, sausage, carrots, garlic, and chilies.

In the coastal regions of Mexico, lentils are stewed with pork; then sautéed apples, underripe bananas, and chunks of fresh pineapple are added with chopped tomatoes and simmered until the flavors are mingled. In Puerto Rico lentils are stewed with slices of chorizo, a bay leaf, chopped garlic, chilies, recao (a pungent herb also known as sawtooth coriander), and tomato sauce. In Cuba, lentils are added to vegetable-rice soup flavored with white wine, basil, thyme, and oregano. Cooked lentils make a delicious salad, tossed with a spicy, cumin-infused vinaigrette.

LIMA BEANS

Butter beans or sieva. These beans originated in Peru over 7,000 years ago and are named after the capital, Lima. The cream-colored, flattish, kidney-shaped beans have thickish, smooth skins and a pleasant nutty aroma, buttery flavor, and starchy texture. Avoid Lima beans that are wrinkled, discolored, or broken, as they tend to be hard and bland.

lima beans

Soaked, cooked Lima beans are good stewed with assertive spices—try cinnamon, garlic, hot peppers, smoked hot paprika—and chorizo or bacon or lamb with chopped eggplant and potato. Cooked, canned, or thawed and cooked frozen Limas are good in salads with chopped celery, red peppers, and onions, dressed with oil and vinegar and sprinkled with toasted cashews.

PIGEON PEAS

Gandules, goongoo, gungu pea, cajan pea, or tropical green pea. A staple of Latin and Caribbean cuisine, pigeon peas are nutritious and high in protein, fiber, iron, and potassium. There are two types—one has a light beige coat and faint rust-colored speckles and is usually called gungo or congo pea. This type is available canned. The other is larger, pale yellowish-tan, and called no-eyed pea or arhardal. Both are somewhat flat and have slightly acrid skins, a nutty taste, and mealy texture.

Dried pigeon peas should be soaked overnight, then cooked 2 to 3 hours. In tandem with rice, they make a complete meal. They are often cooked with rice in coconut milk and spicy seasonings to make arroz con gandule (rice and peas). Pigeon peas are mostly used in the cuisines of Cuba, Puerto Rico, and the Caribbean.

Green pigeon peas are harvested when still green from the pods. These are larger and resemble green peas with a little nub. Green pigeon peas are sold canned and frozen. The large pods filled with peas are in season around Christmas and can be found in some Latin and Caribbean markets. Green pigeon peas are more nutritious than the dried type, containing more protein, sugar, carbohydrates, fiber, and fat, and the proteins are more digestible. They take 1½ hours to cook and retain a slightly chewy texture.

green pigeon peas

PINTO BEANS

Appaloosa or rattlesnake beans. Pintos are medium-sized, irregular, rounded beige beans with brown splotches like splashes of paint dabbed on (the word "pinto" means "painted" in Spanish). When cooked, the mottling disappears and the beans become brownish-pink. Pinto beans have a rich flavor and creamy texture. Closely related are the smaller, plump, pink beans called habichuelas rosadas or pink chili beans. Large Mexican stores also often have pretty, purplish beans speckled with reddish-tan splotches called flor de mayo frijoles, or may flower beans. Both pink and may flower beans have a taste and texture similar to pintos and can be used interchangeably in any recipe.

In Mexico, pintos are the bean of choice, especially for frijoles refritos (refried beans). The beans are cooked with chicharrónes (crispy fried pork rinds), nopales cactus strips, chopped onions, and tomatoes or a sprig of epazote, a pungent, weedlike herb. They are traditionally cooked in earthenware pots called olla para frijoles (special pot for beans) and mashed before frying with wooden, mallet-like mashers. Mexican cooks deem soaking beans overnight as unnecessary and undesirable. It is believed that beans should cook very slowly for several hours with nothing but water and a little lard—salt, other seasonings, and ingredients are added after the beans are soft.

RED KIDNEY BEANS & SMALL RED BEANS

Tolasanas, frijoles colorados, frijoles cortos, or habichuelas colorados pequeñas. Not surprisingly, the difference between red kidney beans and small red beans is the size. Both have smooth, dark maroon skins with a tiny white dot where the seed attached to the pod, a meaty aroma when cooked, and a toothsome, hearty flavor. The thick skins have a slightly sweet taste. The dried beans take a long time to cook, even after soaking overnight, so for convenience you might want to use canned beans. Kidney beans must be carefully cooked as the skin contains a toxic resin. It is eliminated by boiling rapidly for 15 minutes, then simmering until tender and completely cooked. This is a bean for the pressure cooker, if you own one. Both beans are nice for red beans and rice and readily absorb flavors of the seasonings they are simmered with while retaining their shape.

WHITE BEANS

White beans include white kidney beans, navy beans, and great northern beans. White kidney beans are fairly large and slightly squared at the ends with smooth, off-white skins. Great northern beans, similar to cannellini, are medium-sized and more oval-shaped with rounded ends. Navy beans are smaller, oval-shaped, and pea-sized. All three types are more or less interchangeable in recipes. They have a delicate, nutty flavor and creamy texture and hold their shape well. White beans are good conduits for the seasonings they are cooked with and are commonly added to soups and stews or are baked. In Puerto Rico, they are likely to be stewed with the omnipresent calabaza pumpkin and a sweet chili pepper–infused sofrito base.

Starchy Roots & Tubers

The piles of bumpy brown, sometimes scaly, log-like tubers can be a little intimidating (not to mention unsightly). But once you peel the skins off, most Latin roots and tubers can be cooked just as you would a potato—boiled, baked, mashed, or pureed and seasoned with salt, pepper, and butter or olive oil. When deep-fried they produce crisp fries or chips. Added to soups, they contribute creamy texture and earthy flavors. Try them as hash browns, scalloped, or au gratin style. You'll discover a whole new bunch of tubers to play with. For quick cooking, peel and cut into even-sized chunks and boil—most are done in 15 to 20 minutes. Many root vegetables discolor quickly when exposed to air; to prevent this, drop them immediately into cold water after peeling. Look for very firm roots with no shriveled or soft spots. Store at room temperature in a dry, dark, well-ventilated place for up to three weeks. A hanging wire basket in a pantry is ideal. All types are available year-round.

BONAITO

Batata, white yam, and Cuban sweet potato. Depending on where it's grown, this tropical sweet potato may also be called camote, kamote, kumara, or Florida yam. It is shaped like a large, lumpy yam with thin, reddish-pink, patchy skin and creamy white flesh. These can be cooked just like orange sweet potatoes. They have a dryish, mealy texture and delicate, slightly sweet, chestnut-like flavor. To prepare for cooking, just scrub the skins well—no need to peel. If cut into pieces, plunge into cold water as they will quickly turn gray. Bonaito is also sold as a sweet paste, called dulce de batata, and flavored with chocolate or vanilla. It is eaten in slices, often with cheese and fruit or as a spread. Bonaitillo are balls of boiled-down bonaito preserves dusted in powdered sugar, often sold at the front counter of Latin stores in ruffled paper cups.

bonaito

MALANGA

Yautiá, tannier, tannia, or cocoyam. This edible tuber is often confused with its cousin, the taro. Although the two are difficult to distinguish, one clue is the yellow tint to the brown skins of malanga—for this reason they are often called malanga amarilla, or yellow malanga. They also tend to be more potato-shaped than the generally rounder taro. Malanga resemble elongated sweet potatoes covered in shaggy skins with circular ridges. The flesh is slightly slippery but crisp, ranging from pure white to creamy yellow or pale pinkish with darker flecks. It has a nutty-potato flavor with a waxy, starchy consistency when cooked. Malanga are great boiled, fried, or mashed and dissolve into a thick creamy paste with long simmering. If you get malanga and taro mixed up, don't worry, as both work in most recipes.

malanga

TARO

Dasheen, kalo, or araceaa. Taro is found in two varieties. The predominant one found in Latin markets looks almost the same as malanga, but is stubbier and more barrel-shaped. It is banded in brown, shaggy, horizontal ridges and can have white, grayish or pale blue tinted flesh.

taro

Unlike malanga, taro's flesh is usually speckled with tiny brown or gray dots or ragged streaks. But the flavor is comparable, sweetish and nutty.

The smaller type of taro, also called eddoe, is mainly found in Asian and West Indian markets. It's somewhat nutty, but blander than the large type, with a slightly gummy texture. Both types tend to turn gray when cooked.

Taro is good cooked with assertive flavors—boil, slice, and pan-fry in olive oil with garlic, chopped chilies, and hot peppers; add chunks to soups and stews; bake or thinly slice and deep-fry as chips. Before rice was introduced to the Caribbean, taro and malanga served as the main starch.

YAM

yampi

ñame

Igñame, ñame, mapuey, or yampi. Also called tropical and African yam. The taro-malanga mix-up is nothing compared to the sweet potato–yam problem. The sweet orange Thanksgiving tubers often called yams are really sweet potatoes. The true yam came from Africa—the word "yam" derives from the African word "nyami", meaning "something to eat." Yams have bark-like or hairy skins, depending on the type. Log-shaped, they range in size from that of a turnip to 20 pounds and have dense white or yellow flesh. Most weigh close to a pound and are the size of a rutabaga. The type called ñame (ny-AH-may) has crisp white to off-white flesh with a starchy, bland potato taste. When cut, the flesh is slightly slimy. Ñame is good boiled, roasted, or fried but is too sticky to successfully mash or puree. Before cooking, deeply peel it to remove the bitter sap found just under the brown skin. Yampi are more gourd-shaped, bulbous at one end and pointy at the stem end. They have light chocolate brown, deeply cracked skins. The flesh is pale white and fairly dry, and is good baked, boiled, or sliced and fried. Mapuey yams have a very dry texture and are best mashed with copious amounts of butter or garlic-infused olive oil.

All of the most popular tropical tubers are found in frozen form, saving prep time as they come peeled and cut into chunks. Boil and serve with mojo, add to soups or stews, mash, bake, or roast. Cut into smaller pieces and deep-fry or mash and stuff for fritters. You will find yuca, cut into thick fries, ready to be baked and drizzled with oil and salt or deep-fried. There are also bags of mixed tropical roots and vegetables for ajiaco (Cuban criollo soup) and sancocho (beef and vegetable stew).

26

YUCA

Pronounced "yoo-kah" and widely known as both cassava and manioc. In this book, I'll use the name by which it is best known in the country being discussed, for example, cassava in Brazil and yuca in most of South America. Yuca is native to Brazil and widely cultivated throughout Latin America. Yuca are spindle-shaped, about 10 to 12 inches long and 2 to 3 inches in diameter with scaly brown skins. The flesh is bright white, like the interior of a coconut, very hard and dense, and a thin white liquid sap may seep out when cut. Cooked yuca turns pale yellow, is semi-translucent, and has a buttery, slightly sweet flavor with a sticky consistency and chewy texture.

yuca

In recent years, "yuca" has become an acronym for "young upscale Cuban American," but its alternate name, cassava, derives from the Taino Indian word "cacabi." The Tupi, other South American Indians, gave us the word "tipioca", better known as tapioca, for cassava's starchy by-product.

Yuca take some preparation. Both the peel and flesh just under the skin, and the central core have to be removed. To peel, hold the root in one hand, and using a heavy, sharp knife, whittle the skin and underskin off in long slashing motions. Cut the root in half lengthwise and cut away the core. Yuca is best boiled and served hot as it quickly hardens as it cools. Yuca is added to sancocho, the traditional Central and South American pot-au-feu, a boiled one-pot dinner. The national dish of Cuba is ajiaco, a thick potage chock full of chunks of various meats, chorizo, vegetables, green plantain, yuca, and corn, eaten with cassava bread, rice, and beans. The root appears in chip form, French-fried, mashed, roasted, baked, and boiled, cut in chunks and drenched in mojo—the bland pieces soak up the garlicky sauce like a sponge.

You can buy commercially made yuca chips—plain, salted, and with garlic salt—and they're not greasy at all. A recipe for yuca mashed with heart of palm and garlic-chive butter is on page 247.

Corn

Corn is the only native-American cereal grain, believed to have originated in Mexico or Central America over 7,000 years ago. Corn mythology weaves through Mayan, Aztec, and Incan cultures in the form of various gods and goddesses. Corn was also used in worship, as a form of currency, fuel, construction material, and in making jewelry. The silky threads of the tassel were steeped as tea or dried and smoked as tobacco.

Cornmeal is a staple in Latin kitchens and is particularly vital to Mexican cuisine, made into masa dough and slapped into the daily bread, tortillas. You will find a confusing number of cornmeal products in Latin markets. The following is a guide for those unschooled in the controversy over the various types of whole and ground corn kernels. Even more products are covered in the country-specific sections.

HOMINY

Mote de maiz, pozole, or conjiquinha (in Brazil). Mote means "grains peeled with ashes," either wood ash or lye, and the word "hominy" derives from the Algonquian Indian term for corn processed in the same manner.

corn mote

Hominy is made from dent or flint corn, both types with very hard kernels dried on the cob. Once removed, the kernels are soaked in a caustic solution of lime (calcium hydroxide), ash, or baking soda, causing the husks to loosen and kernels to swell. After soaking, the kernels are hulled and the germ is removed by abrasion and dried. Hominy is sold whole, cracked, cooked and canned or frozen, and finely ground into grits. It may be yellow or white. Whole, dried hominy looks like large, smooth popcorn kernels and can be as big as a gumball. It may be labeled "mote" or "pozole." Mote is ground into masa harina and mixed with water into a dough suitable for tortillas, tamales, and empanadas. Whole kernel, fully cooked hominy is sold canned. It has a bland taste and chewy texture and is added to spicy soups and stews, the most famous being pozole, a hog and hominy soup.

Cracked hominy is called maiz trillado (threshed corn). The chunky bits are soaked overnight and drained, then added to soups, stews, and chowders, simmered with vegetables, meats, and seasonings. It adds hearty flavor and thick texture. White cracked hominy is also added to milk-based seafood chowders and used to make sweet puddings, flavored with cinnamon.

hominy corn bits

Hominy grits are available in fine, medium, and coarse grinds in regular, quick, and instant forms.

MASA HARINA

"Masa" means dough in Spanish, but it is generally understood to mean corn dough. Masa harina is the flour made from twice-ground hominy and is essential for making tortillas and tamales. Masa dough is made by mixing the corn flour with water. Tortillas are made from a smoother, soft dough and tamales are made from coarser, stiff dough. Masa harina can be ground from white or yellow corn and looks like fine cornmeal. It is often sold labeled "masa instantanea de maiz," meaning "instant corn masa." It is made from ground, pre-cooked dehydrated corn with lime and is easy to handle. MASECA brand is one of the best, made by the Azteca milling company and sold in 4.4-pound bags. Quaker Oats also makes instant masa harina.

CORNMEAL

Harina de maiz. Cornmeal is made from grinding corn kernels to varying degrees of coarseness. As a general rule, coarse cornmeal is

A nice frozen treat is corn fritters, frituritas de maiz. Thaw and stir the batter, then drop by the spoonful into hot oil, frying on each side until golden brown and crispy. Serve with hot sauce or a dip. Look for the Catalina brand in 13-ounce pouches.

used for breakfast mushes and porridges and as a breading for fried foods and fritters, while fine cornmeal is used for breads, dumplings, and other baked goods. Coarse cornmeal looks grainy, while fine cornmeal resembles powdery sand or flour. Blue cornmeal has a distinctive purple color—coarse blue cornmeal is called harina para tortillas and is used to make breads, including tortillas. Fine is labeled "harina para atole." This is finely ground and roasted and cooked like oatmeal for breakfast and used to make hot, creamy drinks. There is also harina precocida, or pre-cooked cornmeal, made from boiled, dried, and ground white or yellow corn. While this can be used to make tamales and empanada dough, its main use is for arepas—fried or baked corn patties.

Cornmeal lends a sweetish taste and slightly crunchy texture to breads such as pan de maiz (corn bread), pone, and hush puppy fritters. It can be cooked like polenta, cut in slabs and pan-fried, used to thicken soups and sauces, and creates a crispy coating for fried foods.

Goya offers coarse and fine yellow and white corn meal in 12-ounce bags. La Criolla and La Cena brands have both grinds in 11- and 24-ounce bags. Quaker makes ArepArina, pre-cooked cornmeal for arepas in 17.6-ounce (500 g) bags and P.A.N. is a similar high-quality product from Venezuela in 2-pound bags. Goya also has 24-ounce bags of white arepa cornmeal and 5-pound bags of yellow masarepa.

CORNSTARCH

Maizena. This is a fine, white, soft powder made by extracting the starch from the endosperm (inner embryo) of corn kernels. When it is dissolved in water and heated, it turns translucent and is used to thicken sauces and gravies without altering the color or flavor. Majarete is cornstarch pudding, sold as powdered instant mix in small boxes. Brands include Maizena Fecula de Maiz in 13-ounce boxes, Goya, and good old Argo.

3

Chilies

Chilies are the heart and soul (and fire!) of Latin cooking. Chilies are worshiped, adored, and used in abundance to give dishes depth and flavor that varies from mildly spicy to fiery hot. The chili emphatically says "Latin food" to most people, conjuring images of searing salsas and sizzling sauces.

The heat in chilies is concentrated in the interior membranes near the seed heart—not in the seeds themselves. The tip end is the mildest part. Any chili loses some fire when the seeds and membranes it is attached to are removed. To do this, slit the chili lengthwise, then scrape and rinse under running water, being careful to not let the volatile oils irritate your eyes or skin—wearing rubber gloves helps. If you breathe the fumes during this process, really hot chilies can make you choke and your eyes water.

Capsaicin (the heat compound that makes chilies hot) dilates blood vessels to increase circulation and perspiration—you sweat, then feel cooler as even tepid air hits your sweaty skin. Be warned— once you start eating chilies, you can get hooked! Chilies are a stimulant, producing feel-good endorphins (natural opiates) that make you crave more and hotter varieties. If you find a chili is too fierce, gulping water or beer only spreads the oils around your mouth, making it worse. Dairy products neutralize the capsaicin, so try milk, yogurt, or even ice cream to extinguish the flames. Sugar on the tongue also helps.

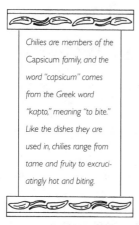

Chilies are members of the Capsicum family, and the word "capsicum" comes from the Greek word "kapto," meaning "to bite." Like the dishes they are used in, chilies range from tame and fruity to excruciatingly hot and biting.

In general, the smaller and greener the chili, the hotter it will be. Red chilies are ripe versions, thus slightly less hot. Thin skins indicate heat, whereas thick skins signal less heat. The jalapeño is in the middle, being smallish with thick skin and medium-hot heat. Anaheim chilies and yellow-green banana peppers are among the mildest, while the tiny pequin are very hot. Hottest of all is the Scotch bonnet, used liberally in Caribbean cuisine (see pages 183–214). Heat levels may vary within the same species, depending on the climate and soil in which they were grown.

Fresh Chilies

Fresh chilies are used in two distinct ways: roasted and used in cooking, or raw in salsas or sliced as a garnish. Some are used both ways. Cooking chilies are usually roasted, peeled, seeded, and de-veined before use. These are the large green types such as the Anaheim, mild New Mexico, poblano, and mulato. The charring also adds to their overall flavor. To roast chilies, place them on a mesh screen (such as a splatter guard) over an electric burner and turn frequently or hold with tongs in a gas flame, moving the chili around so all sides char. Place the blackened, blistered chilies in a plastic bag to steam a bit and cool. Next, start peeling from the stem end, holding the chili under running water. Slit and remove membranes and seeds using a paring knife and wash out any remaining seeds. Peeled and seeded chilies are also available in cans, but they are not as flavorful as freshly prepared ones.

Smaller chilies such as the jalapeño, serrano, and güero are diced and used in fresh salsas. Garnish chilies are not roasted or peeled. You can slit and remove the seeds and membranes for less kick. You should find a fairly large selection of chilies in specialty markets and supermarkets, depending on which region of the country you live in. When selecting fresh chilies, make sure they are firm, smooth, and shiny, with no splits or signs of withering. They will keep several weeks if kept dry in a paper or plastic bag and refrigerated. Chilies are also sold canned, pickled, and frozen. In this discussion, dried chilies follow the fresh.

ANAHEIM

California long green or Rio Grande. Probably the most commonly used chili, the Anaheim was developed in California in the early 1900s for an Anaheim canning plant. This bright green, blunt-nosed, 6- to 7-inch long chili has a mild-to-hot flavor and turns red as it ripens, so it may also be found in a fire engine hue. Green Anaheims are processed and sold as canned California chilies. Anaheims are mainly used in cooking or are stuffed with cheese,

anaheim

dipped in egg batter, and fried to make chilies rellenos. They are also used in salsas, dips, and sauces.

BANANA CHILI

Also known as Hungarian wax pepper, this is a long, shiny, somewhat slender, and slightly curved chili. It ranges from pale yellow to light yellow-green with smooth, waxy skins and vertical creases. There are two types: one is sweet and mild, the other medium-hot and mainly sold pickled in jars. Slice the sweet type into rings to garnish salads, bean dishes, omelettes, stews, and soups. They can also be chopped and used in cooking just like a bell pepper or roasted whole and *banana* used in sandwiches or served as an accompaniment to meats, *chili* potatoes, beans, and fried fish.

CACHUCHA

Ají dulce (sweet chili). Cachucha are tiny, roundish chilies that look like small Scotch bonnets or miniature bell peppers. They vary from light green to yellow and yellow-orange depending on the degree of ripeness. They are not hot, but have a pungent, sharp, peppery aroma and an acidic, slightly sweet flavor. Cachucha are used as a garnish chili, in salsas, and are popular in the cooking of Cuba and the Caribbean. They're delicious halved and pickled with diced red onion in a vinegar, salt, and sugar brine and used as a condiment with grilled or roasted meats and seafood and rice. They are also good diced and mixed with citrus juice for ceviche marinades.

CHILACA

Also called cuernilla (big horns) or chilies para deshebras (chilies to shred). This is a long, slim chili, about 7 inches long and 1 inch wide with blackish-green, shiny skin corregated in vertical ridges. Chilacas vary from mildly hot to hot, have a slight sweet edge, and are used mainly *chilaca* in cooking. They are roasted, peeled, seeded, and shredded in thin strips and added to masa dough for tamales and vegetable dishes. Pasillas are both dried chilacas and very ripe, brown, fresh chilacas.

FRESNO

Bright green (or ripe red), smooth-skinned, short stubby peppers about 2 to 3 inches long. Fresnos resemble the bullet-shaped jalapeño but are plumper and milder, packing only a modestly hot wallop. Fresno chilies are mainly used while still green in salsas, guacamole, seasoning sauces, sliced into rings as a garnish, or pickled. They are also stuffed with cheese and deep-fried to make mild poppers.

GÜERO

Also called Caribe, cera wax chili, or huchiango. Güero means "blonde" in Spanish and this chili is pale yellow to yellow-green, ripening to orange, then dark red like a desert sunset. They range from

1 to 2 inches in length and are somewhat triangular in shape, with a broad stem end tapering to a pointy tip. Most are mild to hot with a sweet undertone. Güero chilies are added whole to stews, sauces, pots of beans, and lentils, or are pickled. They can also be chopped and used like bell peppers.

HABANERO

Also called caballero, or gentleman pepper. There is nothing genteel about these potent chilies, shaped like little Japanese lanterns. These smooth-skinned chilies range from shades of green, yellow, orange, red, and brownish-purple, and resemble mini bell peppers with pointed tips. They are ultra hot with a floral, fruity aroma. For the novice, even a tiny bite can wreak havoc, making your tongue feel blistered with molten lava. On the other hand, I have seen islanders pop whole ones in their mouths and munch them like gumdrops! Fresh habaneros are sliced at the pointy tip end and stirred into sauces to unleash their power. This technique, known as "walking the chili through the sauce," adds pungency and flavor but not searing levels of heat. They are also roasted and used in salsas and sauces.

JALAPEÑO

Jalapeños are the best-known chili, named after Jalapa, Mexico, in the state of Veracruz where they originated. Jalapeños are dark green, smooth, and blunt-nosed, about 2½ to 3 inches long and 1 inch wide. Some may have dark patches or streaks. They ripen to bright red. These bombs are moderately hot but have an immediate bite. They are added to salsas, dips, and sauces and can be sliced in rings to garnish dishes or pickled as a relish. Large, ripened, and smoke-dried jalapeños are called chipotles. Jalapeños are also sold canned and pickled, whole or in sliced rings.

MIRASOL

Mirasols are medium-sized tapering yellow chilies, originally from Peru but widely used in Mexican cooking. The peppers grow pointing to the sun, thus the name. These are mainly used as a cooking chili as they infuse dishes with a fruity, hot flavor and golden color. Good in sauces, soups, stews, meat dishes, and with beans and vegetables. Dried, wrinkled mirasol pods are called guajillo.

MULATO

A large, dark, almost blackish-green, fleshy chili with shiny, slightly wrinkled skin and a pointed tip end. It is about 4 inches long and 3 inches wide and has a mild to medium-hot flavor. This is mainly a cooking chili, but is also stuffed with cheese or spicy ground meat mixtures to make chilies rellenos. Dried mulatos are called mulato pasilla.

NEW MEXICO

Also called chili de rista or California chili. These mild to medium-hot large chilies turn from bright green to scarlet as they ripen and resemble slightly tapered Anaheim chilies. They are mainly used in cooking—roasted, peeled, and blended in sauces. Strips are used in tamale and taco fillings, quesadillas, chili, and stews or with slowly simmered meats such as brisket.

POBLANO

Often mistakenly called fresh pasilla, this big, delicious, fleshy, almost heart-shaped chili has shiny green to blackish-green skin. It's about the size of a bell pepper but tapered at the tip with a deep groove around the base of the stalk. Poblanos have a rich, sweet flavor with just a whisper of heat and are good stuffed or used to make chilies rellenos. The most versatile chili of all, it is always roasted and peeled before using. The deep flavor melds well with cream, corn, cheese, and squash blossoms. Poblanos are good cut into strips and sautéed with cubed potatoes and corn kernels, added to creamy chowders, chili con queso, quesadillas, and cooking sauces. Diced poblano is added to cornbread, omelettes, casseroles, shrimp, and corn salad; scattered over grilled fish; and used in place of bell pepper in any recipe. Dried poblanos are called anchos.

SANDIA

Also called raja, this is a 5- to 7-inch long, skinny, hybrid Anaheim chili with slightly dented, shiny bright green skin and a mild to medium-hot bite. It can be used interchangeably in cooking with the Anaheim. Also sold ripe and bright red, good for salsas and pepper jelly.

SANTE FE GRANDE

Similar in size and shape to the Fresno, these look like triangular-shaped jalapeños. They have a medium-hot heat level and ripen to a sunny yellow hue with a smooth, shiny surface. Can be used interchangeably with the Fresno. They are typically used as a garnish chili or are pickled.

sante fe grande

SERRANO

Also called mountain chili, this popular bright to dark green chili looks like a slender torpedo with a slightly pointy tip. Serranos are about 2 inches long and ½ inch wide. They can be multicolored with patches of orange, turning crimson when fully ripe. Serrano chilies have a sharp, acidic, very picante flavor but the degree of heat can vary. Serrano chilies are not skinned or de-seeded, although they are roasted for tomato and tomatillo sauces. They are mostly used fresh, chopped, and added to salsa cruda (uncooked salsa) and guacamole, or cut into strips and cooked with vegetables, added to soups and stews, or pickled as a condiment. Whole blistered and charred chilies called toreados are served as an accompaniment to meat dishes or soups. Serranos are also sold whole en escabeche (lightly pickled) in cans, sometimes with onions and other vegetables.

serrano

VERDE DEL NORTE

Also called chili magdalena. A long, slender, smooth-skinned bright green chili with a blunt-nosed tip. They ripen to orange, then yellow, and vary from mild to fairly hot and are always roasted and peeled prior to use due to their rather tough skins.

Dried Chilies

Drying chili peppers concentrates their power, making them intensely hot. Some are smoked for a deep, earthy flavor. Dried chilies range from bright red to almost black and are sold in cellophane bags or packets in the spice section of Latin markets. Many supermarkets and specialty stores have them as well.

Some chilies are sold powdered in small packets or spice jars. Always choose chili powder that looks bright colored as it will be fresher than dull powder. You can also make your own by roasting dried chilies on a cookie sheet in the oven until dry and crisp (5 to 10 minutes in a 350-degree oven), turning a few times. Break them into pieces when cool enough to handle, discard stems and seeds, and grind to a fine powder in a blender or spice grinder. Store in a glass jar in a cool, dark place.

Whole dried chilies are prepared for use by toasting gently in a dry frying pan over medium-hot heat until softened. Discard stems, slit, and remove membranes and seeds. Open chilies and spread flat in a saucepan. Weight them down with a small plate or saucer. Add water to cover, bring to a boil, reduce heat, and simmer about 5 minutes. Set aside for half an hour, then pulse in a blender to an even paste. For an even smoother texture, strain through a sieve to remove skin bits. Dried chilies will keep up to a year, stored in a glass jar in a dry, cool place.

ANCHO

Ancho chilies are the dried version of the poblano. They're wide at the stem top and sort of heart-shaped with flexible, somewhat shiny, reddish-brown skins that gradually darken to blackish-maroon as they dry. Anchos have a mild flavor and pungent, sweet aroma and are a key component in moles, the complex Mexican sauces made from a mixture of ground chilies, seeds, and spices. Ancho chilies turn brick red when soaked. To distinguish ancho chilies from mulato pasilla, slit the chilies open and hold them up to a light. Anchos will have a reddish tint while mulato pasillas won't. In the store, anchos will cost less.

CASCABEL

Chili bola. Small, round, reddish-brown chilies with dented or collapsed sides. The name means "jingle bell" because the seeds rattle if you shake them. Fairly hot and flavorful, they are enhanced by toasting to bring out their rich, pungent, and slightly nutty taste. Also used ground, seeds and all (after toasting), in cooked sauces based on tomatoes or tomatillos.

cascabel

CALIFORNIA

These are dried Anaheim chilies and are usually labeled "California dried chilies." They are large, elongated, dark blackish-green and wrinkled. They are soaked and pureed with the liquid for use in cooking and sauces. The flavor is medium-hot and robust.

CAYENNE

Fiery hot, 2- to 3-inch long, bright red, narrow chilies curled at the tips. Cayenne is sold as whole peppers or ground into powder, often just labeled "ground red pepper." Use in sauces or sprinkle over foods—in Mexico, cayenne powder even flavors ice cream! Whole cayenne peppers may be added to soups as well as toasted and ground for cooking sauces.

CHIPOTLE

chipotle

Chilpotle in Mexico. A ripe, smoke-dried jalapeño. They are fairly small with leathery, wrinkled cinnamon-colored skins covered in what looks like a golden cobweb. Chipotles are exceedingly hot with a distinctive fruity-smoked flavor. They are pickled or used whole or in broken pieces to season soups and stews. Most commonly sold canned in adobo (a seasoning paste), adobado (tomato-based sauce), or escabeche (lightly pickled). Another type of dry-smoked jalapeño is the chipotle mora, a small, rosy-purple-colored, very wrinkled chili that is comparable to the chipotle in flavor and heat. Then there is the smallest type of smoked chili, the wine-hued, droplet-shaped morita. It is also flavorful and very hot and is often sold ground. These are combined with ancho chilies to turn up the heat in sauces.

GUAJILLO

guajillo

Also called chilie guaque. The dried form of mirasol chilies. The long, slender, wrinkled reddish-brown or maroon pods are pointed at the tips. In parts of Mexico it is called the travieso, or mischievous chili, as its bite can be quite ferocious. The flavor is fruity-hot with a pleasant sharpness. Another even more slender type are called puya. Guajillos are roasted and ground for sauces or are blended with other ingredients in seasoning pastes or sauces for meats. These are widely available.

MULATO PASILLA

One of the more expensive dried chilies, these have a chocolate-kissed, sweet, pungent flavor. Similar in appearance to the ancho, but darker, resembling a large prune. The best quality are about 5 inches long and 2½ to 3 inches wide at the top and vary from mild to quite hot. Mulato pasilla chilies are toasted and soaked (or just soaked), pureed, and added to cooked sauces and moles. They can also be soaked, slit open and stuffed with cheese, then fried or baked and smothered in tangy tomatillo sauce—delicious.

NEW MEXICO

Interchangeable with dried California chilies, the large, brittle shiny pods are dark red with lighter red highlights and long creases. Garlands of these chiles drying in the sun can be seen all over the Southwest. They are medium-hot in flavor and are usually soaked, then pureed and added to chili, stews, and numerous sauces, imparting a rich red color and deep flavor. Also sold ground as New Mexico chili powder.

new mexico

PASILLA

The dried version of chilaca chilies, these are sometimes labeled "chili negro" as they are very dark. Thin, tapered chilies are 5 to 7 inches long and 1 inch wide with shiny skins creased in wrinkled ridges. They are medium-hot with a rich, sharp flavor. Used as a paste like other dried chilies. Camarónes escorpionados en chile rojo (scorpion-cut shrimp in red sauce) uses soaked pasilla and ancho chilies blended with tomatoes, garlic, oregano, salt, and scallions to make the dark, thick paste served with boiled shrimp cut along the underside so they curl like a scorpion.

pasilla

PEQUIN

Also called chilipiquin or bird's-eye chili, these are very small, oval-shaped, fiery hot chilies that taste a bit like Tabasco sauce. The intense little screamers are soaked and pureed in salsas, soups, and sauces and are pickled in vinegar as a table condiment. Whole ones are added to stews, meat dishes, and pots of beans like Tabasco sauce.

SECO DE NORTE

Chili de la tierra or California chili pod. This is the ripened, dried form of the verde del norte chili. About 5 inches long and 2 inches wide, fuller at the top and tapering to a blunt-nosed tip with dark red, slightly dented, matte skins. Seco de norte range from mild to quite hot with a sharp bite. Sauces should be strained to filter out any tough bits of the chili's skin.

SERRANO SECO

Small, slender, very hot, bright red dried serrano chilies. Use as cayenne or pequin chilies (and with caution if you are tender tongued!).

TEPIN

Devilishly hot, teeny, brick-red chili resembling a tiny berry. Can be used interchangeably with the pequin chili or cayenne pepper. Green, unripe tepins are sold pickled, usually in large jars of brine. Used as a table condiment, as an addition to soups and stews, or munched between bites.

4

Fresh Vegetables & Fruit

Vegetables, known as verduras in Spanish, have a prominent place in Latin cuisine and are often served as a separate course. The produce bins of Latin grocery stores spill with enticing displays—green, yellow, orange, and red bell peppers, onions that look like large scallions, clumps of Swiss chard, corn cobs, potatoes, squash, and green beans as well as pungent herbs and spiky spears of aloe vera.

Vegetables

In the Latin kitchen, vegetables are added to hearty stews, meal-in-a-pot soups, or are simmered with beans. Vegetables are cooked with spices, chilies, and garlic, stewed in coconut milk, or served in sauces made from ground nuts, tomatoes, or cheese. Vegetables are stuffed, roasted, baked, breaded and fried, battered and deep-fried as fritters, made into pudín—spongy baked puddings of grated or sliced veggies, eggs, flour, and cheese—and added to salads raw or blanched. Vegetables may be plain, but never dull or uninspired. Texture, color, and freshness are all important. Seasoning depends on the cook's imagination.

When selecting vegetables, pick firm, unbruised specimens and crisp greens. On the whole, small veggies have more flavor than over-sized giants. Fruit-type vegetables such as bell peppers, eggplant, and tomatoes should be used within a week, refrigerated and stored in open paper or plastic bags (to allow them to breathe). Lettuces, leafy

greens, and herbs should be kept dry and stored no more than four days (some herbs can be kept longer in a glass of water with the leafy tops covered in a plastic bag). Root vegetables such as onions and potatoes will keep several weeks in a dark, cool, dry place.

AVOCADO

Aguacate, palta (in Chile and Peru), or abacate (in Brazil). There are two types of avocados: large, smooth, bright green–skinned ones and smaller, bumpy black-skinned ones. Both are pear-shaped with light yellowish-green flesh. The best of the large type is the fuerte—sweet and moist, it can be distinguished by its matte skin (the other types have glossy skins). Other large types are the zutano and bacon. Both have bright green, shiny skins and are in season from November through May. The giant green Florida avocados are called alligator pears and have a mild, almost bland flavor with firm flesh, good for slicing and cubing as they won't fall apart.

The flesh of the black-skinned Hass is soft, buttery, and slightly nutty tasting. These are good for stuffing and mashing for dips and spreads. Avocados are rich in protein, minerals, and the B-complex vitamins—and fat—but it's the good, cholesterol-lowering kind. Ripe avocados yield to gentle pressure at the stem end (rock hard ones may rot before they ever ripen). Semi-hard avocados can be ripened at room temperature in a paper bag with a banana or wrapped in newspaper.

Avocados discolor quickly once cut open. To avoid this, sprinkle them with lemon or lime juice. Rub unused flesh with citrus juice and wrap tightly in plastic wrap and refrigerate. Avocados serve as both a vegetable and fruit and are best known as the base for guacamole. They are also pureed for soups, diced in salsas, mashed into sauces, sliced into salads, or served as an accompaniment to rice and beans.

BELL PEPPERS

Pimentos verde (green), amarillo (yellow), or rojo (red). Bell peppers are often called sweet peppers to differentiate them from their pungent cousin, the chili pepper. Red peppers are fully ripe, yellow and orange ones are in the stages of maturing. Peppers ripened on the plant are sweeter and more flavorful, with orange and red being the sweetest. Pimentos morrones are roasted red peppers sold in jars or cans, made from the pimento pepper, an elongated variety of red pepper. Choose firm, bright, unblemished peppers with shiny skins and no soft spots. Store in an open bag, refrigerate up to a week.

Raw strips or diced peppers are added to salads and long strips are served with dips. Chopped bell peppers are added to soups, egg tortillas (Spanish frittata), stews, rice, and beans. Whole ones are stuffed. Roasting brings out the flavor of bell peppers and helps in removing the skin. Hold a pepper with a fork and toast in a gas flame or on an electric burner, turning frequently until the skin blisters and chars. Place in a paper or plastic bag for half an hour, then hold under running water. The papery thin, blistered layer of skin will easily rinse off.

Escabeche de pollo is Bolivian-style pickled chicken. Pieces of chicken are cooked in oil and vinegar with slices of carrot, red bell

pepper strips, chopped onions, and minced chilies, then cooled and served with warm tortillas. Moqueca de camarão is a Brazilian shrimp stew made with chopped green and red bell peppers, tomatoes, onions, and chilies. Bell peppers enhance Chinese-influenced South American and Cuban stir-fries, are used in red pepper and papaya chutney, and are good cut in strips and broiled with fish or stuffed with rice and chorizo sausage.

bell pepper

CALABAZA

Also called ahuyama, zapallo, abóboro, Malabar gourd, Cuban squash, West Indian pumpkin, or green pumpkin. Calabaza simply means squash in Spanish, but in English this is generally called a pumpkin or winter squash—even though it's available year-round. Calabaza are shaped like Halloween pumpkins, with greenish, pale tan to orange, hard skins covered in yellow blotches that get larger as the squash matures. They range in size from a watermelon to a cantaloupe, with bright yellow-orange, firm flesh. When buying, check the pumpkin for soft spots and make sure the stem is intact. Very large ones are cut up and sold in chunks, wrapped in plastic. Flesh should be close-grained, neither watery nor dry. Calabaza has a sweet flavor, similar to butternut squash.

Calabaza chunks are added to meat and vegetable stews, baked with beans, mashed with seasonings, deep-fried as fritters, and pureed to make both savory and sweet flan. Meat stews are also baked in whole, hollowed-out calabaza. Carbonada en zapallo is Argentine beef stew cooked in the pumpkin. A lid is cut from the top, with the stem forming a handle; the seeds and fibers are scooped out; and the whole squash baked with lid on until tender. It is then filled with a stew

made from pan-seared cubes of beef simmered in stock with vegetables and canned or dried peaches and baked another 30 minutes. The calabaza is served whole, with diners digging bits of melting soft flesh out along with the stew into individual bowls. Calabaza is also used in custards and cooked in syrup to make a type of glacé.

calabaza

CHAYOTE

Water pear, vegetable pear, merliton, christphine, cho-cho, coko, and xuxu. Chayote resemble plump pears with smooth, thin, celery-green skins and several deep vertical grooves. They vary in size from about 3 to 5 inches in length and 3 to 4 inches wide. To remove the sticky substance they secrete, cut them in half lengthwise and rub the two halves back and forth under cold running water.

The flesh is crisp, watery, and pale with a subtle flavor, sort of a blend of cucumber, apple, and zucchini. There is an edible, soft, white seed in the center. Chayote can be eaten raw or cooked with or without the skin. Chunks or thin strips of chayote are added to soups, stews, stir-fries, soufflés; scrambled with eggs; and made into chutney. Julienned chayote can be added to salads. Thin slices are layered with grated cheese and a mixture of sautéed onion, bell pepper, and garlic and topped with breadcrumbs and baked au gratin. They are also boiled whole or halved, and flesh is scooped out and the hollow filled with a spicy ground meat and tomato mixture and baked. Buy small, firm chayote with no bruises or wrinkles. Store refrigerated, chayote will keep up to a week. For a recipe for a Brazilian chayote, orange, and shrimp salad, see page 239.

chayote

CORN

Maize or milho (in Brazil). Although I discuss corn in chapter 2, I couldn't resist including it here as well. Tender, new corn is best steamed and munched off the cob, slicked with butter. Kernels scraped off the cob are added to soups, stews, succotash, and creamy grits. Cooked kernels go into salsas, salads, bean stews, casseroles, fritters, muffins, and chowders, or are pureed for creamed soup.

To ensure premium flavor when selecting corn, pull a bit of husk away from the top and examine the exposed kernels. Press a kernel—if it is fresh, silky liquid will squirt out. Discolored or shriveled kernels or dried, yellow husks and limp, brown-tinged tassels indicate a lack of freshness. Avoid buying corn displayed in bright sunlight or under high temperatures as the natural sugar quickly converts to starch, making the corn less sweet. Don't add salt to the water you boil corn in as it causes the kernels to harden. Instead, add a pinch of sugar, a little milk, or beer to the cooking water—this will help sweeten the corn. Husked corn can be wrapped in aluminum foil and roasted in an oven or grilled. Eat corn as soon as possible after purchasing—or picking.

EGGPLANT

Berenjena and, in the West Indies, brown jolly. The eggplants found in Latin markets are large to mid-sized with glossy, dark purple skins, shaped like pudgy clubs or squat, plump ovals. Very large ones with more seeds can be cut in slices and sprinkled with salt to "sweat." This reduces the water content and bitterness and prevents them from soaking up huge amounts of oil in cooking. They have a relatively bland flavor and meaty texture. The skin is usually left on—necessary for stuffing or grilling to keep the shape, but it can be removed for adding to stews or sautés. Eggplants are sliced, dipped in beaten egg, cornmeal, or breadcrumbs and fried in oil until golden brown and crisp; or sliced, brushed with

eggplant

olive oil, and grilled. Whole ones are baked or roasted and mashed with seasonings or halved.

Stuffed eggplant is very popular in Latin America. They are cut in half lengthwise and scooped out, leaving a ½-inch thick shell. The flesh is chopped and sautéed with ground beef or pork; cheese and ham; or shrimp, chopped peppers, and tomatoes and packed into the shells and baked. Eggplant "caviar" is made from baked, peeled, and coarsely chopped eggplant mixed with minced onion, red pepper, tomatoes, and cilantro, with a little vinegar or lemon juice. It is served with crackers, arepas (corn cakes), and black olives. Choose firm, heavy eggplants with smooth, evenly colored skins. Press lightly with a finger—if the imprint remains visible, the eggplant is ripe; if the flesh springs back, it is not yet ready for eating. Store up to a week, refrigerated. Eggplant is used to make Venezuelan "caviar," see page 237 for the recipe.

ONIONS

Cebolla. Cebolleta are tender, new onions; cebollino are young onions, and cebollas de rabo, or nob onions, are large scallion-like onions with long tubular greens. Cebollón means a large onion, while cebollitas are tiny, piquant, pickled pearl onions. Onions are used as both a vegetable and a condiment and are indispensable to salsas, sauces, and sofrito seasoning bases. Onions flavor soups, stews, rice, and beans and add zest to salads and ceviche. Half moon rings—called media luna—garnish beans, fish, meats, and many other dishes. Onions are baked au gratin; stir-fried with meats and vegetables; creamed; stuffed; pickled; added to egg tortillas (Spanish frittatas), empanada fillings, and potato salad, are cooked with fish, shrimp, or potatoes, and added whole, slashed with an X, to infuse stocks.

You will find several varieties of onions in Latin markets. All except scallions have thin, dry, papery skins covering round or teardrop-shaped bulbs. As onions dry, the skins change to white, yellow, copper, or reddish-purple, depending on the type. You'll find large, mild, Spanish onions with light, coppery skins; Bermuda onions, which are a mild, white-skinned type with a slightly flat shape; red onions with mild and slightly sweet purplish flesh, and all-purpose yellowish-tan skinned onions with an earthy flavor, firm flesh, and a bit of a bite. The cebolla de rabo, also called Texas scallion, has large marble-sized bulbs, thin transparent skin, and long, hollow, slightly rounded greens. These are sliced, greens and all, and added to pots of beans, soups, and stews. Scallions are small, immature onions

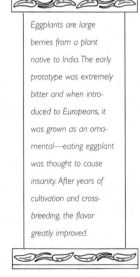

Eggplants are large berries from a plant native to India. The early prototype was extremely bitter and when introduced to Europeans, it was grown as an ornamental—eating eggplant was thought to cause insanity. After years of cultivation and cross-breeding, the flavor greatly improved.

and are mainly used chopped as a garnish. Red onions are minced and added to salsas and bean salads, added in rings to leafy green salads and as a garnish to meat and seafood dishes, or are pickled. White, yellow, and Spanish onions are used in cooking and for stuffing.

When selecting onions, look for firm ones with dry, smooth, crisp outer skins and no sign of sprouting or mold. Store in a cool, dry place up to several weeks. Scallions and nob onions should be refrigerated and used within a week. Chewing a sprig of parsley or mint leaf helps freshen onion breath.

PLANTAINS

Plantains are a part of Latin culture. They're actually a fruit but because they're used mainly as a vegetable, I'm including them in this section of the book. Closely related to the banana, plantains resemble large, thick-skinned green bananas.

Plantains can be boiled, baked, fried, mashed, added to soups and stews, and used in desserts. When green, they are hard, starchy, and rather bland. Left at room temperature, they ripen and slowly change from green to yellow and finally to black, becoming softer and sweeter. The interior flesh changes from creamy white to light yellow-orange. Plantains are usually available in various stages of ripeness, so you will find green, yellow, and mottled or almost black ones. If you buy a very ripe one and don't use it right away, store it in the fridge—the skin will darken even more, which is okay. Store unripe ones at room temperature, away from direct sunlight. Peeled plantains at any stage can be frozen, wrapped in plastic.

The biggest challenge in preparing plantains is removing the thick skins. Ripe ones pose no problem—just cut off both ends and peel as a banana. For green ones, cut the ends off, and make several slits lengthwise down the ribs that cut through to the flesh. Remove the skin in strips with the help of a sharp knife and pull off any stringy fibers. Another method is to put the plantain, with ends cut off and slits cut, into a big pan of warm water (or plug and fill the kitchen sink) for about 10 minutes. After soaking, the strips can easily be peeled by running your fingers under the skin. Plantains begin to discolor when exposed to air—a dip in lemon juice helps. You also may want to oil your hands before peeling plantains to protect against the sticky sap.

Green plantains are known as plátanos verdes or marquitas. They can range from green to yellow-green and are used like a starchy vegetable. They are harder, thicker, and more angular than bananas, and the texture and flavor is somewhat like a sweet potato, but blander. Another variety, the burro plantain from Hawaii, is shorter and stubbier, shaped sort of like a large eggplant with a thick stem attached. It, too, starts off green and yellows with maturity. Unripe plantains (either type) vary from bright green and chartreuse to golden yellow. At each stage they are best suited to certain preparations. When very green and starchy they are boiled or fried. Riper yellow ones are softer, creamier,

burro plantain

slightly sweet and very versatile—they are fried, boiled, sautéed, baked, and grilled.

In the Dominican Republic, bollos de plátanos are fritters made from boiled, mashed green plantain shaped into balls, stuffed with cheese or a spicy meat mixture, rolled in breadcrumbs and fried. Patacones are huge, Colombian-style tostones made by deep-frying whole, peeled green plantains, flattened using a rolling pin to a ¼-inch thickness. They can then be refried whole in a large skillet or cut into any size desired and refried. Traditionally the 11- to 12-inch discs are broken into pieces at the table and piled with shredded beef or chicken, beans, guacamole, shrimp, or grated white cheese. Green plantains are also processed into flour for fu fu (a pounded mash); see pages 216–217.

Ripe plantains are called plátanos maduro. Very ripe, spotted, or almost black plantains are much closer to bananas in taste, aroma, and texture, but are still always cooked, either fried or used in baked desserts. For fried ripe plantains, cut thin, diagonal slices, so you end up with long, angular strips. Fry the slices in hot oil only once, just before serving. Eat with fried eggs, picadillo (spicy ground beef), cornmeal grits, or as a side dish with plates of rice and beans and meat or seafood. By far the most common use for ripe plantains is plátanos al horno, or baked plantain. Whole, peeled ones are studded with a few cloves, dotted with butter, and baked in sugar syrup or a mixture of brown sugar, cinnamon, nutmeg, and sherry. A recipe for semi-ripe plantains or bananas stuffed with curried beef is on page 255.

When you don't have time to wrestle with a plantain, the following frozen products are a quick alternative. Tostones are smashed slices of green plantain. Soak in salted water, drain, and deep-fry for a tasty side dish or snack, dipped in hot sauce or garlic mojo. Plátano maduro are whole, ripe plantains, ready to heat and eat with rice, beans, and

frozen tostones

meats. Whole ones need 20 minutes in the oven or until golden brown, or microwave 1½ minutes per plantain. You may also find frozen platano rallado, or grated plantain. This is used to make plantain soup, casseroles layered with cheese and ground beef, and fritters. Goya and La Fe sell ready-to-fry tostones. Big Banana brand has baked whole plantains in 3.5-pound boxes. Goya has grated plantain in 24-ounce boxes.

SWISS CHARD

Acelgas or silver beet. Swiss chard is sold in large bunches and has broad, tender, spinach-flavored leaves about 6 inches across, either smooth or ruffled. They splay from the tops of long, fleshy, whitish, ribbed stalks, about 1 to 2 feet in length. Another variety, called ruby chard, has beet red stalks and leaf veins. The leaves and stalks of either type are often cooked separately as the tender, crisp stalks take longer to cook than the soft leaves. They both can be chopped and added to long-cooking soups and stews, or braised and used in egg tortillas (Spanish frittatas), lentil and chickpea dishes, or salads. Very tender leaves can be used raw in salads. Swiss chard has to be washed very carefully, like spinach, to get rid of the sand and grit lodged in the bulbous stalk base.

Swiss chard blends well with chickpeas and the two are often combined in hearty stews seasoned with black pepper, paprika, cumin, and parsley. Select chard with crisp, unblemished stalks and evenly colored leaves with no yellowing. Store unwashed and refrigerated in a perforated plastic bag and use within 2 to 3 days.

swiss chard

TOMATOES

Tomaté in Spanish, jitomaté in Mexico. Do not confuse pale green, unripe tomatoes with Mexican tomatillos (green husk tomatoes); see pages 103–104. They are very different.

Avoid pallid, vapid specimens that are devoid of flavor and mealy. If that's all that is available, it is best to use quality canned tomatoes. Tomatoes are eaten raw; sliced into salads, sandwiches, and taco fillings; and are diced for salsas and sauces. They are broiled, stuffed, and baked; added to beans, soups, stews, and casseroles. In Mexican recipes, tomatoes are often roasted, called asado. Roast whole ones under a broiler in an aluminum foil pan for 20 to 30 minutes, turning to cook evenly. The charred skins can be removed, but add flavor and blend into fairly smooth sauces. To peel fresh tomatoes, dip them in boiling water for a minute. The skins will slip right off. To de-seed tomatoes, cut in half and squeeze the seeds out, although many people like the crunch the seeds add. To make tomato pulp for sauces, cut off a thin slice from the top, grasp the tomato in your palm, and rub against the coarse holes of a grater. This creates pulp without any skin.

When choosing tomatoes, vine-ripe are the best, available near the end of summer when tomatoes are at their peak. Select firm, but ripe, smooth, bright red tomatoes with no wrinkles or cracks. They should have a sweet aroma and yield to light pressure when pressed. Use as soon as possible. Slightly underripe tomatoes will ripen if left out a few days. Once ripe, they can be refrigerated, but bring to room temperature before using.

ZUCCHINI

Calbacín. The zucchini is a type of narrow squash, harvested before fully ripe. They range from thumb-sized babies to large cucumbers. Smaller ones are more flavorful and tender. The thin, smooth skin can be tinged with yellow or pale green stripes and specks. Zucchini have a delicate, mild summer squash flavor and are good matched with herbs such as oregano or basil. A small, light-green variety is sold in Mexican markets. Sometimes you can find the yellow fluted blossoms that are used for fillings for quesadillas, added to soup, or battered and deep-fried.

Zucchini are extremely versatile and are used in numerous Latin dishes. They are chopped and slowly cooked in olive oil, battered and deep-fried, baked, stuffed, sliced and grilled, added in chunks to soups and stews, or blanched and added to salads. In Mexico they are cubed and cooked in the Pueblo style—simmered in a sauce of pureed poblano chilies and cream. In Argentina and Chile, large zucchini are hollowed out and stuffed with rice and ground meat or grated cheese mixtures and baked. Choose firm, unblemished zucchini with smooth skins and no cracks or soft spots. Store in a paper or plastic bag, refrigerated up to a week.

Fresh Fruit

Latin American fruit is a feast for the eyes and senses. Markets display a bounty of fruit, with prime specimens cut open to reveal shocking pink, ruby red, or glistening jewel-like flesh. Exotic tropical fruits grow in extravagant abundance in the equatorial regions and craggy slopes of South and Central America and the Caribbean islands. Ripe, delectable fruit is the perfect ending to a hot and spicy meal. In fact, a few fruits are elevated to cult status—the sight of a mamey brings a flood of nostalgia to many islanders who, as children, ate them off the tree. The Mexican artist Frida Kahlo captured the glory of gorgeous fruits in her paintings of custard apples, cactus pears, pitahayas, watermelon, cut open papayas, and pineapples. To discover the luscious flavors, head to the produce section of your nearest Latin grocery. Many tropical fruits are found in Caribbean markets, specialty stores, and well-stocked supermarkets. Some can be obtained by mail order; see appendix 4. Ultimately what you find depends on what is in season.

BABACAO

Chamburo. A hybrid papaya, babacao is five-sided like a starfruit and tapers at the tip. They range from 6 inches to 1 foot long and when cut crosswise form a star-shaped slice. When ripe, they're golden and soft and have pale yellow flesh with an aroma of papaya, strawberry, and pineapple, with a trace of banana. The fruit is eaten as is, cut in slices, diced and added to fruit salad, liquidized into juice, or blenderized in shakes, used to flavor ice cream, and added to meat dishes. Select unblemished fruits and ripen at room temperature until soft and golden. Handle carefully as they bruise easily and can rot quickly. They are also sold whole and in strips in jars of syrup.

BANANAS

Although we generally think of the Gros Michel (Chiquita) type of banana, bananas actually come in three different types. Dessert bananas are sweet, small to medium-sized, and can be eaten out of hand. Cooking bananas, usually called plantains (see pages 43–44), are long and large with drier, starchy flesh. In between are those that are straight and stout and can be eaten as is or used for cooking, such as the burro (also known as dwarf orinoco) and Jamaican red. Besides the familiar Cavendish and Gros Michel, there are many others to look for in Latin and Caribbean markets. A tropical fruit nursery in Florida also sells the rhizomes and baby plants to plant and

manzano bananas

Banana leaves are used to wrap tamales and other foods for boiling, steaming, or grilling. Fresh leaves offer the best flavor so if you live in a tropical climate, pick your own, wash, and cut into pieces. If you don't, buy frozen sheets of leaves. To use, just thaw and cut into pieces. They add a subtle herbaceous flavor to food and keep moisture in meat or seafood.

grow your own exotic varieties—for more information, see page 260.

Squatty ice cream bananas are about 5 inches long with silvery-blue, blotchy skins and creamy flesh that has a frothy ice cream flavor. Manzano, or apple bananas, are short and chubby with pale yellow skins and a hint of apple-strawberry flavor. These come primarily from Venezuela and are best eaten when the skins are almost totally black. Burro bananas are stubby and squared with yellow skins; soft, creamy white flesh with a firm center; and lemony flavor. They are best when fully ripe with brown spots. Niños, also called guineitos, are small, plump dwarf bananas, about 3 inches long and lime green, turning yellow when ripe. They have a rich, super-sweet banana flavor and soft, creamy texture. You may also find squat, dull red bananas that turn maroon when fully ripe with sweet pinkish-orange flesh. These are called Jamaican red, Cuban red, Colorado, indio, or macaboo and are good roasted, the skin split, and sprinkled with cinnamon and brown sugar. Somewhat similar is the pisang raja with yellow skin and yellow-orange delectably sweet flesh.

BLACK SAPOTE

Black persimmon. Tomato-shaped, glossy apple-green to brownish-green. The skins are often freckled with small, light specks and the flesh is dark brown, soft and sweet with a sort of chocolate flavor. To remove the pulp, cut into wedges starting from the blossom end. Gently scoop out the pulp with a spoon, discarding seeds. Use the pulp right away or freeze it. The flavor is enhanced by the addition of a little vanilla, rum, orange juice, or lemon juice. Use in milkshakes, fruit drinks, mousse, ice cream, or sherbet. Also good eaten sprinkled with sugar and served with cream.

CHERIMOYA

Cannona cherimoya or jewel of the Inca. Cherimoya, also called custard apples, have an irregular oval shape and can weigh from ½ pound on up to 5 or more pounds. They have smooth, bronze to light olive green skins, turning yellowish, then almost black as they ripen, covered in fingerprint-like markings. The flesh is white, slightly granular, and very sweet, tasting like a piña colada. Most are sold not yet ripe and can be ripened in a paper bag in a few days.

cherimoya

47

When ripe, the fruit seems swollen and about to burst. To eat, break into pieces or scoop out the pulp with a spoon and sprinkle with orange juice. Don't eat the skin—it's bitter. And don't eat the seeds—they're toxic. Fortunately, they're large enough to separate from the pulp in your mouth—spit them out. Choose firm, heavy ones without any skin blemishes or brown patches. Once ripe, store refrigerated up to 4 days. Best eaten chilled. Cherimoya are available year-round, but peak in July. There is also a pink cherimoya called selma, a rather rare find outside South America. It has smaller seeds and pale pink flesh beneath the green scaly skin.

Sugar apples, also called sweet sops and scaly custard apples, are a relative of the cherimoya, another member of the annonaceous family, fruits with a creamy custard-like pulp. Sugar apples resemble squat yellow-green hand grenades, covered with nubby 3-D crocodile skin. The custardy pulp is rich and sweet with hints of rosewater perfume. There is also a Brazilian hybrid called the fruta do condo, or "Count's fruit."

Lastly, there is the atemoya, a hybrid sugar apple and cherimoya. This is a large, heart-shaped green fruit covered with hooked nubs, much longer than those of the soursop (a distant relative). It looks like a bizarre medieval weapon. This oddity combines the hardiness of the cherimoya with the seductive taste and creamy pulp of the sugar apple. All of these can be used in the same manner as the cherimoya.

COCONUT

Coco seco. Coconuts are the interior nut of the large fruit of the coconut palm tree. Husked coconuts are brown, hairy, and matted with hard, woody shells with three dark spots forming a monkey-like face. The interior is filled with clear coconut water and lined with a half-inch thick layer of firm, white meat. The grated, pressed meat produces coconut milk. Coco verde are whole young coconuts with the nut nestled inside a green or yellow-orange fibrous husk. These are often sold at roadside stalls and by vendors in marketplaces, but some Latin grocery stores stock them. The top has to be whacked off with a machete or sharp cleaver, then you can sip the refreshing water with a straw. Be sure to use a spoon to scrape out some of the tender white pulp lining the coconut.

A mature coconut should be shaken to make sure water is sloshing around inside; if not, it's dry and tough. To crack a coconut open, place newspaper on the floor (cement is best) and hurl it hard—it should smash open. Or pierce two of the black eye indentations with a skewer, drain the water out, and tap firmly around the middle of the coconut with a hammer or back of a cleaver. When a crack forms, insert the point of a sturdy knife and lever the crack open. Use a small knife to pry out large pieces of meat, using a kitchen towel to protect your hands, and peel the brownish skin off with a vegetable peeler. Coconut meat has a sweet, nutty flavor and crisp texture. Unopened coconuts will keep up to a month stored at room temperature. Once opened, store the meat up to a week, refrigerated.

FEIJOA

Pineapple guava, Brazilian guava, and New Zealand banana. The egg-shaped, and egg-sized fruit has slightly bumpy, thin, green skin, sometimes touched with a flush of red. The creamy tan to golden flesh is fragrant, thick, and sweet with a complex flavor of pineapple,

feijoa

strawberry, and eucalyptus with a hint of spearmint. The texture is granular like a pear and the center core is slightly gelatinous with tiny, black, edible seeds. Eat fresh or cook after peeling the bitter skin. The flesh discolors rapidly, so place in water with lemon juice once you slice it. Add to fruit salad or serve with yogurt. Good cooked and made into jam or jelly, poached in sugar syrup, or pureed and used to flavor shakes, ice cream, sorbet, flan, or puddings. Choose aromatic feijoas that are tender to the touch and unblemished. Leave at room temperature until fully ripe, then refrigerate up to 3 days. Also available canned as juice.

GUAVA

Guayaba, guayaru (in Haiti), and goiaba (in Brazil). Guavas vary in shape from round or oval to pear-shaped and range in size from an egg to a baseball. The thin, edible skin varies in color from almost white to green or red and sometimes has tiny pink or black spots. The flesh can be white, pink, or red. There is a ring or central core with tiny, hard, edible seeds. The pulp in the middle is sweet and soft compared to the granular flesh around the seeds. Guavas permeate a room with their distinctive floral fragrance and have an assertive, sweet-tart taste. Some are banana sweet while others are pineapple tangy. Species you may encounter are the cas from Costa Rica with green-to-yellow skins and white, slightly acidic flesh and the apple guava from Mexico, either oval or round with yellow-to-red skins. Brazil exports the araca guava, small and yellow with many seeds, and the cattley, or strawberry guava, a round red or green fruit with vivid dark pink-red flesh. Ripe guava, besides being eaten out of hand, are made into jams and jellies, custards, sorbet, and milkshakes, or are pressed for juice. Choose guavas that yield to gentle pressure in your palm and are aromatic with no brown spots. Refrigerate ripe fruit up to a week in a plastic or paper bag. Guavas are most abundant from October through December.

guava

MAMEY

Mammee sapote, mamey colorado, and chicomamey. This is a large, oval football-shaped fruit with a prominent point, ranging from 3 to 8 inches in length. It has thick, brown skin with a rough, scruffy surface. Inside, the reddish flesh is soft, aromatic, and sweet, a little like a sugary sweet potato or pumpkin. It's also almost fiber free and can be spooned out of the skin, working your way around the large brown central seed. The pulp is made into preserves, fruit drinks, milkshakes, and ice cream. It's hard to tell from outer appearances if the fruit is ripe—try scratching the surface of the skin with a fingernail. If the flesh is deep orangey-red, it's ripe. Allow to ripen at room temperature, then refrigerate up to 5 days. A variety is the St. Domingo apricot, often called mammee. This fruit is egg-sized with brown, rough skin like an Idaho potato and pinkish, sweet flesh that gives off an almond-like perfume when fully ripe. Very ripe ones are eaten out of the shell and underripe, tart fruits are made into preserves.

MANGO

Mangue, mongo, tropical peach, and fruit of paradise. This relative to the pistachio and cashew is found in many delicious varieties. Most average 4 inches in length and can be rounded, oval, or kidney-shaped with leathery skins that range from yellow and yellow-green to golden or reddish, tinged with magenta, pink, orange, or red. The fragrant, thick flesh can be orange, yellow, or peach-colored enclosing a large, flat, white seed. Most mangoes are smooth-fleshed, buttery, and sweet with a spicy, slightly resinous overtone, while others are stringy or fibrous.

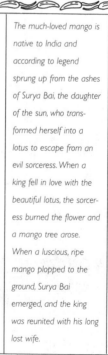

mango

Types of mangoes include the Alphonso—large, plump, and yellow-skinned with a red blush and buttery, smooth, firm orange flesh that tastes like a cross between a peach and an apricot with a hint of pineapple (May through August). Harden mangoes are medium-sized, yellow-skinned with a red-orange flush and slightly fibrous flesh with an apricot flavor (February through June). Kents are large mangoes with greenish-yellow skins, and peach-colored, juicy, sweet flesh (June through August). The Keitt mango is green and yellow and elongated in shape with very juicy flesh and pineapple-peach flavor (July through September). The Tommy Atkin has bright red skin, firm nectar-sweet orange flesh with a small pit, and some fiber. These store well and are in season from April through July and are the most common type in markets here. Look for ripe, aromatic mangoes that yield to gentle pressure. They are past their prime

The much-loved mango is native to India and according to legend sprung up from the ashes of Surya Bai, the daughter of the sun, who transformed herself into a lotus to escape from an evil sorceress. When a king fell in love with the beautiful lotus, the sorceress burned the flower and a mango tree arose. When a luscious, ripe mango plopped to the ground, Surya Bai emerged, and the king was reunited with his long lost wife.

if they have black spots and pitted skins. To ripen, wrap them in newspaper and store in a straw basket. Once ripe, mangoes can be refrigerated up to a week, but let them reach room temperature before eating. Also be aware that many people are allergic to the sap concentrated at the stem end. Take precaution and slice the stem end off before peeling a mango to eat.

MONSTERA

Monstera's fruit is cone-shaped, resembling roasted ears of pale green corn. Monstera taste a little like a mixture of banana and pineapple. When the fruit ripens, the segmented covering of the edible portion begins to separate, starting at the stem end. This is not a commonly found fruit, but I have seen them in some Latin markets and the produce department of gourmet specialty stores and upscale international markets. If not yet ripe, place the fruit in a paper bag. Monstera can be eaten plain or with sugar and cream. Add the pulp to blender drinks and fruit salads or use pureed to flavor sorbet. Diced segments are good added to chicken salad with olives. The fruit can also be cooked and made into preserves. Store ripe ones in the refrigerator.

monstera

ORO BLANCO

"White gold" in Spanish, this is a cross between a grapefruit and a pummelo (a large, pale green cousin to the grapefruit). It may take some searching to find or can be ordered by mail; see appendix 4. Oro blanco are the size of a small grapefruit with yellow skin, a thick whitish rind, and almost seedless pale flesh with a sweet, juicy grapefruit flavor—without the acidity. Eat as is, squeeze into juice, add segments to fruit salad, or pair with slices of avocado and drizzle in a mayonnaise-based dressing. Select oro blanco that feel heavy for their size and store refrigerated up to a month.

PAPAYA

Lechosa and fruta bomba. Papaya are cylindrical or pear-shaped with smooth skins changing from green to yellow-orange as they ripen. Some are blotchy or spotted green and yellow. Most weigh a modest pound or so. The smooth flesh is orange or crimson and tastes like a blend of apricot, melon, and peach. The center contains a mass of shiny, round black seeds with a peppery-cress flavor that are sometimes crushed and eaten as a condiment or garnish, or are crunched for contrast between bites of papaya. In Cuba, always call them fruta bomba, as papaya is slang for female genitalia. Choose heavy, firm fruit that are just beginning to soften. To eat, cut in half lengthwise, scoop out the seeds, peel and slice, and serve with a squeeze of lime juice. You can also just remove the seeds and spoon the flesh out. Unripe green papaya is

papaya

added to curries and stews, shredded for slaw-like salads and pickled. Papaya aids digestion and is considered a system cleanser and detoxifier.

PASSION FRUIT

Granadilla, parch, parchita. Maracuya (in Brazil), curuba (in Colombia), and ceibey (in Cuba). The most common are egg-shaped with thick, lustrous yellow, orange, or dark purple skins that become thinner and wrinkled as the fruits ripen. The inner pulp has a gelatinous texture and ranges in color from pinkish-green to shades of golden yellow, but some are white or almost clear. The sweet, juicy, and slightly tart, aromatic pulp is dotted with small, crisp, edible seeds. To eat, halve the fruit and spoon out the pulp and seeds or use in drinks and desserts. The strained pulp is also sold frozen. Use the frozen pulp or strained juice to make pineapple-passion fruit sauce for roasted red snapper (see the recipe on page 250).

Other varieties of passion fruit include the giant granadilla, a much larger fruit, which has three grooves and a thick rind that is edible along with the pulp. The melon-like rind is rather bland and is usually mixed with the pulp or other fruits. It is greenish-yellow, turning brownish when ripe. Unripe granadilla are cooked as a vegetable. The curuba, popular in Colombia where it grows, is yellow and may also be called banana passion fruit or sweet cup. It is apple-shaped with a thin yellowish-tan rind and has very

aromatic, delicious pulp. The water lemon, or Jamaica honeysuckle, is orange to golden yellow and very sweet. The sweet granadilla is medium-sized, mottled in orange and yellow patterns with distinctive, sweet, juicy pulp. Select passion fruit that are wrinkled, unbruised, and heavy. If the skin is smooth and shiny, they are not ripe. When ripe, store refrigerated up to a week.

passion fruit

PEPINO

Mellow fruit, tree melon, sweet cucumber, and pepino dulce. Resembling a small, elongated melon, pepino have satiny, golden skins streaked with violet and range in size from a plum to a papaya. The mild, delicate flesh is juicy and aromatic, tasting like a mix of cantaloupe and cucumber. There are small, soft, edible seeds in the core. If the skins are greenish, allow to ripen at room

pepino

temperature, then store refrigerated up to a few days. Best when golden and very ripe. Choose ones that are fragrant and yield slightly to pressure. Peel and slice to eat or scoop the flesh out with a spoon. The flavor is heightened with a sprinkle of salt and squeeze of lemon juice. Unripe pepino can be cooked like summer squash.

PINEAPPLE

Anana, nana, piña, or abacaxi (in Brazil). To peel a pineapple, trim off the top and bottom and slice off the skin just below the surface in vertical strips. Trim off any brown eye-spots and cut into pieces, removing the tough core, if desired. The cayenne, large with sweet-tart juicy flesh, is the most common variety. Queens are on the small side with firmer, fibrous flesh, not quite as sweet. Red Spanish pineapples are medium-sized with pale yellow to almost white flesh that is fragrant, acidic, and a little fibrous. Pineapples are eaten fresh, added to salsas, tossed into fruit salads with grated coconut and pureed for drinks, sauces, mousse, and sherbet. They're also used in pineapple tarts, cakes, and candies and made into glazes for meats and seafood. Choose a pineapple that is heavy for its size with a pleasant aroma. It should have deep green leaves and yield to slight pressure when pressed.

SAPODILLA

Naseberry, nispero, neesberry, chico sapota, chiku, sapodilla, sapote, zapote, or tree potato. These fruits are about the size and shape of a large kiwi with rough grayish-brown skins that peel off easily. The flesh is translucent, honey-brown to pinkish-yellow with a grainy texture. The fragrant, brown-sugar-and-pear-flavored pulp melts in your mouth. Naseberry are best eaten when very soft and ripe. When very ripe, the skin softens and when scratched reveals a yellow color. To eat, peel and slice, or cut in half and scoop out the flesh with a spoon, discarding the seeds. Delicious served with thick cream. Can also be pureed to make juice or whirled into a milkshake, cut into fruit salad, and boiled down into syrup and fermented to make wine.

sapodilla

SOUR LIME

Limón chico. In Mexico these small, round, yellowish-green, very sour limes are called limón tequilero. Lime juice adds spark to salsas, guacamole, and chili sauces, balancing sweet and salty flavors. Halved limes are served as a table condiment with salt and pepper, meant to be squeezed over everything from grilled fish and fried fish roe to roasted meats and fried green plantains. Lime juice is sweetened with sugar for drinks and frozen for sorbets. Any lime can be used, but others won't add the same unique sourness and fragrance as the small sour ones.

SOUR ORANGE

Naranja agria, Seville orange, or bitter orange. Thick, baggy, dull orange skins are rough textured with tints of green and yellow. The rind is very aromatic and is used zested in some recipes; in England they cut it into shreds for marmalade. Sour oranges are smaller than sweet oranges with dark orange, dry, and extremely sour pulp. In Latin cooking, the pressed juice is used like vinegar in marinades and glazes for meats, poultry, and seafood. Chicken marinated in sour orange juice, dusted in flour, and fried is deliciously tender. You can add lime juice, garlic, salt, pepper, and ground cumin for even more flavor. If you can't find the oranges, use the handy bottled juice.

SOURSOP

Guanábana, corossol, or prickly custard apple. The largest of the annona family, soursops are elongated, irregular, somewhat heart-shaped fruits with deep green skins covered in fleshy, short-hooked nubs. They range in size from that of a mango on up to 10 or more pounds and are quite soft, darkening as they ripen. The pale flesh is sweet and tangy, like an acidic pineapple daiquiri with a slightly sweet fermented aroma. The thick, icy-looking segmented pulp contains a few hard, shiny, black seeds. These should be removed before eating or pulping as they are said to be toxic. The pulp is very juicy and

soursops make great blender drinks, becoming creamy with the addition of water or milk and a little sugar to offset the tartness. Soursop also flavors ice cream, mousse, custard, and soufflés, and is made into jugo de guanábana—soursop juice mixed with vanilla, sugar syrup, and evaporated milk. Choose heavy fruits that yield to gentle pressure. Store at room temperature for 2 to 3 days, then refrigerate up

soursop

to a week.

STARFRUIT

Carambola or five-finger fruit. Starfruit are 2 to 5 inches long and 1½ inches in diameter with an unusual shape consisting of five prominent ribs running their length. The thin, waxy skin is yellowish-green, turning golden yellow when fully ripe. The edible skin encloses translucent, crisp, slightly acidic, juicy flesh that tastes like a delicate

starfruit

blend of apple and grapes. There are flat seeds in some ribs. When cut crosswise into thin slices, whimsical stars are produced—great as decorative garnishes. A slit starfruit slice adds style slipped onto the rim of a cocktail glass or scattered over appetizer platters. Pureed starfruit goes into marinades and drinks. It can also be made into jelly and chutney. Underripe, sour starfruit is eaten as a snack dipped in salt and chili powder. Despite its fragile appearance, it keeps well. If greenish, ripen at room temperature for several days. Store ripe ones in the refrigerator for up to 2 weeks. Starfruit is used in the sorbet recipe on page 258.

TAMARILLO

tamarillo

Tree tomato. Two varieties of tamarillo can be found. One is golden orange with yellow flesh and the other is reddish-purple with orange flesh. Both are oval and egg-sized with satin-smooth skins. This bitter skin covers firm flesh the texture of plums with a tart gooseberry flavor. The golden variety is milder and less acidic. The dark seeds are edible. To eat, peel with a knife or blanch and plunge into icy water and slip off the skins, then cut crosswise into slices. Good raw, sprinkled with sugar or salt and lime juice. Tamarillos can also be cooked like a vegetable, and can be added to salads or used in sandwiches. Basically you can use them in any recipe calling for tomatoes. Ripen at room temperature out of direct sunlight. Store ripe ones refrigerated up to 2 weeks.

TAMARIND

Tamarindo or tamarin. This is the pod of a large evergreen tree native to India. The cinnamon-brown, knobby pods range from 4 to 8 inches long and contain brown sticky pulp and large brown seeds held together by a fibrous husk. Tamarind is a souring agent, milder than lemon and sweeter than vinegar. The pulp has a tangy apricot-date flavor and fruity aroma. In addition to the pods, tamarind is sold as a sticky mass in plastic bags or small slabs, sometimes pitted, but usually with the seeds. To make an extract from the pulp, soak a hunk in hot water. When it softens, mix into a mushy paste and press through a sieve over a non-metallic bowl using your fingers or the back of a spoon. The fine pulp and juice will pass through, leaving behind the fibers and seeds. Be sure to collect the thick, strained paste stuck to the under side of the sieve. Tamarind extract is used in meat marinades, sauces, and fish flavorings, imparting a sweet-sour tang. It is also used in making preserves, chutneys, candies, ices, and cooling drinks. Jugo de tamarindo is slightly sweetened tamarind juice. Tamarinade is a refreshing alternative to lemonade, popular in Mexico and the Caribbean, spiked with mint. Tamarind is used in the ginger-tamarind chicken recipe on page 254.

UNIQ FRUIT

Ugli fruit. This saggy-skinned fruit is the size of a large grapefruit with wrinkled, pale yellow-orange skin. The inner flesh (not ugly) is juicy and sweet, similar to a mandarin orange with traces of honey and pineapple. Delicious peeled and eaten out of hand, added to fruit salad, and squeezed into juice. Also good in vegetable salads with diced avocado and a creamy dressing. Choose uniq fruit that are heavy for their size, store at room temperature, and use within 5 days or refrigerate up to 2 weeks. Available December through April.

WHITE SAPOTE

Zapota blanco or Mexican apple. These are small, 3 inch in diameter ovoid fruits with thin green skins that turn yellowish when ripe. The pale yellow flesh is juicy with a melting texture and sweet pear-like flavor. To eat, cut in half and scoop out the flesh and serve with sugar and cream, or chop and add to fruit salads, sprinkled with lemon juice and sugar. Also made into a sweet sauce that's good over ice cream. Best when yellowish and very ripe. Store in the fridge up to 5 days.

5

Fresh Herbs
& Herbal Teas

In Latin cuisine, fresh herbs add a bracing, pungent note to foods. They're often blended in sauces with other spices and seasonings. They add a splash of green color and infuse dishes with an essence not found in dried form. Herbal teas are a flavorful staple of Latin food shops.

Fresh Herbs

CILANTRO

Also known as coriander, culantro, culantrillo, coentro, and Chinese parsley. Cilantro has delicate, flat, green, ruffle-edged leaves, thin stems, a distinctive aroma, and sharp, citrusy flavor. It is sold in small bunches, often with the roots attached. Cilantro is used chopped in guacamole, salsas, sauces, sofrito seasoning bases, marinades, salads, stews, and bean dishes and as a decorative garnish, like parsley, adding flavor and color. Cilantro also cools the bite of hot foods. Pollo a gridulce con cilantro is a Cuban chicken dish made by sautéing bite-sized pieces of breast meat in olive oil and butter with chopped garlic, apple, and spices, liberally garnished with chopped cilantro. In Mexican cuisine, cilantro is used in fresh, uncooked sauces for fish and to make mole verde (green mole). Pebre is Chilean hot salsa, made from a mix of minced hot chilies, garlic, onion, lots of cilantro and olive oil and vinegar, served with roasted or grilled meats. Choose fresh, unwilted bunches with crisp stems and no black, mushy leaves. Store up to 2 weeks by standing in a glass of

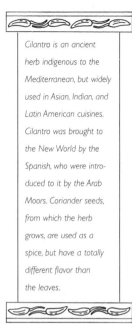

Cilantro is an ancient herb indigenous to the Mediterranean, but widely used in Asian, Indian, and Latin American cuisines. Cilantro was brought to the New World by the Spanish, who were introduced to it by the Arab Moors. Coriander seeds, from which the herb grows, are used as a spice, but have a totally different flavor than the leaves.

water with the tops loosely covered with a plastic bag. The seeds are chewed to neutralize garlic breath.

MARJORAM/OREGANO

Mejorana/oregano. These herbs are very similar and can be used almost interchangeably. Marjoram is more delicate and subtle in flavor than oregano. Marjoram has a mint-sage essence and is used to season veal, pork, and lamb. Oregano, also in the mint family, has a slightly more basil flavor. Both plants have multiple-branched stems tipped with small, grayish-green leaves. Both are used fresh, dried, or ground. Latin markets often have bundles of fresh oregano. The stems are reddish-brown and the soft leaves are oval. There may also be clusters of larger-leafed oregano, which is usually lightly toasted before using. Whole-leaf oregano is much more aromatic than the crushed, dried flakes or powder sold in small packets or shaker jars. Oregano is used in marinades, salsas, stuffings, salad dressings, empanada fillings, tomato sauces, and many meat, poultry, fish, and vegetable dishes. It enhances tuna salad, roasted potatoes, stewed squid, stir-fried shrimp, roasted chicken, and pernil al horno (roasted pork shoulder). Mexican oregano is a particularly aromatic and pungent herb. In Mexican cuisine, oregano is often combined with cumin and cloves as a sort of "holy trinity." The classic balance uses twice as much oregano as cumin and twice as much cumin as cloves. This trio is used to season cooking sauces, stews, marinades, sausages, beans, and picadillos (ground meat hashes). Store refrigerated in a plastic bag and use within 4 to 5 days. To dry the herbs, tie the stems together and hang in a warm, well-ventilated place such as a kitchen window.

RECAO

Eryngium foetidum. Other names for this pungent herb are long coriander, shado beni, culantro, black benny, and sawtooth coriander. This herb has 4- to 5- inch long green leaves with serrated edges. It exudes a strong aroma, similar to cilantro. The roots of recao are cleaned and used as a condiment with rice, soups, and fish. The leaves are added to salads, stews, soups, beans, salsas, and cooking sauces. Shredded recao is added to West Indian green mango chutney. Recao is essential to authentic Puerto Rican sofrito seasoning bases, pureed with cilantro, green peppers, chilies, garlic, and onions. Recao is usually sold in clusters of about 10 to 12 leaves spread flat on Styrofoam trays, wrapped in plastic. Make sure there are no black leaves, which indicate rot.

recao

WATERCRESS

Berro. Watercress has thick, crunchy, pale stems and lush masses of dark green, oval, or round leaflets stemming from small branches off the main stalk. It has a pungent, but pleasant peppery taste and crisp texture. Watercress is sold in fat bunches. In some stores it is found standing in tubs of water to keep it fresh. To use, cut off the roots and

watercress any withered or yellowing leaves and wash thoroughly to get rid of sand and soil. The best way to do this is to cover the cress with water in a large bowl and swish it around gently, changing the water until no grit sinks to the bottom. The juicy leaves have a mustardy tang and are great in salads and sandwiches or pureed for sauces and creamy soups. Watercress is best used the day of purchase as it perishes rapidly. If you have to keep it, store standing in a bowl of water 1 to 2 days and change the water every day.

Herbal Teas

Dried blossoms, leaves, and spices are used to make infusions, sipped for restorative and medicinal purposes. A few are steeped and the vapors inhaled. Some are sold loose in small packets, found in the spice section, others are sold in packets of tea bags. To use either type, boil some water, pour into a teapot or cup and plunk in leaves or a sachet and steep about ten minutes. Strain the loose type. Sweeten with sugar or honey if desired. The following herbal teas are found in Latin markets.

BOLDO

The crushed, dried leaves of this evergreen in the laurel family have a peculiar odor (a little like wormseed weed and turpentine with resinous, pine overtones). They contain a volatile oil and the bitter alkaloid, boldine. The steeped tea is taken as a tonic for the liver, stomach, and gallbladder and is antiseptic, helping ease urinary tract infections. The leaves are occasionally

boldo tea

used as a substitute for bay leaf in cooking, but are very strong so should be used in tiny amounts. Carmencita brand has this tea in plastic-wrapped packets of 10 bags. Add honey to counter the bitterness.

BUENAS NOCHES

A sleep-inducing tea blend of lemon balm, orange blossom, chamomile, linden flower, and fennel seeds, all ground to a powder and packed in tea bags. Lemon balm calms the nerves, reduces overactive thyroid glands, eases anxiety, and alleviates painful menstruation. Orange blossom adds fragrance; chamomile and linden flower aid restful sleep. Fennel adds a sweet licorice flavor and is a digestive aid. Look for Carmencita brand in packets of 10 sachets.

CHAMOMILE

Manzanilla. The dried flowers of this herb look like tiny daisies with fine silky strands instead of petals. Both the flowers and dried leaves

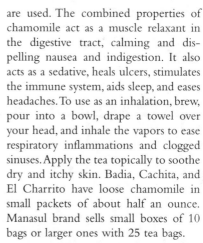

The benefits of chamomile are nothing new. Native to Europe and northwest Asia, chamomile was used by the ancient Egyptians, who called it "the plant of the sun" and made use of it against malarial fevers and in dedications to their gods. Greeks called the herb "ground apple" due to its apple aroma. In Spanish, the name means "little apple" for the same reason. It was once added to sherry and still flavors herbal beers. Chamomile was one of many herbs brought to the New World by the Spanish in the 1500s.

are used. The combined properties of chamomile act as a muscle relaxant in the digestive tract, calming and dispelling nausea and indigestion. It also acts as a sedative, heals ulcers, stimulates the immune system, aids sleep, and eases headaches. To use as an inhalation, brew, pour into a bowl, drape a towel over your head, and inhale the vapors to ease respiratory inflammations and clogged sinuses. Apply the tea topically to soothe dry and itchy skin. Badia, Cachita, and El Charrito have loose chamomile in small packets of about half an ounce. Manasul brand sells small boxes of 10 bags or larger ones with 25 tea bags.

CAT'S CLAW

Uña de gato. The bark of this climbing vine is ground to make tea. Cat's claw is used for inflammations including arthritis, asthma, bronchitis, gastritis, and skin flushes. Certain alkaloids and compounds present in cat's claw have antioxidant, antiviral, and anti-inflammatory properties. The herb is proving to help reinforce the immunological system and is being tried by cancer and AIDS patients to help alleviate side effects from treatment. This treasure from the Amazon is sold in tea bags and in pill form in health food stores. Latin markets have Badia brand tea in packets of 10 bags.

EUCALYPTUS

Eucalyptus leaves are used crushed and steeped as tea or as an inhalation. The leaves have a sharp, resinous, nose-opening aroma. Eucalyptus contains the chemical eucalyptol, which is a decongestant and powerful antiseptic. Eucalyptus tea clears clogged nasal passages and prevents wound infections. The leaves can be steamed and the vapors inhaled, or applied to the skin. To brew, use about 2 teaspoons of crushed leaves per cup of boiled water and steep 10 minutes. Add honey and drink twice a day when you have a cold. To relieve congestion, place a handful of crushed leaves in a pan of boiled water, drape your head with a towel, and inhale the steamy vapors. Look for Badia brand in small packets of 10 bags.

LINDEN FLOWER

Tilo in Spanish, also called lime blossom or lime flower. Tea brewed from the flowers and leaves of the linden tree helps indigestion and stress-related stomach ailments, insomnia, headaches, and symptoms of

linden flower

colds and flu. It also lowers cholesterol levels in people with high blood pressure and soothes nervous tension. Sold loose in small packets—look for Badia and Cachita brands—and in packets of 10 sachets. Also Manasul brand in small boxes of 10 bags or larger with 25 bags.

MINT TEA

Té de menta. Dried spearmint, also called yerba buena, is brewed and taken as a digestive tea. It is often sipped after a meal, sweetened with honey. At the first sign of a cold, drink mint tea to help relieve the symptoms and reduce fevers. Also helps induce sleep when taken at bedtime. Look for Badia brand in packets of 10 tea bags.

· 6 ·

Spices
& Seasoning Sauces

If the heart of Latin cuisine is in its aromatic seasoning sauces, adobos (marinades), and salsas, then the soul must be in the wonderful array of spices that it features. The spices themselves are not particularly unusual to us—it's the role they play in the kitchen that's exotic.

Spices

In Latin grocers, ground spices are called en polvo, powdered spices are molida or molido, and whole ones are entero or entera. Ground and powdered spices are often fried in a little oil to bring out the flavor before they're added to food. Some spices are steeped to make teas. Dried corn husks, used as wrappers for tamales, also fall in this category. Brands that offer a complete line of packets and shaker jars are Badia, Bijol, Cachita, and El Charrito.

ANISEED

Anís. Tiny, khaki-colored seeds that have a slightly sweet licorice flavor with a zesty bite. The seeds can be dry roasted before using to increase the fragrance. Aniseeds are added to sausages, tomato sauces, white bean soups, seafood stews, and clams in wine broth. They heighten the taste of sweet as well as salty dishes. In Peru, aniseed scents and flavors pastel papa, a potato and cheese pie. Layers of cooked, sliced potatoes and slices of cheese are baked in a custardy anise sauce. Anisette and other liqueurs such as pastis, ouzo, raki, arak, and sambuca are flavored with anise. The seeds scent coffee, are steeped as tea, and chewed to freshen the breath.

BAY LEAF

Laurel en hojas. Sold whole and ground into a light olive green powder. Use these aromatic leaves sparingly—one leaf or a small pinch of the powder is enough to impart flavor to a dish. And keep in mind, the longer the leaves cook, the more taste they add. In Latin cuisine, bay leaf is used in meat stews, bean soups, and chicken, vegetable, or fish dishes. A few are added to the marinade for fried, pickled fish called escabeche. Ground bay leaf is added to stuffings and marinades. Whole bay leaves are always removed from a dish and left on the side of one's plate. California bay leaf (long and narrow) can be used interchangeably with Turkish (roundish), but be aware the California leaves are much more powerful.

BLACK PEPPER

Pimenta. Sold as whole peppercorns and ground black or white pepper powders. Whole or crushed peppercorns season meats, stocks, soups, stews, crab boils, pot roasts, marinades, and pickling solutions. Peppercorns are crushed in a mortar with garlic, oregano, and salt and rubbed on meats before roasting or grilling. Ground pepper goes into almost every savory Latin dish, sauce, and marinade and is used as a table condiment. For the best flavor, grind peppercorns as needed. To prevent it from becoming bitter, add ground pepper near the end of cooking. White pepper is made by soaking ripe peppercorns in a saltwater solution to dissolve the outer skin before drying and grinding. While the flavor is in the outer skin, the heat is in the core, making white pepper hotter. It is mainly used in pale sauces and creamy soups to avoid speckling.

Pepper has long been an important spice, used as a tax, currency, and offering to gods. When Rome was being sacked, pepper was used to pay tribute to the invading barbarians. In fact, the insatiable appetite for pepper caused explorers to head out to sea, leading to the discovery of new continents. It was, after all, pepper (and India), that Columbus was after when he "discovered" the Americas.

CINNAMON

Canela entera or canela en rama (whole sticks) or canela molida (powdered). Most cinnamon in Latin markets and supermarkets is actually cassia, the bark of a tropical laurel tree. This is also called Chinese cinnamon and is much harder and darker than true cinnamon. Cassia is also much too hard to grind and will break the blades of a food processor or blender. It dominates the market because it is less expensive to produce, despite having a somewhat bittersweet taste.

Luckily true cinnamon, with its superior flavor, is becoming increasingly available in Latin markets. True cinnamon quills (the inner bark of another tropical laurel) are long—6 inches to a foot—and buff-colored with frazzled ends. Cinnamon's color is a reflection of its quality—the paler the better. It is also soft enough to snap and break into pieces and to grind at home. Cinnamon is used in both savory and sweet dishes. Cinnamon laces many similar cooking sauces throughout Latin America, and has an affinity with beef, pumpkin, and vegetable or oxtail stews. When sticks are added to stews, they should be removed and left at the side of the plate. Whole sticks flavor syrups and milky sauces for

desserts. The sweet side of cinnamon also appears in hot chocolate, creamy rice horchatas (drinks), rice puddings, custards, flans, budín (bread pudding), and cookies.

cinnamon

CLOVES

Clavo. Cloves are sold whole and ground into a russet powder. They're very aromatic with a slightly hot-sweet, sharp flavor. A little goes a long way—too much can overpower a dish. Whole cloves stud roast hams, and are pushed into the onions in boiled dinners and pot roasts. They also flavor and scent marinades, pickling vinegar, and lace syrups with their pungent spiciness. Ground cloves are added to chorizo and blood sausages, beef stews, pickles, marinades, barbecue sauces, vegetables, soups, masa dough for Central American tamales, puddings, fritters soaked in honey syrup, gingerbread, cakes, cookies, and brandy. It is best to buy whole cloves as the powder quickly loses its flavor and fragrance. To check if a clove is good quality, drop it into a glass of water. It should bob vertically; if it floats horizontally or sinks, it is stale. Of course, you cannot tell this until you get home—one reason to buy spices at a store with a high turnover.

CORN HUSKS

Hojas de tamal. These are dried corn leaves for steaming tamales in. The pale, bleached, papery corn husks are sold in the spice section of most Latin markets, in plastic bags of about 18 to 20. Fresh green husks are preferable, but these work when fresh are not available. Dried corn husks have to be soaked before using. Discard any bits of dried silk,

cover with warm water, and steep 30 to 60 minutes. Drain and pat dry. Sort through them and select ones that are at least 5 inches wide across the base and free of rips or holes. They are now ready to pack with prepared masa dough and any fillings you wish to use, from shredded meats in sauce to pieces of cheese. Working one husk at a time, spread flat and place about 2 tablespoons of masa in the center. Push in a bit of filling and with your fingers, pat masa dough up and around the filling. Fold up sides of husks over masa, then lift ends up and over filling. Tie with a thin strip of corn husk or kitchen string to hold it shut.

corn husks

Put tamales, tied ends up and stacked to allow circulation, in a steamer rack set over at least an inch of water. If you have extra soaked husks, line the top of the steamer and sides with them. The goal is to pack the tamales firmly, but not too tight, so they can expand. Steam over medium heat, covered, adding boiling water to the pot as it evaporates, until the masa is firm to the touch and does not stick to the husk—about 45 to 60 minutes. Some cooks prefer to simply drop the bundles of tamales into a pot of boiling water, lower the heat, cover, and simmer for an hour. If made ahead, let tamales cool, wrap in foil or place in a plastic container and refrigerate. Reheat by steaming, about 20 minutes, or zapping in the microwave.

For dried corn husks, look for Badia and La Tamalera in 6-inch bags and La Preferida in 8-ounce packages.

CUMIN

Cumino. Sold as whole seeds or a dark ochre powder. The elongated, curved, pale tan to olive green seeds have a distinctive earthy, cedar-peppery fragrance and warm, toasty, slightly bittersweet flavor. One can hardly imagine Mexican chili con carne or picadillo (spicy ground beef) without it. Cumin seeds flavor sausages, soups, breads, vegetables, meats, and stews. Dry roast and crush the seeds before using them to bring out the full flavor. They can also be sizzled in oil at the start of a recipe with any other spices being used. Ground cumin has slightly less flavor than the whole seeds. Cumin spikes the ground meat mixture for Chilean pasteles de choclo—meat pies topped with corn pudding. Ground cumin also flavors empanada fillings, shrimp and seafood soups, roasted chicken, bean soups, and beef or pork stews.

LINSEED

Linaza, flax, or flaxseeds. Tiny, oval, and shiny brown, linseeds are added to breads and sprinkled over breakfast cereal as a bulking agent and source of fiber in the diet. The seeds can also be boiled, strained, and mixed with honey and lemon as tea to relieve coughs and congestion from colds. Transfer seeds from packet to a jar and store in the refrigerator to prevent oils in the seeds from turning rancid.

NUTMEG

Nuez moscada. Ground nutmeg is called nuez moscada molida. The fragrant nut extracted from the center of the apricot-like fruit of a tropical evergreen gives us nutmeg. Nutmegs are oval, slightly shriveled, and dusty brown. The interior is light brown and speckled. Nutmeg has a peppery-floral aroma and bit-

nutmeg encased in mace

tersweet flavor with fruity overtones. It is best to buy whole nutmegs and grate shavings off as needed—the taste is much superior to the powdered type. Nutmeg seasons both sweet and savory foods, such as sausages, meats, soups, fruit preserves, custards, puddings, and cakes. It adds subtle flavor to potato dishes, eggs, creamed spinach, sauces, onion soup, and marinades, and goes well with milk-based dishes. Avoid combining it with other very aromatic spices or they will clash.

In Argentina, nutmeg and other spices are mixed with vinegar, chopped garlic, peppers, and hot sauce to make a marinade for grilled meats. Try mashing sweet potatoes with a little butter and nutmeg. In Chile, a small pinch of nutmeg is added to cornmeal dumplings cooked in chicken broth. Try to choose nutmegs that are heavy with no visible insect holes—hard to do when dealing with 3 to 4 nuts sealed in little plastic packets. Back home, check for freshness by poking a nutmeg with a needle. An oily droplet should rise to the surface. Grate using a small garlic grater or special nutmeg grater.

PEPPERMINT

Menta. Peppermint is the strongest of all mints so use in small amounts. Dried mint flakes are blackish-green, but some may be brighter green if dehydrated in a microwave prior to packaging. Mint flavors hot and cold soups; sauces; some vegetables, such as fresh fava beans, zucchini, cucumbers, peas, and tomatoes; potato salad; lamb; fish; fruit compotes; ice cream; custards; and juices. It also seasons curries, chutneys, cracked wheat or rice salads, and is steeped and sweetened as tea. In Mexico, pieces of turkey are stewed in a sauce made from pureed chilies, tomatoes, onion, annatto, mint, and cilantro. Try sautéing julienne strips of carrot in butter with a little lemon juice and mint. Steep crushed mint as tea and drink after meals to aid digestion or when you have a cold. Store dried mint in a tightly sealed jar in a dark, dry place and it will retain its flavor up to 2 years.

ROSEMARY

Romero. Dried rosemary resembles short, sage-colored pine needles, has a camphor-like aroma and sharp, resinous flavor. Use sparingly to avoid overpowering the taste of other ingredients. Add to soups, stews, sauce, and marinades, roast with lamb or chicken, and use in creamy seafood dishes. Rosemary is also added to poultry stuffings and sprinkled inside the cavity of whole, cleaned fish before grilling or broiling. Sauté sliced mushrooms and diced boiled potato in olive oil with chopped onions, garlic, and rosemary. Add rosemary to chopped papaya with minced garlic, a pinch of sugar, and a little olive oil as a salsa with grilled fish or lamb.

SESAME SEEDS

Ajonjoli. The tiny, off-white seeds have a nutty, slightly sweet flavor and can be used plain or lightly toasted in a dry skillet. In Latin cuisine, the seeds add crunch sprinkled over various appetizers, salads, slices of cheese, and pasta tossed with butter. Fish fillets can be dipped in

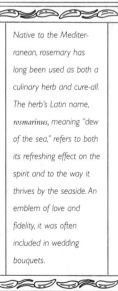

Native to the Mediterranean, rosemary has long been used as both a culinary herb and cure-all. The herb's Latin name, *rosmarinus,* meaning "dew of the sea," refers to both its refreshing effect on the spirit and to the way it thrives by the seaside. An emblem of love and fidelity, it was often included in wedding bouquets.

sesame seeds and pan-fried to create a nutty crust. In Mexico the seeds are ground for cooking sauces such as mole poblano and red or green pipian de ajonjoli. A green pipian is made by frying a paste of ground sesame seeds in oil a few minutes, then adding broth and a pureed mixture of onion, garlic, canned tomatillos, serrano chilies, and cilantro. Poached chicken is then simmered in the sauce. Because more than half the seeds' total weight is oil, they should be stored in a sealed plastic bag or jar and refrigerated to prevent rancidity.

STAR ANISE

Anís estrello. Dried, eight-pointed, star-shaped seed pods. Mahogany in color, each tiny canoe-shaped star point contains a brown bead-like seed. It has an aromatic, anise flavor and is sold and used whole. Star anise is added to meat, rice, curries, and fish soups. The taste is much stronger than aniseed, and only one or two stars are needed to flavor a dish.

VANILLA

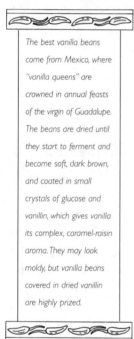

The best vanilla beans come from Mexico, where "vanilla queens" are crowned in annual feasts of the virgin of Guadalupe. The beans are dried until they start to ferment and become soft, dark brown, and coated in small crystals of glucose and vanillin, which gives vanilla its complex, caramel-raisin aroma. They may look moldy, but vanilla beans covered in dried vanillin are highly prized.

Vainilla. Vanilla beans can be used whole, chopped, or ground in a blender. Use vanilla to flavor custards, ice cream, puddings, and sugar syrups for poached fruit. Split them and steep in cold milk or another liquid, then heat the liquid to bring out the flavor. The beans can be used up to four times—remove after each use and store in the fridge in a sealed bag. Vanilla powder or extract is used in tiny amounts in some savory dishes, including black beans in broth and fish soups and with oysters and poultry. Throughout Latin America, fruits are stewed in a dark brown sugar syrup and flavored with vanilla and cinnamon. Vanilla beans are sold in small glass tubes, jars, or pouches. Store in an airtight container at room temperature in a dry place.

vanilla beans

Sauces, Marinades & Salsas

Adobos, Spanish for "marinade," can be wet or dry, and most commercial adobos are the dry, powdered blends. Marinades are always liquid, based on citrus juice, vinegar, or wine. Both are very important elements in Latin cooking and just about every meat, poultry, or seafood dish is prepared in a marinade or adobo prior to cooking. Powdered adobos are used as dry rubs or can be mixed into pastes with a liquid. Sofritos are the base of many dishes, made from finely minced or pureed fresh herbs, garlic, peppers, and onions. Salsas can be made of any combination you can think of. Mojo is a kind of thin salsa, also served with cooked foods, based on citrus juice, minced garlic, and onions. Mojos add pizzazz to bland root vegetables, steaks, roasted chicken, and pork. Mojo criollo is Latin barbecue sauce for seasoning everything from hamburgers to whole roast pigs. Tabasco-like hot sauces are yet another table condiment, used to add extra heat to foods.

ACHIOTE

Annatto. Small, dried, angular seeds used primarily as a food dye. Achiote adds a yellow tint to butter and some cheeses, but has no discernible flavor. To make aciete de achiote (achiote oil), crushed seeds are fried in oil or lard until the oil takes on a bright red-orange hue. The strained oil is used to color rice, paella, stewed or roasted chicken, soups, stews, salt cod dishes, and yuca mashes. Achiotina is a thick, oily paste made from ground achiote seeds, used for frying meats and vegetables or as a base for sofrito.

Achiote is also sold powdered, in small spice jars or packets. Bijol (also a brand of spices) is a bright red-orange powder sold in tiny tins or jars, made from a mixture of fine corn flour, ground cumin, and achiote plus artificial dyes. An even more common product is Sazón and Sazón accent, sold in small boxes containing packets of flavored red powder. This is a powdered form of sofrito with dried herbs and

achiote powder

spices along with achiote for color—but be aware both contain MSG. For achiote seeds, look for Cachita and Badia brands in 1-ounce packets. Goya sells achiote paste in 5- and 10-ounce jars. Goya makes Sazón in small boxes with 8 packets of seasoning powder. Many commercial brands of ground achiote are available.

ADOBO

A seasoning paste or marinade usually made of chilies, garlic, and vinegar. Another type is simply a mix of crushed black peppercorns, oregano, and garlic rubbed on meats, poultry, and fish before cooking. Commercial powdered adobo is made from dehydrated ground onion, salt, garlic, and vinegar. Adobado means marinated and cooked in an adobo sauce.

In Mexico, adobos are dark red, thick, and piquant, made from pureed, dried, and soaked chilies; spices; and just a touch of vinegar. Chunks of pork are marinated in an adobo paste, then grilled over coals. Diluted with broth, the paste can also be used for simmering meats. A mixture of cilantro, bay leaves, cumin, dried oregano, and thyme with chopped onion and garlic pureed with vinegar makes a great adobo. Whisk in some vegetable oil and use as all-purpose marinade for meats. Commercial adobos available in Latin markets pale next to homemade ones. To use, coat the meat or fish in oil then roll it in the mixture or just sprinkle directly on the food. You can also mix the powder with water or broth to make a thick paste and rub it on the meats. Allow it to marinate (dry or paste) a while before cooking to allow the flavors to penetrate. Brands to look for in various-sized shaker jars are Goya, Iberia, El Charrito, and Knorr. Read the labels for specific ingredients in the blends.

MOJO

A citrus juice–based sauce associated with Cuban cuisine, but variations are found throughout South America and the Caribbean. A mojo can be made with grapefruit, lime, sour orange, or lemon juice; chopped herbs; minced garlic; shallots or onions; with additions of salt; ground cumin; red pepper flakes; diced papaya, mango, or pineapple; and olive oil. For a lighter mojo, eliminate the oil. When making a mojo, add the herbs just before serving or the juice will dull the bright color by leaching out the chlorophyll. Mojos are used as marinades, dipping sauces, salad dressings, and as accompaniments to grilled and roasted meats, fried fish, cold seafood,

mojo marinade

and with yuca and other bland root vegetables. Mojo criollo, also called Spanish barbecue sauce, is made with sour orange juice and has a tart and tangy taste. Mojo marinade is similar but thicker, made from a blend of grapefruit and orange juice with vinegar. Mojo is the classic, very thick and chunky sauce with flecks of floating onion and garlic in a tart citrus, vinegar, and olive oil base. This is served as a condiment with boiled or fried yuca, plantains, and roast pork. Commercial mojo criollo, mojo marinade, and thick mojo are all available in bottles.

RECAITO

A thick green sauce made from pureed cilantro, recao, onions, garlic, green peppers, and black pepper. Recaito is used as part of a sofrito base and is also good as a marinade for grilled chicken. To make, process or blenderize half a green pepper, half an onion, 2 cloves of garlic, a hefty pinch of black pepper, and a clump of fresh cilantro with 2 recao leaves (or substitute parsley). The mixture will be a beautiful, bright green color with a slightly coarse texture. Bottled recaito is less flavorful and may contain MSG, modified food starch, and dehydrated garlic and onion. Goya offers it in 6- and 12-ounce jars and frozen in 14-ounce tubs. Conchita, Chef Cesar's, and Iberia are in 12-ounce jars.

recaito seasoning

SALSA

Salsa cruda (fresh, uncooked salsa) or salsa frita (cooked salsa). A table condiment of finely chopped ingredients. Salsas are made from chilies, fresh herbs, tomatoes, roasted corn kernels, black beans, cucumber, cheese, peppers, peanuts, papaya, pineapple, plantain, mango, and coconut in endless combinations, some mild, others fiery hot. Salsas can also be cooking sauces based on tomato, cream, coconut milk, citrus juice, rum, wine, and butter with seasonings. Hot sauces and dipping sauces are salsas.

While every Latin country has some form of spicy salsa, the Mexican markets have the widest range of hot sauces and south-of-the-border salsas. Look for Goya salsa verde (green, based on tomatillos and chilies) in 7-ounce jars. Frontera has hot chipotle, hot roasted tomato, mild jalapeño, and medium-hot tomatillo salsas, all in 16-ounce bottles.

SOFRITO

An aromatic mix of herbs, peppers, and spices. A few tablespoons of the mixture are sautéed in a frying pan or pot and cooked for a minute or so to mingle all the flavors. Next a tablespoon of tomato paste, tomato sauce, or some chopped tomatoes are added. Any sofrito is cooked over low

heat 10 to 15 minutes, and then it is ready to use or store. This serves as the base for countless dishes. The basic Puerto Rican sofrito is made from pureed green bell peppers, garlic, onion, recao, and cilantro. Some cooks also add tomatoes. The benefit of commercial sofritos is their long shelf life—some brands are Pamplona Spanish-style sofrito in 14-ounce cans and Goya in 6-ounce jars and frozen in 14-ounce tubs. Some stores offer freshly made sofrito in the deli case in plastic containers—the next best thing to making your own.

sofrito seasoning

SOUR ORANGE MARINATING SAUCE

Naranja agria. A bottled sauce made from very sour, small oranges, also known as bitter oranges. Mainly used as a marinade for meats, poultry, and seafood, but also splashed into soups and stews and used to season beans, rice, and paella. Can also be mixed with lemon or lime juice in ceviche marinades and is used in mojo and barbecue sauces. Commercial sour orange marinades have sugar, salt, preservatives, and yellow dyes. Some brands include La Lechonera, Kirby, Goya, and Conchita in 12- and 24-ounce bottles. When possible, try to find fresh sour oranges and squeeze your own juice.

sour orange marinade

7

Meat, Fish
& Cheese

Any South American or Mexican store worth its salt will have dark chunks or strips of carne seca, or dried beef. Sausages are in the deli or meat case, in fresh, semi-cured and cured, and dried form. There are dark red chorizo, black blood sausages, and fat salami-like salchichón to select from. If you really don't want to cook, look no further than the freezer cases. Here you'll find ready-made empanadillas, tamales, and croquettes. When it comes to fish, salt cod—those pale, crystallized planks that look sort of fossilized—is a staple of the Latin diet. And all Latin markets have queso blanco, a type of mild, fresh white cheese.

Dried Meat —
Carne Seca

Also called carne de sol, cecina, charque, charqui (pronounced "sharky"), or tassajo. In spite of the ready availability of fresh meat today, salted, dried meat continues to be relished. Meat for carne seca is cut, with the grain, from a lean piece of beef. The meat is liberally salted and dried until stiff and hard. The type most commonly found in Latin markets is sold in small slabs wrapped in cellophane on a tray, resembling petrified wood. The slabs are about an inch and a half thick, often coated in a thin layer of pale yellow beef tallow. The hard, dark meat may have crystallized salt on the exposed sides, giving it a frosted look. Cecina is Mexican beef jerky. The elongated strips are salted and hung in the sun until the surface is dry, then the meat is coated in a mixture of lime juice and crushed black pepper, re-hung, and left to dry completely.

Dried beef has to be de-salted and reconstituted before using. To do this, place meat in a saucepan, cover with water and bring to a boil, and cook about 5 minutes. Depending on the saltiness, repeat the process 3 to 4 more times, using fresh water. During the last water change, reduce heat and simmer 20 minutes or until meat is tender. It can then be cooled and shredded with a fork. Prepared, cooked carne seca has a pleasant chewy texture and somewhat salty, concentrated flavor. Throughout Latin America, dried meat is added to sancocho especial, a boiled dinner similar to pot-au-feu, made for festive occasions—the more ingredients the better. It is always added to feijoãda completa (black beans and mixed meats), the national dish of Brazil. Shredded carne seca is often cooked with potatoes and eggs, and is added to bean dishes.

Most dried meats come in unlabeled packaging, or are sold by the piece at the meat counter. You may have to ask for it if you don't see it. One widely available brand of dried slab beef is Montevideo tassajo from Uruguay, coated in beef tallow and tied with string. Cans of Kirby brand tassajo aporreado include dried meat in tomato sauce. It's heated and served with rice and fried eggs and used as a pizza topping.

Picadillo was the forerunner of a dish you probably ate as a kid, sloppy Joes. This is a mixture of ground beef and tomato sauce served on a squishy hamburger bun. If you thought they were named sloppy Joes because they were messy to eat, guess again. Picadillo, a much spicier take on ground beef with sautéed onions, garlic, raisins, olives, capers, and tomato paste was first served in a Havana bar, then one in Key West, both of which Hemingway frequented. The name of the Key West bar is Sloppy Joes, thus the name of the childhood favorite.

Sausages

Some types and brands of cured Latin-style sausages are nationally distributed, and some stores have a butcher who will make them on site. The following are sausages you may find.

BUTIFARRA

Catalana or Cuban butifarra, these are pale, fresh sausages made from ground pork and spices. They resemble veal bratwurst but are softer, marbled with bits of pork fat and spiced with thyme, parsley, cinnamon, and cloves—but no paprika, so they are considered "white" sausages. Grill, pan-fry, add to bean soup, or casseroles, or fry and slice as part of an appetizer platter with cheese and other sausages. Look for Los Gallequitos, distributed from Union City, New Jersey.

CHORIZO

Chorizo is the famous Spanish-style, rusty red sausage found in various sizes. The spicy, rich flavor comes from ground smoked pork mixed with heavy doses of paprika and garlic. Other seasonings may include ground cumin, crushed coriander seeds, red wine, oregano, ground peppercorns, and crushed red chilies. Chorizo is sold freshly made, semi-cured (semi-soft), and cured (hard). In general, soft chorizo is used in cooked dishes and the hard variety is sliced for cold cuts.

Fresh chorizo can be cooked and eaten right away or dried for later. Semi-soft ones, called semi-curado, are sold in tins or wrapped in plastic on Styrofoam trays. There are catimpalo (cocktail sized) and larger plump, stubby links. These are mainly used in cooking, added to soups and stews, as they sort of melt into the other ingredients. The tiny links, called choricitos, are often fried as an appetizer.

Cured chorizo comes in strings of links, usually dangling from hooks above the meat or deli counter. Longer, cured links are behind glass, laid out in the deli case and sliced by the pound, best served spread out on a plate with cheese, olives, pickles, and bread or used in sandwiches. Mexican-style is made from freshly ground pork, chilies, and paprika and has to be cooked before using. Squeeze the sausage mixture out of the casing, crumble, and sauté with diced potatoes, use to stuff empanadas and quesadillas, or scramble with eggs.

chorizo

When choosing chorizo, look for bright color and store refrigerated once you have opened a vacuum-sealed package. Such packages include Corte's famous "El Baturro" chorizo, sold in a looped link and El Niño, Rio Jano, Diana, Fiesta, Goya, and Quijote brands, all in 3½-ounce packages of 2 links. Quijote also offers chorizo "Exquisito" in a vacuum-sealed link and chistorra-style, long skinny chorizo with 2 looped links. Los Gallequitos has 8-ounce packages of 4 links and offers low-fat chicken chorizo, also with 4 links to a package. El Mino brand has tins of chorizo packed in lard as well as vacuum-sealed packs containing 4 links.

MORCILLA

Blood sausage. Blackish to blackish-red cured sausages made from coarsely ground pork fat, pigs' blood, and rice, seasoned with cinnamon, cloves, and nutmeg, and sometimes onion, aniseed, or fennel. The ones in vacuum-sealed packages have the right dark color, but are a pale imitation in taste. They are always fried or boiled before eating and are often served with fried eggs and hot sauce or are added to boiled one-pot meals, bean soups, beef and chickpea stews, or lentil dishes. Look for El Ebro brand in both 3- and 13-ounce cans, packed in lard, or two small links in vacuum-sealed packages. Also El Asturiano in 12-ounce sardine-type cans.

SALCHICHÓN, LONGANIZA & SALCHICA

Salchichón is a semi-soft, cured log-like sausage. Also called farmer's sausage, this is made from ground pork, pork fat, beef or beef heart, and spices. Slice and serve as an appetizer with cheese or use as a cold cut in sandwiches. Longaniza is a longer, slimmer, version of salchichón. Some Latin markets may also have freshly made longaniza, which has to be cooked before eating. Either type can be cut in pieces and added to soups, bean dishes, or stews. Also good fried or grilled. Sometimes called Argentine sausage, salchicha is a similar mixture of minced pork and spices. It is a fresh sausage, sold in plump links ready to toss on the grill, pan-fry, or use as any Italian sweet sausage. Los Gallequitos brand has 15-ounce, fat 2-inch wide batons of salchichón, and High Top brand sells 14-ounce salchichón sticks. The deli case may have La Primera (and other local brands) salchichón, sold sliced by weight, or salchichón "Lugareno," a classic Spanish-style sausage sold in 8- and 16-ounce vacuum-sealed packages. You might also find La Cena brand smoked salchichón in small stubby sticks.

Frozen Meats

CROQUETTES

Breaded morsels of chicken, cheese, or minced ham. They are deep-fried before freezing and just need to be heated in an oven or microwave. Serve with hot sauce, mustard, or ketchup. Look for Goya and El Sembrador brands in 9.6-ounce boxes, each containing 8 small croquettes.

EMPANADILLAS

Small empanadas, also called pastelillos. These are baked pastry turnovers stuffed with spiced ground beef or American cheese. Heat in an oven or microwave. Look for Goya in 9.6-ounce boxes with 4 beef pies to a box or 12 mini cheese pies.

PAPA RELLENOS

Stuffed potato puffs. Mashed potato dough is filled with a spicy ground beef mixture ready for deep-frying. There are 4 balls to a box. Look for Goya in 11-ounce boxes.

TAMALES

Tomalitos en hoja. Masa dough stuffed with pork and steamed in corn husks. Sold individually and in boxes of 4. Reheat in a steamer for 20 minutes or zap in the microwave. Unfold the corn husk wrappers to eat and serve with hot sauce. Look for Goya, El Sembrador, La Milpa, and Catalina brands.

YUCA RELLENOS

This is sort of a yuca tamale. The plump rolls are made from mashed yuca, stuffed with spiced ground beef or pork. Bake or microwave and serve with hot sauce and garlic-laced mojo. Sold individually wrapped in 5-ounce packages. Look for Catalina and Goya brands.

Dried Fish

DRIED SHRIMP

Camarón seco. Tiny, peeled shrimp preserved in salt brine and dehydrated in the sun, with the heads and tails removed. They are hard and should look plump and be a bright pinkish-orange. Very small ones are fried and sprinkled over rice, vegetable dishes, and salads as a crunchy garnish. Larger shrimp are toasted until crisp to bring out the flavor—to do this, toast in a low oven or in a dry skillet over low heat. They can then be pulverized in a food processor or blender and used to thicken and flavor soups and stews. Whole toasted shrimp are also added to soups, fritters, and vegetable dishes.

Charales are tiny, silvery-white dried fish, mainly used to make fish stock for use in soups and sauces. The fish come from Lake Patzcuaro in Mexico, caught in the wings of butterfly nets manipulated by fishermen on small wooden boats.

Mexican groceries also sell camarón molido—shrimp powder. This pinkish-tan powder is mixed with beaten eggs,

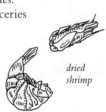

dried shrimp

fried into pancake-like patties, and served with salsa. It is also used as a thickener. Once packets of dried fish, shrimp, or shrimp powder are opened, transfer to a tightly sealed container and store in the refrigerator.

SALT COD

Bacalao or bacalhau in Brazil. Many folks who did not grow up eating crispy salt cod fritters or eggs scrambled with shredded salt cod are put off by the mysterious looking, salt-encrusted pieces and strong smell. But after soaking in several changes of water over a 24-hour period, a transformation takes place. It loses its pungent odor and saltiness and swells up to almost the size it was when fresh. After a brief poaching, it becomes firm, succulent, and tasty.

At one time inexpensive, bacalao now costs about as much as sirloin steak. It ranges from semi-moist to really stiff. The fish in plastic pouches are the moister type and are usually skinless and boneless. The stiff specimens are sold by weight in plastic-wrapped trays. These usually have to be boned after soaking—flake and use your fingers to pick out the bones. After soaking and cleaning, salt cod can be poached and pureed with olive oil, garlic, nutmeg, milk, salt, and pepper as a spread; flaked, seasoned, and blended with flour and deep-fried as fritters; shredded and fried with rice; or sautéed with shrimp and vegetables.

When choosing salt cod, look for whitish pieces as yellowish ones are old and less flavorful. The best quality are not sheathed in plastic, but in the meat/fish counter, sold by the slab. Arctic Moon offers the semi-moist type in 16-ounce bags labeled "sin espinas, sin piel," meaning boneless and skinless—but check the label as some is cod, some Alaskan pollack. Look also for Labrador from Canada in 1-pound bags and La Fe in 14-ounce bags (boneless). You may also find prepared bacalao in cans, ready to use (no soaking). There's also prepared bacalao in 6-ounce sardine type tins in various sauces—garlic, Viscaya-style, and tomato.

SMOKED HERRING

Fillet de arenque. Brownish-gray, salted, smoked herring fillets—no head or tails—about 4 to 5 inches long. The pungent aroma dissipates when soaked and cooked. The fillets are sold by weight, wrapped in plastic on trays. To use in cooked dishes, place several fillets in a saucepan and cover with water, bring to a boil, lower heat and simmer about 10 minutes. Or soak them overnight, changing water once or twice, and boil as described above. Drain, remove spine and small, fine bones—don't worry if some remain, they are soft and can be eaten. Flake the fish and add to soups and stews, mix into steamed rice or sauté in oil with chopped onion, garlic, and tomatoes. To use in salad, do not boil, just remove bones and mash with chopped tomatoes and cucumber, and serve with lettuce.

Cheese —
Queso Blanco

Queso blanco is the ubiquitous farmer's cheese of Latin America. It's a fresh, unripened cheese made from whole or partially skimmed milk. Good quality queso blanco melts easily and looks shiny. It's used for stuffing, layering, and garnishing—stuff pieces into chilies and fry; tuck into tamales; crumble in fillings for empanadas, stuffed bell peppers, enchiladas, and hollowed-out zucchini; and slice and use in quesadillas. Crumble over soups, stews, beans, vegetables, dips, and grilled meats. Slices of queso blanco are paired with cured meats and olives as an appetizer and with fruit preserves or pastries after a meal. Store refrigerated up to a week. Bulging, puffed packages should be avoided—the cheese has started to ferment and turn sour.

If you like cheese that's a little firmer than the traditional queso blanco, look for queso para freir. This fresh, white cheese is sliced and fried or grilled until golden brown—without breading or melting into a messy ooze. It's delicious as a snack, an appetizer with slices of chorizo, or as an accompaniment to a main dish. There are locally made brands of both types of cheese as well as nationally distributed brands.

Notes on other cheeses can be found in the following chapters.

queso para freir

8

Sweet Things

Latin Americans wake up to cups of foaming hot chocolate and often end a meal with sweet fruit preserves and cheese. In between, they snack on caramel-stuffed cookies, and quench their thirst with exotic fruit smoothies. Romance your taste buds with some Latin sweetness—soon you will be licking your lips and saying "bien me sabe," or "it tastes good to me"!

Dulces

CARAMEL

Dulce de leche. Also known as arequipe, cajeta, manjur, and dolce de leite. This is sweetened milk boiled down to a rich, caramel goo that evolved as a way to preserve milk in the days before refrigeration. Made from either cow's or goat's milk or a combination of both. Goat dulce de leche has a rich, slightly musky-caramel flavor. To make caramel, milk and sugar are mixed together and cooked, stirring constantly over low heat until thickened and amber colored, about two hours. Caramel is sold in jars or plastic tubs and used as a dip for sliced fruit; a spread for toast, crackers, and pancakes; and is sandwiched between cookies; stuffed into pastries; or swirled into ice cream.

caramel

Cajeta is a Mexican caramel made from a blend of cow's and goat's milk. Originally packed in thin, slat-wood boxes, travelers bought the boxes of caramel as souvenirs and it became so famous that it was called cajeta de leche quemada, or "boxed burnt milk candy" to differentiate it from all others. Soon the name was shortened to cajeta, which came to refer to all types of Mexican caramel. Brands to look for include Nela in 15-ounce jars, Coronado cajeta made from goat's milk in 11-ounce jars, Coronado wine caramel in 10-ounce jars, and La Paila from Argentina in plain, coconut, and banana flavors in 15-ounce jars. There's also Conaprole, Chimote, and Veronica brands from Argentina.

CHOCOLATE

chocolate tablets

Also called chocolate a la taza (chocolate for the cup). You'll find two kinds of chocolate in Latin markets: bitter, made from refined chocolate liquor and pure cocoa butter, and sweet, with sugar added. Mexican chocolate is flavored with cinnamon and vanilla or ground almonds. The slab type is sold in large, thin bars, scored into tablets to ease breaking, or two ½-inch-thick scored bars packaged back-to-back and wrapped in waxy paper. Mexican chocolate is also sold in six rounds stacked in a stop sign–shaped yellow-and-red box. Cut or break a tablet from a bar of bitter chocolate and add to one cup of water or milk in a saucepan. When the chocolate melts, sweeten to taste with sugar, and whirl in a blender until foamy. To use the sweet type, melt a round or about 6 tablets with 4 cups of milk and sugar to taste, and blenderize.

Chocolate flavors champurrado, a hot beverage made from masa harina (page 28) mixed with water, warm milk, cinnamon, and brown sugar and beaten with a molinillo until thick and creamy. It also appears as an ingredient in Mexican mole poblano and the famous black mole of Oaxaca, both complex sauces made from pureed chilies, nuts, seeds, tomatoes, garlic, cinnamon, and chocolate, used to cook turkey and chicken in. Bitter chocolate is offered by the Corona and Luker brands in thick 8.8-ounce bars. For sweet chocolate, look for Corte, Goya, Menier, Sobrino, and Valor in 8-ounce scored slabs. Corona also makes 17.6-ounce bars. Mexican chocolate is made by the Abuelita and Ibarra brands in 19-ounce boxes of rounds and Popular in 8-ounce flat white boxes of scored tablets.

PANELA

Dulce de atado, panelin, and raspadura. An unrefined, dark brown sugar; in Mexico it is also called piloncillo, and in Chile and Peru it goes by chacaca. Panela una bola means little cones or slabs. Dulce quemando is a brown sugar paste from Colombia. Also sold "dehydrated," ground into a coarse powder. Panela tastes like a mix of molasses and brown sugar and has a dark caramel color. If you can't find it, substitute brown sugar blended with a little molasses. Very hard slabs or cones of panela have to be broken into pieces with a hammer. The chunks can then be grated,

panela

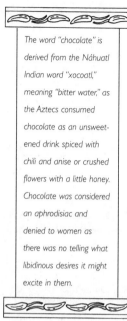

The word "chocolate" is derived from the Náhuatl Indian word "xocoatl," meaning "bitter water," as the Aztecs consumed chocolate as an unsweetened drink spiced with chili and anise or crushed flowers with a little honey. Chocolate was considered an aphrodisiac and denied to women as there was no telling what libidinous desires it might excite in them.

crushed with a rolling pin in a plastic bag, or pulsed in a blender or food processor. To make syrup, melt pieces in water in a saucepan over a low flame with a cinnamon stick. This is drizzled over pancakes, or used to poach fruit in.

The rich flavor of panela blends well in desserts with bland, starchy foods such as yuca, plantains, and bananas. In Puerto Rico, bananas are coated in melted butter, sprinkled with lime juice and grated panela, then drizzled with a liqueur such as Amaretto or Grand Marnier, ignited with a match and brought to the table flaming. Look for Goya piloncillo in 1-pound squares or round cakes, Iberia panelin in 1- and 2-pound blocks, and 8-ounce cones of piloncillo from Mexico. There's also El Sembrador in bags of coarse powder, and San Vincente in 32-ounce lumps, wrapped in dried leaves from El Salvador.

Preserved Fruit

Latin American preserves are also known as dulces and ates or pastas (pastes). There are two types of preserved fruits: chunks, slices, shreds, or shells (cascos) in a clear sugar syrup and pureed, jam-like pastes or translucent jellies.

FRUIT IN SYRUP

These preserves are made by cooking chunks of fruit in a water and sugar syrup until the fruit is soft and the syrup thick. Alimbar on the label means "in syrup." You will find chunks of both green and ripe papaya (fruta bomba or trozos de lechosa), pineapple, mango slices (tajadas de mango), orange segments, guava shells (cascos de guayabana), orange shells (cascos de naranja), and coconut shreds (coco rallado) all packed in syrup. Some are labeled marmalade, but should not be confused with the citrus type we're familiar with. Preserved fruit chunks are poured over ice cream, custard, and puddings. Fruit in syrup is offered by the Ancel and Batey brands in 18-ounce cans, Delifruit is in 20-ounce cans, and Conchita is packed in 16- and 34-ounce cans. Conchita also has dulce de tomate, made from tomatoes.

PASTES

Fruit pastes are pureed fruit cooked with sugar until thick. These are sold in slabs, sealed in plastic; some in cardboard boxes, others in tins or jars. Fruit pastes are also mixed with milk and boiled to make light-colored creams. There are also the creams made from strained fruit pulp, corn syrup, and pectin that resemble slabs of Jell-O—cream in this case meaning paste, not blended with milk. Many are labeled as cajeta and can be clear jellies or milk and fruit creams, not caramel. There are plain bars of guava paste, (guayaba mechada); milky guava paste slabs with a jelly center, jalea de guayaba (guava jelly slabs); and napolitanos, 1-pound triple-layered bars of mango and guava paste with milk cream or guava cream, orange cream, and guava jelly. There are also mango paste and milk cream slabs, called cajeta de mango, and cajeta de leche. Quince paste (membrillo) is packed in decorative round tins as well as in jars and plastic-wrapped slabs. All of these products are eaten as dessert, plain or with cheese or cream. Sliced pieces of guava paste and queso blanco cheese is charmingly called "Romeo and Juliet." Look for La Cubinata brand in 8- and 15-ounce slabs, including milk creams, jellies, quince paste, and napolitano, all in 14-ounce bars and 1-pound boxes. Guava and quince pastes and creams are offered by Ancel, Conchita, Goya, Goiabada, and Versailles brands in various-sized slabs and tins. Castipan brand from Colombia has bocadillo de guayaba, which are bite-sized cubes of guava paste packed with 18 to a 22.8-ounce box. The same brand also has small pieces of guava paste sandwiched between thin sugar wafers. Dulce de batata (white sweet potato paste) is made by Noel and Orienta brands, both in chocolate and vanilla in large round tins.

Fruit Pulps

This is one of the best buys in Latin grocery stores—for less then two dollars, you get 14 ounces of pure, tropical fruit pulp. Just thaw the jewel-toned slabs of pulp and whirl in a blender to make milkshakes, cocktails, or aguas frescas, Mexican-style coolers, literally meaning "fresh waters." To make drinks at home, blenderize a thawed fruit pulp of choice with water and crushed ice and a little sugar or lemon or lime juice. Try mixing and matching fresh fruit and pulps. Watermelon and mamey are delicious together as is fresh cantaloupe with soursop, or strawberries with blackberry pulp. You can select from annon (soursop), grated coconut (good blended with pineapple for drinks or for making puddings, cakes, and other sweets), guava, mamey, mango, morro (blackberry), papaya and passion fruit (often labeled parchita or maracuya), pineapple, tamarind, and tomato de arbol (tree tomato).

The slabs of pulp are about 4 inches by 6 inches and ½ inch thick. Brands to look for are Canoa in 16-ounce packages and Frupa, La Fe, El Sembrador, and Goya in 14-ounce slabs.

Pulps are also a way to experience unusual fruits that are rarely found fresh, and some particularly interesting fruit pulps follow.

frozen fruit pulp

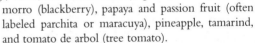

BOROJO

Borojoa patinoi. These coffee-colored, small round fruits have fleshy seeds and dark orange pulp with a sweet-tart flavor, sort of like lemonade mixed with sugarcane juice. Very refreshing as a cooler, blended with water, sugar, and ice; or whirled with mango, pineapple, or strawberries. Borojo is only exported as a pulp or as jalea (jelly). This is a dark blackish-brown paste sold in 18.5-ounce jars under the Borovalle label.

CURUBA

Also called banana passion fruit and known as banana poka in Hawaii. It is called curuba de castilla in Colombia, tasco or tausco in Ecuador, parcha in Venezuela, tumbo in Bolivia, and tumbo delnorte or tintin in Peru. These are a large type of passion fruit that grow on climbing vines. The aromatic pulp, salmon to yellow-orange in color, tastes like a tart cross between passion fruit and mango. Blenderize curuba pulp with sugar and milk or use in gelatin desserts or to flavor ice cream or sherbet. Delicious whirled with pineapple or blended into whipped cream. The sweetened pulp can also be boiled down into a sauce for topping ice cream.

LULO

Also called lulu and naranjillo, meaning "little orange" or lulun in Mexico and naranjita de quito in Peru. This fruit's flesh is translucent green or yellowish, very juicy, and slightly acidic with a floral-citrus aroma and pineapple-lemon flavor. Add the green pulp to blender drinks, mixed with a little sugar and apple or pineapple juice. Also good whirled with banana or honeydew melon. The fruit is also sold canned—look for the Solo Fruta brand from Ecuador in 20-ounce cans; Tropifruit in 26-ounce jars, halved in syrup; and La Fe in 18-ounce jars.

lulo

Part 2

CUISINES BY COUNTRY

9

The Mexican Market

Mexican food is a culinary fiesta, a celebration of flavors born in the collision of two cooking worlds—the native Indians and the Spaniards. While Mexican food may be the most popular Latin cuisine in America, it is also the least understood. Combo plates smothered in goopy melted cheese and sour cream do not represent the incredibly complex and varied repertoire found in Mexico and sophisticated Mexican restaurants in this country. In addition to native fare, products from Central America and Colombia are often stocked in Mexican grocers, and I'll discuss them in this chapter. With the vast supply of ingredients found in Mexican markets, and a sense of adventure, you can recreate authentic Mexican flavors in your kitchen.

Masa —
Mexico's Dough
of Life

MASA DOUGH

This is the mixture of ground hominy used to make tortillas and tamales. You can make it yourself from soaked mote (page 28), but it is much easier to buy pre-cooked masa harina labeled "harina pre-cocida" and mix it with water into a soft dough. You can also find masa para tamales, used to make tamales in Mexican markets. There is plain masa as well as chili, pineapple, and strawberry flavored.

PINOLE

Harina de pinol. Another cornmeal product popular in Mexico and Central America, made from dried, toasted, and ground corn kernels. The pale powder is used to thicken sauces for cooking chicken and turkey. Pinolillo is cornflour with spices added, used as a thickener and to make drinks. Pinole is also sold blended with cinnamon, sugar, and spices. To use, mix a few teaspoons in a glass of water or milk to make a creamy drink. Look for Proinca brand pinolillo instant spiced corn mix in 12-ounce bags. Pinole Mexicano is sold in 15-ounce bags, flavored with cinnamon, cloves, and allspice and sweetened with sugar for hot or cold drinks.

CORN TORTILLAS

Tortillas de maiz. Good corn tortillas should be a creamy off-white or pale yellow. If they are very thin and floppy, the masa was cut with wheat flour to help them stay soft and flexible. Cook the tortillas on both sides in a dry skillet or griddle and keep warm in a tortilla warmer.

corn tortillas

Fresh corn tortillas are used to make tacos. A taco can be soft, made from a warm cooked tortilla, or can be fried in a little oil until softened, folded with a filling, and fried on the other side until crispy—then shredded lettuce, sliced avocado, onions, and tomatoes or sour cream can be slipped in. Tacos can also be filled with steamed, flaked fish; crab; or shrimp. Enchiladas, meaning "chilied tortillas," are tortillas rolled up with a filling, covered with sauce and baked, sometimes topped with cheese. Tortillas are also layered with chili sauce, grated cheese, shredded chicken, and tomato sauce to make casseroles. Day-old tortillas are used to make chilaquiles, meaning "broken sombreros." The tortillas are torn into pieces and fried until golden (but not crispy), layered in a pot with crumbled cheese and tomato sauce, and simmered in chicken broth with hot sauce until the liquid is absorbed. They can be served garnished with sour cream, crumbled fried chorizo, onion rings, and lime wedges. To make chips, cut tortillas into quarters and allow to dry for a day or two, then fry in hot peanut oil and sprinkle with salt.

Did you know that tortillas have two sides? They have a distinct inside and outside that determine which direction the tortilla is best folded around a filling. The side with the thinner layer, called the pancita, or belly, should face the inside when folding the tortilla. If the outside of a tortilla cracks with pieces flaking off, it has no doubt been folded with the pancita on the outside, not inside.

Corn tortillas are sold in stacks of about 36 five-inch circles, wrapped in paper if fresh from a tortillería, or in sealed plastic or twist-tied bags. Check your nearest Mexican market for locally made brands. Pre-made, folded taco shells are also widely available, but are never as good as freshly fried ones. Use finely cut, fried tortillas in the tortilla-lime soup recipe, page 242.

Antojitos

Corn tortillas or masa dough are also used to create many Mexican antojitos, or "little whims," served as appetizers or snacks. Some favorites follow:

HUARACHES

Large, flattened corn cakes filled with a layer of pureed black beans and fried, then topped with a spicy sauce and crumbled cheese. The name refers to the sandal-like shape.

PANUCHOS

Small tortillas cooked until they puff into little balloons, slit and stuffed with mashed beans, hard-boiled egg slices, shredded meat, and pickled onions.

TAMALES

Packets of masa dough wrapped in corn husks or banana leaves and steamed or boiled. Breakfast tamales are stuffed with fruits, nuts, sweet beans, or caramel, while others hold bits of meat, cheese, olives, pork cracklings, cactus strips, fresh corn, chilies, or seafood. Tamales are party and festival fare, made anytime family and friends gather together. For tips on making tamales, see pages 63–64.

TORTILLAS RELLENAS

Stuffed tortillas. A meat mixture is rolled up in a corn tortilla, secured with a toothpick, dusted in flour, dipped in beaten egg batter, and deep-fried, served with salsa and avocado slices.

TOSTADAS

Also called totopos, these are fried corn tortillas topped with refried beans, shredded meat, grated cheese or sour cream, lettuce, tomatoes, onions, and avocado slices—sort of a meal on an edible plate. You can make your own or buy them pre-fried (or baked), in stacks, wrapped in cellophane. The Charras brand sells 36 tostadas to a 14-ounce package, offering plain, jalapeño, and chipotle flavors. Los Pericos brand with three parrots on the 5-ounce packet has 10 crispy plain tostadas.

tostadas

FLOUR TORTILLAS

Tortillas de harina de trigo. Flour tortillas are usually larger than corn tortillas, averaging 7 to 8 inches across with 10 to a package.

Fajita-size are smaller, about 6 inches, and burrito-size range from 8 to 10 inches. Flour tortillas are the bread of northern Mexico, where wheat is the main crop.

Flour torillas should be served warm with a meal for tearing and scooping up foods. They're used for fajitas—filled with strips of grilled steak, and served with salsa, grilled onions, and guacamole. Burritos and chimichangas are tubular "sandwiches" made from flour tortillas folded up with beans, rice, shredded meat, and cheese. The difference is that chimichangas are deep-fried, and usually smaller than burritos. Both are served with salsa, avocado slices, sour cream, and radish slices. Quesadillas are two flour tortillas with a layer of cheese and chilies in the middle, cooked on both sides in a dry skillet until the cheese melts, then cut in wedges. Nationally distributed brands of flour tortillas include Azteca in 14-ounce packages of 8 super size or 10 larger burrito-size and 13-ounce packs of 10 fat-free tortillas labeled "buena vida," or the good life. Check for locally made brands in your area. To make your own, invest in Quaker's Harina Preparada para Tortillas, or prepared tortilla flour, in 4-pound bags. All you do is add water. Flour tortillas are used in the fajitas recipe on page 257.

Sauces & Condiments

MOLE

Pronounced molay, this is considered the national dish of Mexico. Mole is a smooth sauce made from a ground paste of many ingredients, but which always includes chilies. Modern Mexican cooks buy pre-made mole pastes in mounds at the central market or in handy jars off the shelf. Moles made from scratch are always sizzled in hot lard or oil before making the cooking sauce. This tempers and blends the flavors, and assures the sauce will not have a raw taste. To cook with store-bought mole pastes, thin with broth or water and constantly stir before adding the poached or boiled meat, lower the heat and then simmer 10 to 15 minutes until the sauce and meat are melded together. While most are used for cooking, some are used as a marinade. Brands to look for are Adelita, Doña Maria, La Costana, La Preferida, and Rogelio in 8-ounce jars. Also Juanita's and Embasa in 15- and 17-ounce jars—these are ready to use, already mixed with liquid. You just need to heat and add cooked meat.

ADOBO MOLE

A thick, dark reddish-brown paste made of ground ancho chilies, sesame seeds, peanuts, cracker crumbs, sugar, garlic, onion, and spices. Adobo mole is thinned with broth and a little vinegar and used to marinate pork chops or other meats before grilling or roasting. Warm tortillas are dipped in adobo mole sauce and rolled up with meat or cheese to make enchiladas.

GREEN MOLE

Mole verde or mole verde de pepitas. Based on toasted, ground pumpkin seeds (pepitas), sesame seeds, peanuts, poblano chilies, tomatillos, cilantro, toasted bread crumbs, salt, and spices. Blend a few tablespoons of paste in broth, adding a little sugar if desired (many Mexicans like their moles quite sweet), bring to a boil, stirring constantly with a wooden spoon, lower heat and simmer with pre-cooked chicken or turkey meat. Meatballs and duck are also good simmered in green mole sauce. You may also find hot green mole, kicked up a notch with the addition of ancho chilies.

green mole

RED MOLE

Mole rojo or pipian rojo. This is a dark mahogany paste made from ancho, pastilla and mulato chilies, ground sesame seeds, toasted bread crumbs, cinnamon, and spices with a hot, rich flavor. Thinned into a sauce, this is good for seasoning beans or for simmering cooked pork, beef, chicken, or meatballs in. Use on enchiladas or top with fried eggs.

PIPIAN

pipian mole

A reddish-brown, thick paste made from roasted, ground pumpkin seeds, ancho chilies, peanuts, sesame seeds, breadcrumbs, salt, sugar, cumin, cinnamon, garlic, and onion. Thinned with broth, pipian sauce is used to simmer cooked chicken, turkey, or pork in. It is also mixed into masa dough for spicy tamales, as an enchilada sauce, and to season both rice and beans. You can also whip up a quick pipian by simmering a large can of Mexican hot tomato sauce with a tablespoon or two of creamy peanut butter and a pinch of sugar, salt, and cinnamon. Add cooked meat and simmer for about 10 minutes.

MOLE POBLANO

This is the famous chili sauce of Puebla, the most complicated mole of all. Commercial mole poblano is a dark chocolate brown color, made from mulato, ancho, and pasilla chilies; ground almonds; peanuts; sesame seeds; cracker crumbs; cinnamon; cloves; anise; salt; sugar; and cocoa. Mole poblano is thinned with broth and used to simmer poached chicken and turkey in, often with raisins added. This mole is associated with festivals, and no posada (Christmas celebration) would be complete without turkey cooked in mole poblano and tamales. If you buy only one type of mole, get this one.

HOT SAUCE

Salsa picante. If you like hot zing, most any hot sauce will fire up your taste buds. Shake a few drops into soups and stews; dribble over rice, beans, eggs, chicken wings, grilled meats, and seafoods; blend into sour cream for dips; drizzle into tacos, tostadas, fajitas, and ceviche. Serve at the table with empanadas, tortilla chips, tamales, and fritters. Hot sauces are made from a thin puree of hot peppers with salt, herbs, spices, sugar, and often vinegar for tang.

mexican hot sauce

Some brands to try are Cholula in 2-ounce and larger bottles. This is a thin, bright orange sauce and has a pleasant, lingering after-taste once you recover from the initial jolt. Tapatío is in 5- and 10-ounce bottles and has a tangy, spicy flavor. Valentina is another vivid orange salsa picante, a little like wing sauce, sold in 12-ounce bottles—there is also a brick-red extra hot type. Bufalo brand offers dark red jalapeño hot sauce in 13.8-ounce bottles and a smoky chipotle hot sauce in 5.8-ounce bottles. Other generic hot sauces are offered by the Country Sweet and El Rio Grande labels.

ENCHILADA & TACO SAUCE & SALSA

All of these are sauces based on red chiles and tomato sauce or green chilies and tomatillos (green husk tomatoes) and range from mild to hot. Taco sauce is a slightly coarse thick puree; enchilada sauce is thinner and smoother and is best heated in a saucepan before dipping warm tortillas in it, filling and rolling them up and covering in more sauce prior to baking. Enchilada sauce can also be used in tacos, burritos, flautas, and any other sauced Mexican dish or on hamburgers, roasted chicken, rice, and scrambled or fried eggs.

green salsa

Salsa is a red or green chunky sauce made from chopped chilies and tomatoes or tomatillos. Serve with chips, fried foods, soups and stews, pasta, and fajitas; use in enchiladas or tacos; toss with pasta; or use as a pizza topping. Salsa verde is a blend of jalapeños and tomatillos. Salsa casera, or "homestyle," is a mix of tomato, onion, serrano chilies, and seasonings—sometimes this type is labeled as salsa ranchero or "country style." Salsa de chili fresco is Mexican tomato sauce laced with chili, onion, garlic, and spices. Chili ancho salsa means a hot tomato sauce, made with ancho chilies. Any of these products can be used interchangeably in many Mexican recipes. La Victoria,

chili salsa

Pace, and El Paso brands have green and red, mild, medium, and hot taco sauces in bottles. Frontera Gourmet brand has tomatillo salsa made from roasted green husk tomatoes, slow-cooked garlic, serrano chilies, and cilantro, great with grilled fish or meats. La Preferida offers chipotle chili cooking sauce and salsa and milder ancho sauce in 8-ounce bottles. Check for other brands in your region.

CANNED CHILIES

A handy alternative to fresh or dried chilies, canned chilies are pureed for sauces and moles. Some are packed in thick spicy adobo sauces for extra body and flavor. Whole serrano, chipotle, and jalapeño chilies are widely available in cans. There are also canned large green chilies, good for stuffing to make chili rellenos. Goya brand has whole chipotle chilies in adobo and jalapeños in brine, both in 7-ounce and larger cans. Adelita has whole serrano and chipotle

canned chilpotle peppers

chilies in small cans. El Pato has green jalapeños in sauce in 7-ounce cans while La Costena offers 7-ounce cans of jalapeños in brine.

Pickled & Brined Goods

PIQUIN PEPPERS

Also called chiltepe or chili pequin, these are tiny green, oval-shaped chili peppers, less than ¼ inch long, but plump for their size, packed in a vinegar and water brine. These are very hot—use with caution! Pickled piquin adds provocative tang and heat when added with a splash of the vinegar solution to soups and stews. They are served as a table condiment or tucked into tacos and tamales. Look for Miguel's brand in 8-ounce jars and Goya in 2-pound jars, also Maria's in 16- and 32-ounce jars.

NOPALITOS

Peeled, processed nopal cactus pads, cut in thick strips and preserved in brine. They have a somewhat oily texture and tangy green bean taste. The type in jars is superior to canned strips, which have a stronger briny flavor. Both need to be drained and rinsed well. Add to taco and quesadilla fillings, salads, pork stews, and egg dishes. Chop and sauté in butter with onions, tomatoes, and whipped eggs, and serve with a sprinkling of crumbled queso blanco. My friend Roberto once made a cactus cake with nopalitos and cactus liqueur mixed into the batter. In addition to the store-bought, you can prepare your own from fresh cactus paddles sold in the produce section; see page 102. For a cactus and tuna salad recipe see page 240.

Dry Seasonings

PICO DE GALLO

A mix of powdered chilies, salt, and spices. It is used to make a highly seasoned relish—blended with chopped onions, fresh chilies, and tomatoes—served as a table condiment. Pico de gallo is also the name of a relish made from sliced jícama and oranges seasoned with chili powder and salt. The powdered type can also be used to season salsas and guacamole or sprinkled on slices of jícama or green mango with a squeeze of lime juice as a snack. Look for Durango brand in 4-ounce shaker jars or make your own by blending together chili powder or hot paprika with salt and a dash of toasted and ground cumin seeds.

POLLO ASADO MIX

A blend of chili powder, salt, cumin, and garlic powder sold in shaker jars. It is sprinkled on chicken, seafood, and meats before grilling or roasting. It is very similar to powdered adobo (see pages 66–67). Look for Durango brand in 4-ounce jars.

RECADO

Also spelled as reaudo, this is a crumbly brick or sticky dark square of paste wrapped in plastic. In Mexican markets, it is found in the spice or mole section, often just labeled with a sticker. All types are based on sour orange juice or palm vinegar mixed with ground oregano, ancho or poblano chilies, annatto seeds, garlic, and salt. There are three main types: recado rojo, red and rich with annatto, used in soups, stews, and masa for tamales; recado bistec, a grayish-green seasoning for beef and fried, pickled chicken called escabeche Oriental; and the black chilmole, also called recado negro. The last is the most commonly found type and is also labeled recardo. This flavors and colors soups, stews, sauces for simmered meatballs, and stuffings for turkey.

To use, dilute a little of the crumbly paste with vinegar and rub it on chicken or meats before stewing to add color and flavor to the liquid.

Nuts & Seeds

Known as nueces and semillas in Spanish. Both nuts and seeds are toasted and finely ground to thicken sauces. They also are used in baked goods, candies, drinks, and desserts. Shelled nuts and seeds are sold in bags or small packets and are widely available in Mexican markets, supermarkets, and health food stores. Refrigerate nuts and seeds to keep them from going rancid.

ALMONDS

Almendra. Almonds are sold whole and in blanched slices and slivers. Powdered almonds are used in horchata, a sweet drink made by grinding blanched almonds, soaking the mixture in water with lemon or orange peel 3 to 4 hours, straining through a cloth, squeezing the almond pulp to extract the milky liquid, and sweetening to taste. It is best served chilled over crushed ice. Some markets sell amendrado, almond-flavored gelatin pudding, in clear plastic cups in the dairy case.

PECANS

Pecana. Pecans are used ground in sauces, toasted or candied in salads, and in various sweets and baked goods. Ternera en nogada is veal stew meat cut in pieces, simmered in stock, drained, and cooked in a sauce made from toasted pecans pureed with the seasoned stock, with sour cream whisked in just before serving. Ground pecans flavor rich butter cookies called pastelitos de boda, or bride's cookies.

PINENUTS

Piñones. In Mexico, pinenuts are often paired with pineapple or are toasted and pureed with broth for meat sauces. The nuts are chopped and folded into sweetened whipped cream with candied cherries and pineapple chunks, spooned into hollowed-out pineapples and refrigerated a few hours before serving so the cream can set. Ground pinenuts are also mixed with condensed milk, sugar, and egg yolks and baked in custard dishes with a layer of carmelized sugar and decorated with pinenuts to make a creamy flan.

PUMPKIN SEEDS

Pepitas. Very small ones are called chincillas. The smooth, oval green seeds are toasted and ground for moles, pipians (a type of mole), and thickening sauces, and are added to corn gruels called pozoles. Cooked pork is simmered with cactus strips, green beans, and zucchini in a puree of tomatillos, pork broth, chilies, onion, garlic, and pumpkin seeds. Whole shelled seeds are mixed with boiled sugar syrup to make palanqueta, a hard candy similar to peanut brittle. Brilliant pink and orange bars made from soaked, ground pumpkin seeds, grated carrots, and milk simmered with sugar and cinnamon can be found in the sweets box at the check-out counter.

pumpkin seeds

WALNUTS

Nuez de castilla. Walnuts are finely ground for sauces, often mixed with other nuts, and also flavor cakes, candies, and cookies. The best known Mexican dish using walnuts is chiles en nogada—large, roasted, peeled, and seeded poblano chilies (or bell peppers) are stuffed with a spicy ground meat mixture and baked, served in a white sauce made from softened cream cheese blended with milk, chopped walnuts, and almonds, and garnished with ruby red pomegranate seeds.

The Butcher Counter

In Mexico, no part of any animal is wasted, so be prepared to view various innards in a Mexican market. Mexican meat cutters traditionally slice with the grain, making the meat easier to shred lengthwise after cooking. Meat is used sparingly in most dishes. Party food, however, goes whole hog, meaning roasted pigs, kid, and huge hunks of marinated and roasted meats.

Remember all meats and poultry have to be USDA inspected to be sold in the U.S. The same standards apply to the Mexican market as to any supermarket. Just the type of cut and names are unfamiliar. In Mexico, as anywhere, the tenderest cuts of meat are grilled in a simple, straightforward manner, but a cook's ingenuity is displayed in the preparation of tougher, but often more flavorful cuts.

Beef

In Spanish, beef is called carne de res. Commonly found cuts of beef are listed below, including organs and innards. You can also ask to have large pieces cut to your specifications.

AGUAYON

Top butt steak (rump) cut into thin steaks—ask for any thinness you want, indicating with your index and thumb if language is a problem. Pan-fry or grill with barbecue or hot sauce, cut into strips for fajitas, or bread and fry for steak sandwiches. This is one of the lean cuts used to make cecina (Mexican beef jerky).

ARRACHERA

Inner skirt steak. A 16- to 20-inch-long flank steak, about ¾ inch thick. Cut into small pieces and sauté with onions and peppers and use to fill tacos and burritos. Flank steak is good for making ropa vieja ("old clothes"). Stew and shred the meat so it looks like tattered rags and sauté with chopped onions, tomatoes, chilies, and beaten egg. Serve with rice or rolled up in tortillas.

ARRACHERA CON CUERO

Outer skirt steak, cut outside the rib and muscle dividing the lung and liver. Cuero means skin, or the thin tissue (also called entrada) covering the diaphragm. This cut has a lot of marbling, is not as tough as inner skirt steak, and is cut crosswise into varying degrees of thickness. Best used cut in thin strips for fajitas or brushed with a spicy sauce and grilled, pan-fried, or charbroiled.

BOLA ENTERA

Whole sirloin tip cut from the hind part, about 7 to 8 inches in width. This is sliced into very thin "minute" or sandwich steaks called bistec de bola. The steaks are sold pre-cut, or you can have the butcher slice them for you. As this is a very lean cut, grill or pan-fry the steaks quickly, seasoned with salt, pepper, chili powder, and a squirt of lime juice.

CALLOS

Tripe. Cows have three stomachs, each producing a slightly different tripe. From the first comes the smoothest, called regular or callo (pronounced "cayo"). The smaller second stomach produces honeycomb tripe—probably the most familiar, and also called corral. From the third stomach comes libro, or "book tripe," which looks a bit darker than other tripes. All three kinds are blanched, thus partially cooked. Look for white or creamy off-white tripe with a pleasant aroma. Before cooking, soak 10 minutes in cold water, rinse, roll up, and cut into 1-inch squares. They can be marinated and grilled as an appetizer or added to soups and stews.

CHAMORO

Arm roast. Cut from the upper shoulder and is a type of chuck, sold in thick slabs with a piece of bone and some marbling. Good for pot roast or stews. Cover the meat with cold water, bring to a boil, cover, and simmer about 3 hours. Save the broth and chop or shred the meat and use in any number of recipes.

chamoro

COJONES

Also called huevos de toro ("bull's eggs"), creavillas de toro ("balls of the bull"), or calf fries. These are the testicles of a bull, resembling small pink, smooth eggs. Considered a delicacy, they are thinly sliced and deep-fried or added to soup. They are tender, delicate, and taste a little like sweetbreads. Each testicle is enclosed in a sac of skin with a tiny opening. Pull the opening apart to expose the soft membrane-covered part inside. Cut the skin away with a knife, leaving the membrane intact.

COLA DE RES

Oxtail. These are the sliced, round segments of steer and cow tails, mainly used in soups. The oxtails are simmered in water with a little vinegar, cinnamon, garlic, allspice, salt, and pepper for about 2½ hours, then chopped tomatoes and several chorizo sausages removed from their casings are added and the soup is cooked another 30 minutes with a few tablespoons of masa harina stirred in as a thickener just before serving.

CORAZONES DE BECERRO

Veal hearts. Smaller and more tender than beef hearts. Trim and cut into small pieces and marinate overnight in sauce made from ground, soaked chilies, garlic, cumin, salt, pepper, wine vinegar, and a little oil. Grill the hearts, brushing with sauce as they roast. Beef hearts, called corazones de res, are larger, weighing almost 4 pounds. They are also cut into small squares, marinated, and grilled.

COSTILLA DE RES

Beef ribs. The three middle ribs, also called short ribs, cut very thin.

GUISAR

Lean chuck cut in chunks for stew. Also used to make chili con carne.

guisar

HÍGADO DE RES

Beef liver. Usually cut into small slices and seasoned with salt, pepper, and crushed garlic and left to marinate in red wine at room temperature for several hours. It is then drained, saving the marinade, patted dry on paper towels, and sautéed in melted butter for a few minutes, making sure both sides are cooked. The marinade is reduced in a small saucepan and served over the liver on a bed of steamed rice.

HUESO DE RES

This simply means beef soup bones. Boil and strain the liquid for beef stock and sauces.

LENGUA

Beef tongue. Wash the tongue and cover with water in a large pan. Add sliced onions, a bay leaf, and pinch of salt. Bring to a boil, skim off any foam, lower heat, cover, and simmer until the tongue is tender, about 3 hours. Leave in the broth until cool enough to handle, lift out and remove skin and any bones or bits of fat, and cut into slices. The slices can now be simmered in any number of sauces, from a hot chili sauce to a complex mole.

LOMO

Rib eye steak. You can have the butcher cut slices off the steak to any thickness. The thin slices are fairly tender, good for grilling or cutting into small strips and sautéing with onions and seasonings for fajitas or taco and burrito fillings.

MOLLEJA DE RES

Sweetbreads. This is the thymus gland of calves consisting of two parts, a central lobe known as the heart sweetbread and two lateral lobes known as the throat sweetbread. They have a delicate flavor and are very tender. To prepare them, soak 2 to 3 hours in lightly salted water, changing the water several times. Blanch 6 to 7 minutes in boiling water to firm them up for easier handling. When cool enough to handle, remove the membranes, veins, and any surrounding fat, and pat dry. Sweetbreads can be grilled, sautéed, braised, or breaded and fried, then served in a hot sauce or creamy almond puree. Don't overcook or they will dry out.

PULPA

Inside round, similar to top round. A lean cut, large pieces can be marinated and roasted. Thin slices are good grilled or cut in small strips and stir-fried with onions and seasonings for taco, burrito, and fajita fillings. Bistec de pulpa are steaks. These are prepared country style (ranchero), seasoned with salt and pepper and minced garlic, seared on both sides, then placed in an ovenproof dish. The steaks are covered with sliced potatoes and hot tomato sauce is poured over the meat and potatoes. Strips of roasted, peeled Anaheim chilies are laid on top. The dish is baked, covered, for 30 minutes, then uncovered for another hour, until the potatoes are browned and the sauce reduced.

RINONES

Kidneys. Multi-lobed, knobby, dark reddish-brown organs. Calves' kidneys are lighter in color, smaller and more tender, while the large beef kidneys can be tough with a strong, bitter taste. They should be plump and shiny with no ammonia-like smell.

SESOS

Beef brains. Pale grayish-pink crenulated lobes with fine red veins. They have a delicate flavor and soft, slightly chewy texture. To prepare, soak the brains for 30 minutes in cold salted water, changing the water several times. Remove the thin outer membrane and fine veins and blanch 15 to 20 minutes in salted, boiling water with a little lemon juice or vinegar added. Plunge brains into cold

In Mexico, ground beef is used to make albóndigas (meatballs), often mixed with ground pork, breadcrumbs, an egg, and seasonings. The meatballs are gently simmered in broth, green mole, or tomato and chipotle chili sauce. The poaching gives them a delicate, springy texture and they absorb the flavors of the sauce or broth they are cooked in.

water, remove, and pat dry. Blanched, chopped-up brains are stuffed into soft tacos with sliced onions, chopped cilantro, and hot sauce.

Pork

The Spanish name for pork is carne de cerdo but it is also called puerco. Common cuts of pork found in Mexican markets follow. Although pork loin is probably the favorite, shoulder is just as good and more economical, although it needs a little longer cooking time.

BUCHE DE PUERCO

Pork stomach. Cleaned, pale white, soft folds of the pig's tummy is often called Mexican soul food. It is cut into small squares and added to hearty stews, pozole, and carnitas—pork bits and pig parts cooked in lard until soft inside and crusty on the outside. Small pieces can be marinated and grilled.

CHULETAS DE CENTRO

Center cut pork chops. Pan-fry and serve in creamy nut sauce or green mole, also good brushed with hot sauce and grilled. In the coastal regions along the Gulf of Mexico, pork chops are browned in lard, then simmered in sherry and meat broth with chunks of pineapple and fresh mint.

CHULETAS DE PUERCO

Thinly cut end pork chops. Thin pork chops can be seasoned and pan-fried or added to stews. Very thin chops are breaded and fried for sandwich fillings.

CHULETA CON CUERO

Pork steaks with the skin on. A thick, rubbery rind and layer of white fat surrounds the edges and becomes crunchy when the steak is fried. Deep-fry or pan-fry in at least an inch of oil and serve with a sour orange sauce to counter the fattiness along with sliced onions, pickled chilies, and sliced radishes.

chuleta con cuero

COSTILLA DE PUERCO

Spare ribs. Simmer with a chopped onion, garlic, peppercorns, and salt, then cook in a green mole until very tender. Have the butcher cut them into serving-size pieces.

LOMO DE PUERCO

Also called lomo de cerdo, these are butterflied pork loin chops or steaks. They are sautéed in oil or lard and baked in almond sauce. Poblano-style means pork loin marinated in a puree of chilies, mint, oregano, garlic, cumin, cinnamon, and dry red wine, then simmered in the sauce over low heat until tender, about 2 hours. They can also be stuffed and baked in a creamy nut sauce or spicy salsa. Make the stuffing from breadcrumbs with grated cheese or apple chunks, raisins, and olives.

PATA DE PUERCO

Pork feet. The feet are boiled, the bones removed, and inner muscles dipped in egg and fried to make lampriados. You will find pickled pork feet (labeled patas en vinegre) and pickled pork skin in jars of brine. These are often nibbled with drinks or tossed into the soup pot.

PORK SKIN

Cuero de puerco. Pieces of fresh pork skin are added to carnitas meaning "little meats," pickled or dried, and deep-fried to make chicharrónes, or pork cracklings. Most stores sell homemade ones or bags of commercially made, curled, puffed crisps.

PUERCO PARA FREIR

Literally, "pork to fry," this is used to make carnitas. Various cuts are used, including fresh or picnic ham, ribs, butt, and shoulder cuts. The meats are cut into 3-inch cubes, salted, and placed in a pot of hot, melted lard—the lard completely covering the meat. With the heat high, a bottle of cola is added, along with a head of garlic cut in half, the juice of two oranges, plus the peels of several limes, a big chopped onion, and a few crushed bay leaves. This is stirred every so often, so the meat doesn't stick, and cooked about 1½ hours or until the liquid becomes concentrated. The meat bits are removed and drained and should have a dry, crispy exterior with a moist, succulent interior. Carnitas are served hot with rice, beans, pickled onions, salsa, and fresh tortillas or can be used as a filling for tacos and burritos. Most Mexican groceries make their own.

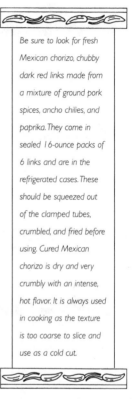

Be sure to look for fresh Mexican chorizo, chubby dark red links made from a mixture of ground pork spices, ancho chilies, and paprika. They come in sealed 16-ounce packs of 6 links and are in the refrigerated cases. These should be squeezed out of the clamped tubes, crumbled, and fried before using. Cured Mexican chorizo is dry and very crumbly with an intense, hot flavor. It is always used in cooking as the texture is too coarse to slice and use as a cold cut.

Chicken

In Mexico, chicken (pollo) is quite expensive, but here it is very popular. Mexican markets sell chicken by the piece, piled in heaps on beds of ice. The pieces are selected with tongs—or point to what you want and a plastic-gloved clerk will place them in a bag for you. Of course, whole chickens are for sale too. There may also be whole turkeys (pavo) or turkey parts.

Chicken is added to soups and stews, cut up and cooked with rice to make arroz con pollo, fried, grilled, roasted, pickled, and poached, then cooked in any number of moles and sauces. Pollo con chorizo is chicken simmered in seasoned stock with chopped onions and tomatoes, then cooked in a sauce made by pureeing the stock solids with chopped chorizo sausages and chilies. Chicken is marinated in thick adobo sauces and simmered in dry white wine with raisins, ground cinnamon, cumin, garlic, olives, and sliced almonds to make pollo borracho (drunken chicken). It's also stewed with canned chipotle chilies, tomatoes, chunks of chorizo, and garlic in stock, and served with sliced avocados. Pollo pibil is pieces of chicken smeared with a spice paste and roasted wrapped in banana leaves. Turkeys are stuffed with a mixture of ground pork, sliced bananas, chopped apples and tomatoes, toasted almonds, chilies, and spices and roasted.

Dairy Products

Fresh farmer's cheese (queso blanco) is the most common cheese in Mexico, but Mexican markets have a wide range of fresh, semi-soft, stringy, and aged cheeses. Cheese is sold by weight, cut or sliced from large, long bricks or huge wheels at the deli counter. Smaller pre-packed cheeses are in the dairy case, where you will also find jars and pouches of crema Mexicana, a tangy sour cream used in sauces, as a topping and like tangy mayo in tortas (sandwiches). Widely distributed brands of Mexican cheeses include Cacique, Chaclo, Del Caribe, El Caporal, El Tapatio, Mexica, and Supremo in slabs or rounds, sealed in plastic.

AÑEJO

Aged, white, crumbly and very dry, sort of like dry feta. Great for grating and using in enchilada fillings and to garnish tacos and tostadas or sprinkle over cooked beans, vegetable stews, cooked greens, shredded meat, and salads.

AÑEJO ENCHILADO

Fresh añejo cheese. A semi-soft, round-shaped, mild cheese, a bit like Muenster, and coated in an orange spice brine made from salt and paprika. Crumble and grate over beans, tacos, and tostadas; use to stuff chilies for chili rellenos; and include in tamales and empanadas.

ASADERO

Very mild, like provolone with a buttery texture and slightly tangy taste. Excellent for melting.

CHIHUAHUA

A mild, pale butter yellow, semi-soft cheese. This cheese has a high fat content, making it a good melting cheese with a flavor reminiscent of mild cheddar. Good for chili rellenos, enchiladas, tamales, quesadillas, burritos, and for grilled cheese sandwiches and nachos.

COTIJA

Also called anejado, or "aged" cheese. This is a very hard, dry, off-white cheese with a slightly sharp, pungent flavor. It is sold in irregular shaped blocks for grating and in plastic bags, both coarsely grated and finely powdered and is a little like Parmesan cheese. Sprinkle over salads, soups, stews, pasta, and beans, use to garnish tacos and tostadas and roll sour cream–smeared grilled corn on the cob in it. Other, very similar cheeses are queso rallado, a hard, dry, roughly grated cheese from Honduras, and queso seco ahumado, a hard, dry, smoked cheese from Nicaragua.

CREMA MEXICANA

Also called jocoque. This is tangy, thin sour cream. Crema ranges from white to a pale creamy butter tint and varies in levels of "bite." Elote con crema is fresh corn kernels sautéed in butter with chopped onions, garlic, tomatoes, and roasted chili strips with crema stirred in. The mixture is simmered until thickened, about 5 minutes. Crema is pureed with crumbled cheese and chilies, and the sauce is layered with lightly fried

crema mexicana

tortilla pieces to make chilaquiles. Mexican brands are sold in glass or plastic containers and Central American types are in jars or plastic pouches—clip a corner off with scissors and squeeze it out. Look for Cacique brand in 15-ounce jars, Crema Pura, E & V, and La Preferida brands in 1-pound jars. Also Perfecta butter blend crema Latina from Nicaragua in 1-pound pouches. Store refrigerated up to several weeks. Once opened, some cremas become tangier with age.

OAXACA

Mexican string cheese. Slightly tangy, white mozzarella-type cheese popular in the state of Oaxaca. When heated the cheese melts into skein-like strands, good in roasted meat sandwiches and quesadillas or for topping beans. This is sold in plastic-sealed lumpy balls.

PANELA

Also called queso blanc panela. Mexican-style basket cheese—fresh curds are pressed into baskets, leaving the trademark woven imprints on the rind. It is a mild, white, semi-soft cheese with a smooth, firm texture. Good cut into chunks and served with drinks, sliced chorizo, olives, and bread. It is also used in chili rellenos and enchiladas and is also excellent for grilling or sliced and served with sliced apples or guava paste.

QUESO FRESCO

Another name for queso blanco (see page 75). In Mexico, it's crumbled over beans or finely chopped for tacos, chili rellenos, and enchiladas or sliced and paired with quince paste.

queso fresco

RANCHERO SECO

Strongly flavored, dry farmhouse cheese, similar to cotija or Romano cheese. Grate and sprinkle over beans, fried plantains, pasta, soups, stews, and fried meats, or grilled corn spread with mayonnaise or sour cream.

REQUESON

A soft, spreadable cheese similar to ricotta with a milky taste. Use in casseroles, as a filling for enchiladas, or whipped with sugar for desserts. Mix with grated cheese and chili powder as a dip with chips or with jam as a spread for crackers or bread.

Starchy Stuff

Rice and beans are indispensable to Mexican cuisine and no meal is complete without the duo. For a complete description of the types you'll find in markets, see chapter 2. Here, I'll talk about common preparations of rice, beans, and pasta in Mexican food.

RICE

Rice is rarely served plain in Mexico; even white rice is first sautéed in oil with garlic and onions, then steamed in water with a pinch of salt. Yellow rice is tinted with annatto seeds fried in oil or the powdered type is used. Mexican rice—the dish by which good cooks are judged and the reddish rice so often served in restaurants—is made by soaking the rice in hot water for 15 minutes, draining it and sautéing in oil, then adding stock mixed with a puree of tomatoes and onions, bringing to a boil, then lowering the heat, covering the pan, and steaming until each grain is separate. Peas, chopped bell pepper, strips of pimento, or olives can also be added. Arroz verde, or green rice, is prepared in the same manner, but with a puree of poblano chilies, cilantro, onions, and garlic.

Rice also plays a role in sopa seca, "dry soup," a traditional Mexican dish. At dinner, sopa seca follows the sopa aguada, or soupy soup, as a separate course. But sopa seca is not really soup as we know it. It is a dish made from rice, or strips of fried tortilla or pasta, cooked in broth until the liquids are entirely absorbed.

BEANS

In the Mexican kitchen, beans are never soaked. For best flavor, cooks add dried beans to cold water and simmer them over low heat for 2 to 4 hours, depending on how dry the beans are. Traditionalists stir beans only with a wooden spoon. They taste better a day or two after cooking as the flavor develops—cool and refrigerate, then bring to a boil to reheat. The bean liquid becomes thick, soupy, and delicious. Refried beans are not fried twice, but cooked, mashed, and fried with onions in melted lard or oil. Small pieces of side pork, pork rinds, or other pig parts are often added to beans, infusing them with a rich, smoky porcine flavor. Plain beans or refried beans can be jazzed up by adding sautéed onions, green peppers, ground cumin, and chili powder. Popular brands include Adelita, Ducal, Goya, Miguel's, La Costeña, La Mexicana, La Preferida, La Sierra, and Verde Valle in 15- to 29-ounce cans.

PASTA

The coiled nests of thin vermicelli, also called cabello de angel (angel hair), are used in Mexican cuisine. The dried nests are browned in oil and added to chicken or beef broth with seasonings to make sopa de fideo, served piping hot with small cubes of cheese. Sopa seca de fideo is a dry "soup," made by crushing the pasta with a rolling pin (leave the pasta in the package), and frying the bits in oil until golden, stirring constantly to prevent them from scorching. The pasta is then pushed to one side, and finely chopped onions, garlic, bell pepper, and tomatoes are added, followed by boiling stock. The pan is covered and cooked over low heat until all the liquid is absorbed. This is served in place of rice, with a dab of Mexican crema or sprinkle of grated cheese and avocado slices. It becomes a main course with the addition of chicken, seafood, pork, chorizo, or other sausage and vegetables. Other small pasta shapes such as stars, tiny tubes, shells, or rice-shaped orzo are used to make sopa seca or are added to soup. Larger pasta twists, elbows, or shells are good cooked and tossed with hot Mexican tomato sauce or tomatillo sauce, served with grated cheese. Brands of fideos (noodles) include Golden Grain, Goya, Iberia, and Molinera in 10- to 12-ounce bags.

A pasta-like food found in Mexico are duros, also called pasta para chicharrónes, doritos, and chicharróne harina. It's a type of dried dough produced in various shapes, mainly ridged chips and flat wagon wheels. Made from wheat flour, cornstarch, salt, coloring, and baking soda, duros resemble shiny orange bits of molded plastic. To eat as a snack, drop into hot oil or microwave 20 seconds until they puff up. They're light and crunchy and taste like pork cracklings, thus the name "chicharrónes." The chips can also be boiled like pasta, served with a sauce, or added to soups. Look for La Mexicana brand in 8-ounce packets.

Vegetables

The produce section of Mexican markets overflows with a profusion of vegetables and greens called quelites. Cheek by jowl are potatoes, corn, tomatoes, beets, bell peppers, and pungent weedy looking greens, pods, tubers, cactus paddles, and pears, and small green tomatoes encased in sticky, paper-thin husks. Depending on the size and location of the market you might also encounter multiple-pronged Andean tubers, squash or bean blossoms, tiny yellowish limes, and a variety of herbs. Many vegetables found in Mexican markets are covered in the Latin basics section (see chapter 4). The ones here are less familiar types or are typically Mexican.

ARRACACIA

Pronounced ar-a-catch-a, this is also called Peruvian carrot or parsnip, white carrot, aymara, apiocriollo, sonarca, or batata baroa. The type exported from Puerto Rico are called apio—a confusing name because it also means celery in Spanish. Botanically related to carrots and celery, arracacia looks like a knotty, misshapen rutabaga or celeric (celery root). Most are pale yellowish with patches of brown; some are off-white or violet tinted. They have a crisp texture

arracacia

and taste like a blend of celery, parsnip, cabbage, and roasted chestnuts. To prepare for using, scrub, peel, and cut in chunks, then boil, roast, add to stews, or boil and puree. Thinly sliced rounds are fried into crisps or the root can be grated raw for salads. Arracacia have a delicate, yet earthy pleasant flavor—worth the effort of tackling the cumbersome root clumps. Peeled chunks can also be found frozen, often mislabeled "yellow cassava." Look for the La Fe brand in 14-ounce bags.

CALABACÍTA

Also called calabacíta criollo. Mexican squash about 3 to 4 inches in length. They can be round and plump or stubby and slightly elongated with rough-edged pale green and cream-colored striations. The soft fleshy interior is delicate with a slightly sweet flavor and absorbent texture. They are cooked in countless ways—chopped and simmered in chili or cream sauces; baked with eggs and grated cheese; added to soups and stews; and split, hollowed out, and stuffed with creamed corn, eggs, grated cheese, and seasonings and baked. Calabacítos con crema is diced squash and chopped tomatoes simmered in thin cream with a cinnamon stick, peppercorns, cloves, and several whole serrano chilies until soft and all the cream is absorbed. The chilies and spices are discarded and the mixture is served with meat or fish. Rinse and trim before using and choose firm, unblemished squash. Store refrigerated up to a week.

GUAJE

Also spelled cuajes. These are long, flattish pods filled with small lentil-shaped green seeds that exude a peculiar, garlicky aroma. When the pods are fresh and green, chop up the whole pod with the seeds and add to meat stews. If the pods are brown, pull apart and scrape out the seeds and add to salads, soups, stews or eat as a snack—they have a slightly sweet, grassy flavor and can be eaten raw, fried, or pickled. Guaje seeds combine well with other strong flavors such as garlic, chilies, adobo pastes, or curries. Look for fresh green pods and store refrigerated up to two weeks—the pods will begin to darken but you can still use the seeds.

guaje pod

HUITLACOCHE

Pronounced weet-lah-COH-chay and also spelled cuitlacoche and called corn mushrooms or corn smut. This is a naturally occurring fungus that forms on ears of corn, producing a large gray mass, black on the inside and glossy on the surface. It looks like a little brain and is considered a great delicacy, especially as a filling for quesadillas. While you may occasionally find the fresh fungus at farmers' markets, most Mexican markets sell it prepared and canned. If you find the fresh type, chop it and sauté with minced onions, garlic, and chilies until the black juice it exudes evaporates (about 15 minutes), and use in quesadillas or serve topped with creamy melted cheese and warm tortillas. The canned kind has been cooked in oil with chopped jalapeño, onion, epazote, and salt and just needs gentle reheating. When you open the can you will find inky, sac-like swollen kernels entwined in the herb leaves. Heat with cream for soup, scramble with eggs, or roll up in crêpes and serve in a cream sauce. Look for Adelita brand corn mushrooms in 7.6-ounce cans. Some stores sell the fungus frozen.

huitlacoche

JÍCAMA

Pronounced HEE-kama. Native to Mexico, this is also called Mexican potato and yam bean. Jícama is shaped like a large turnip and covered in a thin, leathery tan skin. The flesh is pale, juicy, and crisp with a mild, sweet taste. To prepare, peel off the skin with a potato peeler or sharp knife. Jícama is usually eaten raw as a snack and in salads and relishes. Street vendors sell paper cones of sliced jícama tossed with salt and chili powder, served with orange or lime wedges. Pico de gallo is a traditional relish from Jalisco made from peeled and diced jícama, oranges, chili powder, and salt, served as an appetizer. Sliced jícama can be tossed in any salad, even fruit salads, adding contrasting crunch. Jícama is also

jícama

diced and tossed with cubed avocado, chopped onion, cilantro, orange juice, and salt. Or toss with tart green apple slices, tomatillos, crumbled cheese, and lime juice. Coarsely grated jicama is combined with shredded coconut, sugar, and orange juice, cooked into a sticky paste and shaped into little mounds to make candies called dulces de jícama y coco. Jícama will keep 1 to 2 weeks, refrigerated and wrapped in plastic.

NOPAL CACTUS

These are the beaver tail–shaped paddles, or "leaves" of the prickly pear cactus. They are thick, fleshy, and dotted with sharp thorns or small nubs, depending on the variety. Choose the smallest, thinnest, palest ones, as they will be the most tender and flavorful. If you get the thorny kind, hold with tongs and scrape out the spines with the tip of a knife. Shave off the nubs if it is thornless. Either way, try not to remove too much of the outer green layer. Cut off the fibrous base and cut the paddle into small pieces or strips and cook until tender in boiling, well-salted water—about 10 to 20 minutes. Add a pinch of baking soda (if you add too much it will foam up and boil over) to dispel the slippery substance the cactus exudes. Cooked nopales may have a slightly slimy texture like okra. To minimize this, rinse and drain in a colander and cover with a damp towel to prevent them from drying out and let stand for 30 minutes.

Nopales have a tart, green bean–bell pepper flavor and are added to salads, scrambled eggs, quesadillas, and pork stews. Store refrigerated up to a week. Nopalitos (strips) are also available in jars and cans, packed in brine; see page 89.

RADISHES

Rábanos. Mexican markets sell bunches of bright red radishes with the leafy greens attached. Trim off the roots and leaves, wash, and drain. The greens can be cooked like spinach, added to moles and soups, or chopped and added to mashed potatoes. In Mexican cuisine, radishes are a popular garnish, sliced and floated on soups and stews, and in tacos, tostadas, and sandwiches. Carved rosettes decorate platters of flautas, roasted and grilled meats, seafood, and rice and bean combos. Radishes are diced and added to salads or minced for fresh salsas. Choose small, firm, smooth-skinned ones without any cracks. Store unwashed in a perforated plastic bag with the greens cut off—these should be used right away as they wilt rapidly.

SQUASH BLOSSOMS

Flor de calabaza. The large, deep yellow, fluted flowers of large squash or calabaza pumpkin. The blossoms have a delicate, slightly sweet flavor and velvety texture. To prepare for cooking, remove the stems, pluck out the pistils, and strip off the stringy green sepals, leaving the bulbous calax at the flower's base, which adds a slight crunch. Chop and sauté the blossoms with chopped onions and chilies and stuff into quesadillas with cheese. Whole blossoms are stuffed with cheese, battered, and deep-fried. The fragile blossoms are best used right away as they wilt rapidly.

squash blossom

TOMATILLO

Tomaté de cascara. Also called fresadilla and Mexican green husk tomato. A small grape-sized variety is called milpero. The average tomatillo is about the size of a golf ball, encased in a paper-thin, light green husk. They have a fruity-tart flavor and are usually cooked before using. Remove the slightly sticky husks and rinse in warm water. Place in a pan of water and simmer over low heat for about 5 minutes or until somewhat translucent, then drain. Tomatillos are also sold canned—whole, husked, and cooked as tomatillo entero or tomaté verde, and as a thick sauce (salsa). They are added to green mole in which meatballs and pork are cooked. Chopped, cooked tomatillo can be added to guacamole and other dips. The tiny milpero has an acidic, lemony flavor and must also be removed from their

husks. They are then chopped and added to salads, guacamole, and meat stews. Either type should be firm when purchased and can be stored for several weeks, refrigerated in the crisper bin. Roasted tomatillos are used in salsa; see page 234.

tomatillo

TUNA

Prickly pear. These large berries of the paddle-leafed nopales cactus are about 2 to 4 inches long, oval-shaped, and succulent with skin that varies in color from yellowish-green, orange, or pink to dark magenta. The skins are studded with tubercles encasing thin, often invisible spines that can give you an alarming prick. The juicy pulp ranges in color from pale green to yellow-orange and red with a sweet-tart flavor and contains numerous black, edible seeds. To remove the skin, cut off a slice at one end, then make shallow lengthwise incisions to make it easier to peel off, or cut in half and scoop out the flesh with a spoon. Most are sold de-spined—if not, remove them before peeling. Rub the skin with a thick cloth or scrub under running water wearing rubber gloves for protection. Eat as is or sprinkle with lime juice. Dice and add to fruit salad or puree in blender drinks. Select smooth tuna with unblemished skins. They ripen at room temperature and are ready to eat when they exude a sweet fragrance and yield to gentle pressure. When ripe, eat at once or store refrigerated up to 3 days.

tuna

Quelites

Pronounced keh-LEE-the, this word means Mexican greens in general as well as one specific one, known in English as lamb's quarters. Store all greens loosely wrapped and unwashed in paper or plastic bags, refrigerated for a few days. Greens are best used right away. Many grow wild.

FLOR DE FRIJOL

Bean blossoms. The small flowers of green, snap, wax, white, pinto, or red kidney beans, along with the tendrils and leaves, are sautéed with chopped onion, garlic, and tomatoes and stirred into bean soups and stews. They can also be chopped and added to fresh salsas.

HUAUZONTLE

Also called guauzoncles. The bunches of greens resemble elongated broccoli spiked on top with thick clusters of small dark seeds. Another very closely related species, *Chenopodium berlanderi,* has thicker, black side coats. Both types have stalks about 3 feet tall and taste a little like broccoli when cooked. To use, remove the rough outer leaves and trim the stalks so they will fit in a large saucepan. Boil in salted water for about 20 minutes, or until tender. They can now be sautéed with chopped onion and garlic or stuffed with bits of cheese between the small stems, dusted in flour, and dipped in a fluffy batter made from whipped egg whites with the beaten egg yolks folded in and fried in hot oil until golden. When fried like this, they are usually served with a green tomatillo sauce. To eat, pick up by the woody stems and nibble off the tender leaves and seeds with the oozing cheese.

QUELITES

Lamb's quarters, fat-hen, pigweed, or goosefoot. The leaves of this green are cooked like spinach. Wash the stripped-off leaves before cooking. Buy or pick a large amount since they reduce when cooked. Try the leaves sautéed with chopped onion and green salsa or ground pumpkin seeds with roasted chili strips. Boil a few minutes and serve with butter and salt, garnished with slices of hard-boiled egg and crumbled bacon. Add to sauces, soups, rice, beans, potato, or pasta dishes.

ROMERITO

Long, slender, succulent leaves resembling ragged rosemary with an herbaceous flavor. The leaves are made into a mole with other seasonings and spices for the Lenten and Christmas specialty, tortas de camarón—dried shrimp and egg fritters served in a broth made from the thinned mole. Chopped romerito leaves can also be cooked in various chili sauces for shredded meats or served garnished with chopped hard-boiled eggs.

VERDOLAGES

Purslane. The small, oval leaves have a sharp, lemony flavor and unctuous texture. When young and tender, add the greens raw to salads. When mature, larger leaves and light green stems can be briefly blanched and added to meat, bean, or vegetable dishes. Espinazo con verdolages is a traditional pork stew with purslane simmered in a tomatillo and chili-based sauce. Add the purslane near the end because it becomes slippery when overcooked. It's also added to spicy lentil or chickpea stews.

Cooking Herbs

AVOCADO LEAF

Hoja de aguacate. Spear-shaped, glossy leaves of the avocado tree—the trees with the poorest quality fruit seem to bear the tastiest leaves. Most Mexican groceries sell the dried, dull green leaves in bags or small packets. Fresh or dried leaves are usually lightly toasted to bring out the flavor and can be used whole or ground. They have a hazelnut-licorice aroma and anise flavor—and are added to soups, tamales, pork, chicken, fish, and bean dishes. Chicken in pumpkin seed pipian sauce is seasoned with a large fresh or dried avocado leaf. Toasted, ground avocado leaves are often sprinkled over refried beans.

EPAZOTE

Mexican tea, sweet pigweed, and wormweed. This herb with tapering, serrated leaves grows wild in Mexico and the United States, especially California. It has a pungent scent and can seem a little overpowering

epazote

when sniffed the first time. In Mexican cuisine, chopped, fresh epazote is essential to a good pot of black beans and is also added to salsas, cream sauces, soups, fillings for quesadillas, omelettes, and mushroom dishes, lending a sharp, peppery, anise flavor and lemony aftertaste. The herb also seasons mukbilpollo, a Yucatan tamale pie filled with a spicy mixture of chicken and pork steamed in banana leaves.

Epazote is cooked with meats or eaten on the side, chewed between bites, as it is thought to help digest meats and cleanse the system of toxins. This herb also helps reduce the gas associated with beans—one reason why it is often cooked with beans. This is the most commonly found fresh herb in Mexican groceries and is also sold dried in small packets.

HOJA SANTA

Also called sacred pepper, tlanepa, momo, and yerba santa. A large, valentine-shaped, velvety green leaf with a light green underside. It has a strong anise scent and an anise, nutmeg, and black pepper flavor. This delicious herb makes a fragrant wrapper for grilled or steamed fish and it flavors green moles, pipian verde, beef, chicken, and shrimp dishes. Fresh leaves are not readily available. Dried leaves are sold in large, flat, plastic packets under the Gromex label but are not as flavorful. They are best ground for sauces as they are too brittle to use as wrappers.

PAPALO

Also called papaloquelite. A pungent, citrusy-flavored leaf resembling a small butterfly—oval with a center crease forming two wings. The name comes from papalotl, the Náhuatl word for butterfly. Sprigs of the leaves are tucked raw into tacos and Mexican subs, called cemitas, piled with meats and string cheese. The leaves are also cut in fine strips and added to guacamole and salads. The flavor grows stronger as they get older.

PEPICHA

Also called pipicha, this is an annual herb, similar to cilantro but with a much stronger flavor. It is chopped and added to green salsas and quesadillas filled with squash blossoms and cheese or huitlacoche (corn fungus).

PEREJIL

Mexican flatleaf parsley. It is finely chopped and used in soups and stews, added at the end of cooking; in salsas, moles, and salad; or as a garnish for everything from grilled fish to clear chicken broth.

Drink Mixes & Concentrates

Mexicans have enjoyed hot, thick beverages made from masa or powdered, toasted corn with spices, chocolate, or fresh fruit since pre-Columbian times. Pinole, a toasted corn gruel, was the field ration of early Indian warriors and is still popular today. Atoles are made from masa harina mixed with water, strained through a sieve, and boiled with milk, sugar, and flavorings until creamy. Flavorings include ground almonds, vanilla, cinnamon, and cloves or crushed fruits such as strawberries, blackberries, raspberries, and guava. Mexican grocery stores sell instant powders, based on cornstarch, milk powder, and flavorings to make atole. There are also mixes and liquid concentrates for horchata and fruit concentrates. These are mixed with 1 part concentrate to 12 parts of water with sugar to taste.

CHAMPURRADO

Chocolate atole. A powdered instant mix flavored with cocoa. Cornstarch replaces the strained masa harina used in the traditional preparation made with Mexican chocolate tablets, cinnamon, brown sugar, and vanilla. To use, add 2 to 3 tablespoons of instant mix per cup of hot water and stir. It is even better frothed in a blender. Look for La Mexicana brand in 12-ounce bags of a slightly pinkish-tan powder.

HORCHATA

Horchatas are chilled drinks made from steeped and strained ground nuts, grains, and a tuber called chufa. It's time consuming to grind, soak, and strain almonds or rice to make horchata, thus the popularity of instant mixes and liquid concentrates. Although horchata looks creamy, it is dairy free and low in fat. To use the powder type, dissolve a packet in one quart of cold water with sugar to taste, add ice, and stir. Besides the traditional cinnamon-laced rice horchata, there are other flavors including tamarind, strawberry, mango, guava, orange, piña colada, and Jamaica flower (sorrel). Look for Klass brand in 1.2-ounce packets and Natura's in 12-ounce bags (directions are on the label). Delicia brand has 32-ounce bottles of horchata concentrate. To use, dilute a few tablespoons in cold water.

MAIZENA

Fecula de maiz. A flavored cornstarch used as a shortcut to make a type of atole. To use, mix one packet of powder in 1 cup of water and set aside. Bring a quart of milk to a boil, blend in cornstarch mixture, and simmer, stirring constantly for about 2 minutes. Sweeten to taste. Each 1.76-ounce packet makes 5 cups. Look for the Maizena brand and choose from chocolate, cinnamon, coconut, strawberry, almond, and vanilla.

maizena

The Central American & Colombian Corner

Most large Mexican stores and Latin supermarkets have some nook set aside for products from Central America—mainly Guatemala,

Honduras, and El Salvador. Some are quite unusual and delicious (well worth a try!) and many are also used in Mexican cuisine.

Products imported from Ecuador and Colombia are also stocked in this section.

Pickled & Syrup-Packed Products

BABACAO

A five-sided, hybrid papaya from Ecuador. These are poached, cut in vertical slices, and packed in syrup. Babacao has a tart-sweet flavor and soft texture, and is good added to fruit salad and blender drinks. Chunks are also added to meat stews. Look for La Cholita (little Indian girl) brand in 1-pound jars.

babacao

CHIPILIN EN SALMURA

Chipilin in brine, also known as cepil or chipil. The flowers, tiny brown pods, and leaves of a shrub are boiled (to remove toxins) and preserved in a saltwater brine. To use, drain and lightly sauté in a little oil. It has a tangy asparagus, green bean–like flavor. The leaves are also tucked into the famous tamales de chepil and are cooked with rice. These greens are used like lettuce as a garnish for beans, salads, tostadas, grilled fish, and meats and in quesadillas and sandwiches. They are also sold frozen. Look for Goya and Delicia brands in 32-ounce jars or Miguel's from Guatemala in 16- or 32-ounce jars and El Sembrador brand in 14-ounce bags, frozen.

chipilin en salmura

COYOLES

Palma de vino. The fruit of the coyol palm, also known as spiny palm, packed in a thick, dark brown sugar syrup. The syrup-packed fruit is very hard and fibrous with not much flesh surrounding a big seed. It tastes almost totally of brown sugar and is sticky with a texture like the coating of a soft taffy apple. About all you can do is nibble at the flesh and lick off the syrup, but the syrup is delicious poured over ice cream, minus the coyoles. It is also added to fruit-filled punches. Look for Miguel's brand in 16- and 32-ounce jars.

CURTIDO SALVENDORENO

Pickled cabbage salad, El Salvador–style. Shredded white cabbage with carrot slices, onion, and red pepper strips in a salt brine seasoned with oregano. Drain and use as a garnish in tacos and sandwiches or a relish with tamales, pupusas (stuffed cornmeal pies), grilled or roasted meats, and fried plantains. Look for Goya in 32-ounce jars.

ELOTITIOS TIERNOS

Baby corn in brine. Tiny ears with a slight crunch. The corn is picked when immature and has a mild taste. Drain and rinse and add sliced in rounds or whole to salads, soups, stews, and stir-fries. It is the same as the baby corn found canned in Asian grocery stores. Made by Miguel's, Loty, and Tucan.

ENSALADA DE VERDURAS/VERDURAS ENCURTIDO

Mixed pickle salad from Guatemala and El Salvador. Each brand differs slightly, but most contain halved onions, pieces of carrot, and cauliflower florets packed in a vinegar brine. Some add spices, whole jalapeños, and red pepper strips, others include broccoli, pacaya (palm "flowers"), and loroco flowers. Drain and serve as an appetizer, add to salads, and use as a table relish with soups, roasted meats, rice, beans, tamales, or other foods. Goya, Tucan, and Milios brands have variations in 32-ounce jars.

ensalada de verduras

GUAYABA WHOLES

Whole, peeled guavas in syrup. Eat with the syrup, chilled; chop and add to fruit salads or meat stews; whirl in blender drinks; add to fruit punch; or serve over ice cream. Look for El Gallito brand in 31-ounce jars.

HIGOS EN ALIMBAR

Whole green figs preserved in light syrup. Plump, soft, and sweet, these are delicious as is or served in the syrup or with cream. Serve as an appetizer with proscuitto, chop and add to fruit compotes, or pair with queso blanco and wine. Brands include Miguel's in 1-pound jars, Respin and Doña Paula from Colombia in 28-ounce jars, and La Cholia from Ecuador in 20-ounce jars.

JOCOTE

Cashew apples. Also called jocote rojo, Spanish plum, maranon, cajueiro, and acaju. Cashew apples are bell-shaped and yellowish-pink to rose-colored, sweet, and juicy when preserved in syrup. Native to Brazil, cashew apples are also grown in Guatemala and El Salvador. Eat in the syrup or with cream, add to fruit salad, or liquidize into a thick juice. Look for Goya and Tucan brands in 32-ounce jars and El Sembrador in 14-ounce bags, frozen.

LOROCO

Also called floroco and quilite (in El Salvador, when cooked). A popular edible flower that is either flash-frozen or pickled in a saltwater brine. Loroco tastes like a cross between asparagus and green bean with a slight bite and pleasant tartness. The flowers are chopped and cooked with rice, chicken, or eggs; added to empanada stuffings with crumbled cheese; and folded into batters for fritters. The buds, unopened flowers, and vine tips are also cooked as a green, often just sautéed with garlic and onions as a side dish. In El Salvador loroco are stuffed into a lump of masa dough with bits of salty cheese, pressed flat into a thick patty, and cooked on a griddle to make pupusas; or the flowers are finely chopped and mixed into masa dough with grated cheese for tamales. In Guatemala, chopped, boiled loroco are sautéed in butter with chopped tomatoes, tomatillos, onion, and sweet peppers

and mixed into mashed potato, garnished with sour cream and grated cheese. There is a growing craze in Central America for pizza topped with loroco and even loroco lasagne! The pickled flowers taste better than the frozen, which have a mushy texture. Look for Delicia, La Fe, and Tucan brands in 32-ounce jars as well as Goya with the addition of onions and carrot slices. El Sembrador brand has the frozen flowers in 6- and 14-ounce bags.

loroco

NANCES

Also called nanche de perro and nantzin (in Mexico), nancito or cabo (in Honduras), nance verde (in El Salvador), tapal (in Guatemala), and nanzi (in Colombia). Resembling golden cherries, these fresh fruits have a juicy and slightly oily pulp, with flavor ranging from sweet and acidic to that of ripe cheese. Nances packed in brine have a mealy texture with a sort of musty smell and taste like a mix of apple and cheese. Fresh nances are often sold at street markets in Mexican neighborhoods and are eaten raw or boiled in sugar syrup. They also go into some soups and stuffings for meats (de-pitted). In Mexico, nances are cooked with olives and rice with stewed chicken. They flavor carbonated beverages, and are fermented into chicha (wine). In Costa Rica, nances are distilled into a rum-like liquor called crema de nance. The nances in brine work best in savory dishes such as meat and vegetable soups and stews. They are also sold frozen, which are tastier and sweeter and can be used to make jam and jelly. Look for El Sembrador frozen in 14-ounce bags. Miguel's brand has them in 1-pound jars and Delicia in 1-pound and 32-ounce jars.

nances

PACAYA

Also called bandejas and pacayitas. These are the male inflorescence of the pacaya palm. They look like elongated, mutant chicken feet or scaly, baby corn splintered from a thick, central stem and have a delicate flavor similar to heart of palm. Pacaya are sold in jars of brine or frozen. Chop and add to salads, fry with eggs and potato or rice and other vegetables, and add to soups, like baby corn. It is also pickled with other vegetable salads (encuritidos) and served as a table relish. Delicia, Goya, and Tucan have pacaya in large jars and El Sembrador sells it in 14-ounce bags, frozen.

PALMITO ENTERO

Heart of palm—the inner portion of the stem of several types of palm trees. They are slender, ivory-colored, and resemble white asparagus without the tips. The flavor is reminiscent of artichoke and the texture is firm and smooth. Canned heart of palm are ready to eat and delicious sliced into green salads, or served whole as an appetizer on a bed of lettuce with a mayonnaise or vinaigrette dressing. They can also be sautéed in butter or olive oil with salt and pepper and other seasonings, sliced and stir-fried with shrimp and leafy greens, or cooked with shrimp in tomato sauce. Some brands include Nosara, Roland, and King of Hearts in 7- to 8-ounce cans, and Miguel's pickled heart of palm in 16- and 32-ounce jars. Also IVALI brand from Brazil in 6.5-ounce and 1-pound cans. For a recipe including heart of palm and mashed yuca, see page 247.

*palmito
entero*

PAPA CRIOLLA

Creole potatoes. Also called papa amarillo. Yellow potatoes grown in Colombia, cooked and packed in water brine or frozen. The flesh is light yellow, firm, and buttery flavored. The little spuds are added to soups and stews with other softer potatoes that fall apart, thickening the dish. Use them as any firm, waxy potato, roasted, sliced, and pan-fried with chorizo or other sausages, in potato salad or tossed on the grill with meats. La Fe and De Colombia brands offer them in 16- to 32-ounce jars and El Sembrador in 14-ounce bags, frozen.

PECHICHE

Wild cherry. A blackish-purple cherry. These cherries have a fig-custard flavor. With their large stones, they're best nibbled as is. They're also pressed through a strainer to separate the pulp from the stones. Eat with thick cream or over ice cream or custard. Look for Fiesta brand in 14-ounce jars and La Cholia in 1-pound jars.

*pechiche
preserves*

PEJIBAYE

Peach palm. Also called pejivalles (in Costa Rica), pijuayo or chonto (in Peru), chontoduro (in Colombia and Ecuador), and pupunha (in Brazil). These are the fruits of the pejibaye palm tree, resembling large acorns, about 2 to 2½ inches in length. They are rather hard with shiny skins that range from a mottled yellow to reddish-orange. The flesh is slightly sweet and starchy. Whole clusters are boiled, and the fruits scooped out when they float off the central stem. They are then canned or packed into jars in a salty water brine. The bright orange ones tend to stain your fingers as the rich oil rubs off on them while handling. You can eat them straight from the jar but they are mainly eaten as a starchy vegetable, roasted or boiled and served with butter and salt, or pureed with stock and cream for soups. They are added whole to stews and before processing can be ground into flour for use in breads and pastries. The simplest preparation is to

pejibaye

boil for about 45 minutes, cut in half lengthwise (base side down, slicing through the pointed end) discarding seeds, and mash with olive oil or butter, and season with salt and pepper. Look for Goya and La Fe in large jars.

PONCHE DE FRUITOS

A type of Mexican-style fruit punch, made for parties and at Christmas. Ripe guava, tejecotes (little apples), plums, peaches, and pineapple are preserved in a thick, heavy syrup made from panela (brown sugar) flavored with cinnamon and Jamaica flower (sorrel). To use, pour contents of the can or jar into a large pan and gently heat, but do not allow to boil, and serve. This is really a dessert, ladled into bowls and eaten with sweet breads or pastries. Garmex has large 35-ounce jars with sugarcane. Huge 101-ounce party-size cans are offered by Zunimex brand.

TEJECOTES

Mexican hawthorn. Also called manzilla, meaning "little apple." This fruit gives off a peculiar odor of decaying fish when young, but when fully open, it smells like balsamic vinegar. The fresh fruits look like tiny, blush-tinted apples. Cooked and packed in syrup, they resemble bruised, slightly speckled, golden hawthorn apples. Mealy textured yet juicy, they taste sweet and tart and are added to Christmas punch and fruit salad or enjoyed with queso blanco or with cream and syrup. Fresh ones make good jam or jelly and go into piñatas with candies. Look for Goya and Tucan brands in 32-ounce jars and Del Carmen in 1-pound jars.

TOMATE DE ARBOL

Also called tamarillo, these resemble large, golden cling peaches, but are peeled and poached tree tomatoes (see page 54–55) in syrup. The syrup has a tart flavor and the tree tomatoes are soft with the texture of canned peaches and tart apricot flavor. They can be used in both sweet and savory dishes, chopped and added like tomatoes to soups and stews, pureed for tangy sauces and with other fruits in blender drinks—delicious whirled with pineapple, mango, banana, or cantaloupe; or with sugar and lemon juice. Look for La Chilia brand from Ecuador in 16-ounce jars, La Fe brand in 28-ounce jars, and Yerba Buena in 17-ounce jars.

Dry Goods from Central America

Most of the following products are offered by the Amazonas label.

ATOL DE SHUCO

Purple corn flour mix. Made from a finely ground corn called maiz negrito (purple colored corn) from El Salvador. To use, bring 1 teaspoon of flour per 2 cups of water to a boil, removing from heat the instant it boils. Strain to remove any lumps from the thin, milky liquid, sweeten to taste with sugar, and refrigerate for a refreshing drink. Sold in 12-ounce packages.

AYOTE SEEDS

Whole pumpkin seeds in the shell. Toast and sprinkle with lemon juice, salt, and chili powder for snacking; or toast and grind and use as a thickener in sauces for chicken, turkey, and tamales. Pepitoria sells shelled whole pumpkin seeds in 4-ounce packets.

CACAO BEANS

Another name for cocoa or the beans from which chocolate is made. Resembling coffee beans, when toasted they have an intense and rich nutty flavor with a slight bitter edge. Before using, toast until fragrant in a hot, dry skillet. Toasted cacao beans can be crushed and added to cookie dough and other baked goods as an alternative to nuts or chocolate chips—and makes quite a sophisticated adult cookie. Sprinkle crushed bits in salads for interest, especially baby greens dressed in balsamic vinegar and a virgin olive oil, and on top of hot chocolate, cappuccinos, and lattes. You can also grind toasted beans in a coffee grinder to a fine powder and use to make hot chocolate with milk and sugar. Available in 8-ounce bags. Nibs removed from the shell are also available in gourmet specialty stores and can be used in most of the same ways or just munched as is.

CEBADA

Barley flour. Use to thicken soups and stews for a barley essence, combine with wheat flour in breads and other baked goods, or try as a refreshing Central American drink—boiled, strained, and mixed with water, lemon juice, and sugar. Use a few teaspoons of flour per cup of water. Super Abrosa is a strawberry-flavored barley and rice powder drink mix. Proinca brand has both plain barley and the flavored blend in 12-ounce bags.

GUASCAS

Also spelled huascas and known as gallant soldier, quickweed, and water weed—as like water it spreads everywhere once it gets a foothold. This herb is sold dried and crumbled. It has an earthy flavor, sort of a cross between parsley and very mild oregano. The herb is added to soups and stews, especially ajiaco, the chicken and potato soup from Bogotá. Look for Kiska brand in small packets. You could substitute fresh parsley and dried oregano.

guascas

HARINA PARA CHILATE

Corn flour drink mix. Used to make a Salvadorian refreshment called chilate. Dilute 2 tablespoons of the flour in 1 cup of water, strain and add one allspice berry. Cook over medium heat, stirring constantly until thickened, and add sugar to taste. Sold in 12-ounce bags with an attached sealed pouch of allspice berries.

MASARICA

Instant masa, a prepared cornmeal for making Central American tamales. You just add water and knead into a soft dough. Sold in 32-ounce packages.

MORRO SEEDS

The small seed from the breadnut tree (not breadfruit), called arbol de pan. Other names are ramon tree, corntree, or snakewood. The dark brown, heart-shaped seeds are about the size of a small lentil with a white interior. When toasted, they give off a rich, nutty aroma and are finely ground to make horchata de morro. They can also be toasted and ground in a coffee grinder and used to brew an organic, caffeine-free type of coffee with a slightly fruity aroma and nutty flavor. To make horchata, pulverize 1 cup of seeds in a blender as finely as possible. Mix with 6 cups water and 1 cup sugar with a pinch of cinnamon and let stand 4 hours. Strain through a damp cloth, squeezing hard to extract all the milky liquid from the seeds. Serve the strained liquid over ice. You can also buy horchata Salvadorean, a powdered drink mix made from ground morro seeds, peanuts, sesame seeds, almonds, and rice, flavored with cinnamon and sugar. Mix

morro seeds

a few tablespoons with water or milk, and add sugar to taste, stir, and serve over ice. Look for LYA brand in 12-ounce bags for the horchata powder, also Amazonas horchata de morro, a blend of ground morro seeds, pumpkin seeds, cloves, sugar, cinnamon, and allspice. Morro seeds are found in 8-ounce packets from Amazonas and Doña Lola.

SEMILLA DE CHANG

Chia seed drink mix. A gritty mixture of tiny black and gray chia seeds and colored sugar. In Central America, chia seeds are called chang-chia. They are soaked an hour or so until they swell and are mixed with fruit juice or lemonade. To use, mix 2 tablespoons of mix into about ¼ cup water, then add fruit juice to make a cup. For the sugar and seed mix look for the 10-ounce bags with a white-and-green label from El Salvador. Amazonas and Doña Lola brands sell the seeds in 4-ounce packets, which can be mixed with sugar to make the drink—it just won't be tinted reddish.

TRIGO PELADO

Peeled green wheat kernels. Young, green wheat—the smooth kernels are brownish-green with a pleasant fresh flavor and slightly chewy texture. It is cooked much like rice. Add wheat to cold water, bring to a boil, then lower heat and simmer, covered until soft, season with salt, pepper, and hot sauce, and serve with vegetables. To make what is called chambar, add chicken or other meats to the wheat as it cooks, with seasonings. Sold in 15-ounce bags under the Amazonas label.

Colombian Starches

All of the following flours and starch mixes are offered by the Colombian La de Banderita brand in 14-ounce boxes. Most contain a blend of cornstarch, sugar, baking powder, yuca starch, and wheat flour in varying proportions and can just about be used interchangeably to make a variety of fritters and baked goods.

ACHIRA

A tuber similar to yuca, about the size of a large carrot. The starch is extracted from it to make various biscuits, small crunchy breads, and cookies. It's not always available, but yuca starch, called yuca harina, can also be used to make these savory, salty treats.

ALMOJABANA

A blend of rice flour, corn flour, yuca starch, tapioca starch, and baking powder. It is used to make almojabanas, soft round cheese biscuits. Add 3 cups of grated queso blanco to 2 cups of mix with ½ cup milk, a tablespoon of butter, and an egg. Blend together and shape into rounds and bake until puffy. They are soft and chewy, best while still warm. Form the dough into little doughnut rings and you have pan de queso. Without the cheese and formed into small crescents or rounds, they are called bizcochuelos, and any of the boxed mixes can be used to make these.

BUÑOELINA

A basic corn flour and yuca starch blend mainly used to make small fried fritters. Mix 2 cups of grated cheese with 2 cups of the powder and 2 eggs and shape into balls. Deep-fry until golden brown and serve hot with hot sauce as a snack or appetizer.

buñoelina

MAZAMORRO

Also called peto, these are the large, dried corn kernels known as mote or hominy. Used to thicken porridge, eaten hot for breakfast, or cooled and mixed with panela (brown sugar) as a refreshing snack. To use, wash the corn thoroughly and simmer about 1 cup of kernels in 3 quarts of water with a teaspoon of baking soda in a large pot, 45 minutes to an hour, or until soft. Then add a teaspoon of cornstarch and cook until thickened, being careful not to cook for too long or over too high a temperature. Add salt and any seasoning or cool and add sugar. Banderita has 1-pound bags of mazamorro.

Palitos de queso, little cheese sticks, can be made with any of the mixes. Strips of dough are stuffed with cheese and baked. They are flat, like a pastry strip with the dough folded over the filling.

PAN DE BONO

Literally "good bread," this is one of the most popular Colombian breads. The mix contains cornstarch, yuca starch, sugar, and baking soda and is mixed with grated cheese to make dense and chewy puff balls with a crisp crust. Most South American bakeries sell these—but make sure they are fresh as they harden into lead.

YUCA HARINA

Pure yuca starch used to make pan de yuca, crispy round or half moon–shaped breads. Mix one box of the starch with ½ pound softened butter, ½ cup sugar, and 1 egg yolk. Shape the dough and bake the breads about 15 minutes at 350 degrees or until golden on top. These slightly sweet breads are best when warm and soft. You can also add grated cheese to the mixture. Besides the Banderita brand, there are the Yucarina brand in 12-ounce boxes and Del Maiz brand in 14-ounce boxes of pure yuca and cornstarches.

Mexican Pan Dulce & Sweets

Besides countless varieties of sweet breads known as pan dulce, Mexican panaderías specialize in bread and bolillos, dinner rolls somewhat like a hard-crusted French roll, and sweet and savory stuffed empanadas (turnovers). Most Mexican groceries also sell an assortment of pan dulce in clear plastic boxes with tongs to select what you want. The cardinal rule is to never touch the breads with your fingers—always wait your turn and use the provided tongs.

Basic pan dulce is made from flour, yeast, shortening, milk, sugar, and egg dough. The dough is kneaded and shaped, left to rise, smeared with a creamed butter, sugar, and egg yolk topping—often tinted pastel colors—and baked. It has a flaky texture, is not overly sweet, and tends to dry out quickly. Mexican groceries and panaderías also sell pastries, cookies, fritters, churros, and doughnuts. Following are just some of the treats found in a panadería or Mexican market.

Barra de mantequilla is a slice of baked, buttered bread sprinkled with sugar; bizochitos are anise-flavored cookies; and buñuelos are puffy fritters made from egg-enriched, deep-fried dough sprinkled with cinnamon sugar or served in warm sugar or honey syrup. Some buñuelos are made in fancy shapes, resembling crispy wheels of lace, dusted in powdered sugar. Campechanos are flaky, sugar-glazed rolls; canelitas are little cinnamon cookies; and cantutillas are puff pastry horns filled with custard. Churros are breakfast fritters made by squeezing batter through fluted tubes into hot oil, forming loops or long ridged sticks that are sprinkled with sugar.

Conchos are shell-shaped pan dulce with a sugar, butter, and egg glaze raked

In Mexico, at every fiesta, vendors set up huge cauldrons bubbling with hot oil and pipe churro batter into large loops which are threaded on sticks for easy transport through the festive throngs. Churro makers also work the dawn hours, selling long ropes of crisp golden brown churros for dunking into mugs of hot chocolate or café con leche. Hollow churros are often stuffed with dulce de leche or jelly.

with a fork in a cross-hatch pattern. The glaze is often tinted pink or yellow. Cortados are oval-shaped sweet breads with slashes cut in the surface before baking, usually in a cross-hatch pattern. Powdered sugar–coated cake doughnuts are donas; and doraditas are fried squares of puff pastry with a sugarglaze. Empanados, also called

churro

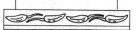

turnovers or hot pockets, are half moon–shaped pastries stuffed with pumpkin or sweet potato paste and strawberry, guava, or pineapple jams. Some panaderías also sell savory empanados with meat and cheese fillings. Ensalimadas are snail-shaped sweet rolls, sometimes topped with a sugar glaze or powdered sugar; galletas amarilla are triangular-shaped sugar cookies; and gaznates are cornets of thin, fried dough stuffed with pineapple or chocolate paste. In the spring, look for hornazo, Easter bread stuffed with chorizo or chopped ham. Huernos are sweet bread horns shaped to form a crescent; while huesitos are pastry horns filled with jam—the name means "bones" as the jam resembles marrow in a bone.

Mantecadas are corn muffins; molletes are anise-flavored sweet rolls with a thin, crackly brown sugar topping; and orejas are large, crispy elephant ear pastries. Pan de muerto, or bread of the dead, is one of the offerings on All Souls' Day, November 2, also known as the day of the faithfully departed. It is brought to ancestors' graves or eaten in their memory and is a special round coffeecake decorated with alternating dough teardrops and bone shapes with a knob in the center, sprinkled with pink sugar. The bread is eaten after an all-night vigil, served with coffee, beer, tequila, and pulque (fermented sap of the century plant) with tamales.

Pan para capirotada are bags of toasted bread slices used to make bread pudding, especially popular during Lent. The bread is layered in a buttered casserole with apple slices, raisins, nuts, and grated cheese with a cinnamon sugar poured over the layers before baking. Pastel rosa are slices of pink-tinted cake;

pastellitos are flaky pastry rectangles with a spicy fruit filling; and polvorones are strawberry, vanilla, or chocolate shortbread cookies tinted to match their flavor. Puros are yeasty, cigar-shaped sweet rolls; puros cortados are cut strips of sweet bread twisted into a roll and sprinkled with sugar; rebanadas are crème-filled toast sandwiches; and rieles are crunchy pastries with strawberry jam or pineapple jam fillings. Rocks are thick, round cinnamon cookies; and roles de canela are cinnamon rolls glazed with sugar syrup.

rosquilla

Rosquillas are anise-flavored, ring-shaped cookies made from an olive oil and flour dough, rolled into thin ropes, shaped into circles, and deep-fried in hot oil until golden and crisp. Sopaipillas are fat, pillow-like fritters made of fried bread dough. They can be split and stuffed with cold cuts to make a sandwich or served with sugar or honey syrup, dusted in powdered sugar. Suizos are sugar-topped, yeasty sweet rolls; and torteles are small bread rings filled with sweet potato paste, almond paste, or jam. Pan dulce shaped like a triangle is a triangulo; round-shaped pan dulce is a yoyo.

FROM THE SWEET BOX

Sweet treats include afajor de coco, thick slabs of grated coconut coated in a thin, hot-pink coconut paste and camote dulce cubierto, orange slabs that are lacquered with a sugar glaze. Acitrón is candied biznaga cactus. There's also calabaza de azucarado, lumps of candied pumpkin; bright orange, shredded coconut patties called cocadas; gummies (slabs of fruit jelly covered in sugar crystals); and jamoncillo, caramel-colored milk fudge made from sweetened condensed milk formed into little logs or round swirls topped with a walnut. You'll find mazapan, Mexican marzipan made from finely ground peanuts, powdered milk, flavorings, and honey, sold in little round discs wrapped in cellophane. There's also chocolate-dipped mazapan skulls on sticks; paleanquetas, little bars of pumpkin seed or peanut brittle; and picon, lumps of candied sweet potato. Calaveras de dulces, also called alfenques, are sugar and egg-white candies made for the day of the dead. The most famous are the sugar skulls on which you can have your name—or your dearly departed's—piped on in sugar icing. For the less squeamish there are candy lambs, ducks, fruits, doves, donkeys, and bulls.

Stocking Up

A lover of Mexican cuisine would load up on rice, dried or canned beans, both flour and corn tortillas, tostadas, mole and other cooking and seasoning sauces, salsa, pumpkin seeds, a soft white fresh cheese and an aged añejo. He would also buy some nopalitos cactus, jicama, tomatillos, epazote, carnitas or other roasted or steamed meat, and a selection of pan dulce. The adventurous would also try one of the Central American greens or fruits in brine or syrup and Colombian cheese bread mix.

10

The Andean Market: Peruvian Provisions

Peruvian food is a melange of European, ancient Incan, Asian, and African influences—it could be called one of the first fusion cuisines. Despite a long history and healthful reputation, this sublime cuisine remains relatively unknown, even secret. Once you explore the ingredients and learn to identify and use them, the mystery is removed.

Peru probably has the most extensive and varied menu of any South American country. The dual Incan and Spanish heritage is reflected in seafood soups, meat stews thickened with whole wheat kernels, fried fish pickled in vinegar, ceviche, and stuffed mashed potato cakes. Japanese, Chinese, and Italian influences also weave through the cooking of Peru, so stir-fries, rice, and noodle dishes are a part of the melting pot along with Spanish elements. From the hearty, spicy hot dishes of the highlands to the fish-based cuisine of the coast, Peru offers a delicious variety of flavors as international foods mingle and meld to create new riffs on ancient themes.

Potatoes & Tubers

Peru's gift to the world. There are more than 200 varieties of Peruvian potatoes and they are round, elongated, twisted, and nobbed, the size of grapes on up to grapefruits, ranging in hue from coral, tan, and yellow, to bright red and purple, shaped like gumdrops, cherries, and caterpillars. Peruvian grocery stores have freeze-dried, canned, and frozen potatoes and tubers—but rarely a fresh one in sight! Following are what you will find.

CHUÑO

Dehydrated whole potatoes. Newly harvested potatoes are frozen and thawed several times, then stomped on to remove the skins and press out any remaining moisture. The finished product is chuño negro, grayish, dry nuggets about the size of small stones. They are hard as wood but very light and will keep for many years. To produce chuño blanco, also called tunta or moraya, larger potatoes are used. White chuño are reserved for feast days in the Andes while black chuño are a part of the everyday diet.

Chuño is sold dried and whole or whole in cans and ground into flour. The canned type is reconstituted and ready to use. Dried chuño needs to be soaked in 6 to 8 changes of water before adding to soups, stews, and other dishes. White chuño is crushed to flour. It has a slightly sour smell, bland taste, and somewhat dense yet porous texture. Chuño swells a little after soaking and readily absorbs the flavors of

chuño

whatever it is cooked with. It softens in about half an hour of simmering and is popular in chupe (chowder) and stews. Chuño is perfect camping food—light, portable, and needing only water to reconstitute. Black and white chuño are found in 20-ounce cans under the Amazonas label. Dried white chuño, called chuño blanco seco, is in 1-pound bags of the Huascaran brand. Phoebe brand has harina de chuño (chuño flour) in 1-pound bags.

PAPA SECA

Cooked and freeze-dried potato bits. Made from yellow potatoes, also called papa amarilla sancochada (yellow stew potatoes), prepared in a similar way as chuño. The potatoes are peeled, cooked, and cut into small cubes and left to freeze and dry into hard little bits. To use, toast the bits in a dry skillet over low heat, about 5 minutes, stirring to prevent scorching. Remove from heat, place in a colander and rinse under cold water, drain, and and place in a bowl, covered with water and soak overnight. Drain and rinse again. The potato bits will have swelled a little and are now ready to add to soups, stews, and meat or vegetable dishes. Carapulcra is the best-known dish using papa seca. To make it, toast the dried bits in a dry pan, then soak half an hour, drain, and lightly mash or grind in a blender with some water. Sauté some chopped onions, garlic, salt, black pepper, chili powder or hot sauce, and ground cumin in oil, then add strips of chicken or pork and fry until browned. Add the mashed potato with some water or stock, some sweet wine, and toasted, chopped peanuts, and simmer over low heat until the potato mixture is soft. Stir once in a while so it doesn't stick or burn. Serve on a platter surrounded with boiled, sliced yellow potatoes or yuca and garnish with hard-boiled egg slices, olives, and chopped parsley. This is usually accompanied with rice and hot sauce. Commercially made carapulcra is sold in 20-ounce cans under the

Amazonas label. Papa seca is offered by Amazonas, Andina, Doña Isabel, La Casita, La Fe, and La Ollita brands in 15- to 16-ounce bags.

OCA

Also called ruba in Colombia and papa roja and papa extranjero in Mexico. When dried and frozen, they're called khaya or, if washed prior to freezing to make them lighter, okhaya. These small tubers resemble small, bumpy baby carrots with thin, shiny candy-colored skins, ranging from almost white, light yellow with reddish spots to magenta and violet. The flesh is pale and firm and juicy. Some are very sweet while others can have a slight tang. Oca tubers are found canned in brine or frozen. Fresh ones are available by mail order; see appendix 4. Most are slightly sweet with a pleasant, somewhat bland flavor. They can be boiled, baked, roasted, mashed, added to soups and stews, or candied as a sweet. Look for Piemco Inca's Food and Amazonas brands in 20-ounce cans or frozen in 1-pound bags. Andes Foods also has canned oca in 8- or 13-ounce cans.

OLLUCO

Also called melloco and ullucu. Olluco look like small, bumpy fingerling potatoes with thin, rainbow-splotched or speckled skins. They can be white, yellow, light green, pink, yellow-orange with green spots, or purple. The firm flesh is yellow and they taste like new potatoes. Some varieties have a slightly sticky consistency—if so, parboil to remove it. Ollucos are added to soups, chowders, meat and vegetable

olluco

stews, or are boiled and sliced for salads. Olluquito con charqui is one of the national dishes of Peru. Onions, garlic, chili sauce, and spices are sautéed with chopped tomatoes, strips of olluco, and shredded beef jerky and served with rice. Strips of chicken, pork, or beef can be substituted for the jerky. Ollucu cook very quickly. The tubers are sold in brine or frozen. Look for Amazonas, Piemco Inca's Food, and Phoebe brands in 20-ounce cans and Andes Foods in 8-, 13-, and 20-ounce jars. Frozen olluco look like French fries. Amazonas and Tambo de Oro brands have them in 1-pound bags.

Corn

The most sacred of all Incan crops was corn, which is found in many colors and varieties. For the Incans, corn was not just food and drink, but an important commodity used in trading. Types of corn available in Peruvian grocery stores include frozen cobs of pale jumbo kernels, purple corn, mote, and corn for popping.

CANCHA

Popping corn. Also called maiz para tostada, meaning "corn for toasting." There are several types, all partially dehydrated kernels used to make the Peruvian equivalent of popcorn. The kernels are fried in a little oil in a covered pan that is shaken as the kernels begin to make a

cancha

popping sound. Unlike popcorn, the grains do not explode into flowers but puff up and turn a toasty golden-brown color. Cancha is crisp, yet slightly chewy, and is delicious sprinkled with salt or chili powder as a snack. Cancha amarilla, also called cancha chulpi (or chulpe) is yellow corn, often labeled "frying corn." The large tooth-shaped kernels are very wrinkled, but puff up into crispy, smooth-skinned pellets when popped. Use only a tiny amount of oil and be sure to cover the frying pan or hot kernels will fly all over the place. Cancha kernels are irresistible hot out of the pan, and unlike corn nuts are not saturated in fats. Cancha chulpi is offered by Amazonas, Doña Isabel, and Tambo de Oro brands in 15-ounce bags. There are often small snack-size packets of maiz tostada near the front counter, but pre-popped cancha is not as tasty as freshly popped and can be stale or slightly rancid.

CHOCLO CUZQUERO

This is the large, white corn grown in the Cuzco region. Choclo means fresh on the cob, as opposed to dried, which is called mote (hominy) or cancha (popping corn). In Peru, fresh, giant choclo cobs are sold as snacks, boiling hot with slices of cheese and chili sauce. Here, it is found frozen on the cob, cut into segments (discos) and as kernels cut off the cob, labeled "choclo desgranado," and in jars of brine. The juicy jumbo kernels are sweet and delicious. Boil the whole cobs, slather with butter and sour cream, and sprinkle with salt and chili powder; or serve plain like sweet corn as a side dish. Loose kernels are added to soups, stews, and vegetable casseroles, and are thawed and grated to make humitas (fresh corn tamales). Grated kernels are also good in corn bread and corn pancakes. The sliced segments go into soups and stews and are boiled and served with ceviche. Look for Amazonas cobs, kernels, and segments in 1-pound bags. Tambo de Oro brand has 15-ounce bags of the kernels, and Andes Food has 8-, 13-, and 20-ounce jars of whole choclo kernels in brine. Drain and rinse before using.

MAIZ JORA

Dried, crushed, fermented sprouted corn. This unusual product is used to make chicha de jora, a non-alcoholic, but lightly fermented beverage. Maiz jora sold in Peruvian markets is fermented, crushed, and dried, recognizable by the hairy, purplish-yellow flattened grains—and strong sour smell. To use, boil in a large pot of water with sugar and a few cloves for about 3 hours, then allow to sit a few days, covered, and strain. The liquid is yellow and tastes like a slightly sweet and spicy "lite" cider, but is not carbonated. Chicha de jora is sold ready-made in bottles (used only for cooking, not drinking) as it is more of a fermented corn sauce than cider. Doña Isabel brand offers the chicha de jora sauce in 32-ounce bottles. La Hacienda and Piemco Inca's Food brands have the dried type in 1-pound bags.

MAIZ MORADO

Purple corn. This corn is naturally dark purple and native to the Andean valleys of Peru. It is mainly used to prepare a refreshing beverage called chicha morada (a spicy cider) and in a fruit jelly dessert. Dried purple corn is found in whole or broken cobs with small, purple-black hard kernels. To make chicha morada, boil the cobs for 15 minutes, strain, and mix the purple liquid with sugar and ground cinnamon and cloves. You can also add pineapple or apple juice. Chill before drinking. The cider tastes like spiced grape juice and is considered good for high blood pressure. To make the dessert called mazamorra morada, simmer one bag of purple corn cobs in 12 cups of water with some crushed pineapple and chopped apple, a few cloves, a cinnamon stick, and a pinch of anise for about 45 minutes or until the kernels start to burst open. Strain, discard cobs, and pour liquid into a large pot.

chica morada mix

Add soaked dried apricots, prunes, and raisins and about 1½ cups brown sugar. Stir to dissolve sugar and add a cornstarch slurry made from 2 tablespoons cornstarch mixed in ¼ cup water and stir well. Chill several hours and serve in bowls sprinkled with cinnamon. Whole purple corn cobs are sold by Amazonas, Loty, and Tambo de Oro brands in 15-ounce bags. Prepared chicha morada is found in the fridge case in plastic bottles—look for La Cholia brand. Amazonas, Negrita, and Phoebe brands also have instant mazamorra morado dessert mix in 8-ounce packets.

Grains & Flours

While corn and potatoes are the mainstays of Peruvian cuisine, grains also play an important role. Most grains and flours should be stored in airtight containers in a dry, cool place up to 6 months.

ARROZ DE CEBADA

Husked, cracked bits of barley used like rice. It is added to hearty soups and stews or cooked as pilaf—sautéed in oil with spices, chopped onion, and garlic, with water or stock added, and steamed. Nuts, meats, or vegetables can also be added to the steamed barley. Look for Doña Isabel brand in 15-ounce bags.

CEBADA ENTERA

Whole barley grains in the husk. This can be used in soups, but the barley needs to be soaked several hours to loosen the husks. Some husk will remain, making this form hearty and chewy with high roughage. Cebada pelada is "peeled" barley. The outer husk has been removed, but most of the nutritious bran coat is intact. Cebada tostada is whole, husked, and toasted barley with a delicious nutty taste. Hulled and toasted barley types can be cooked like rice, used to make porridges (savory or sweet) and added to soups and stews, usually with meat, potatoes, and spicy seasonings. Barley is also added to fermenting corn to make chicha (beer). Healthy and tasty barley water is made by boiling, steeping, and straining whole barley, adding sugar and lemon juice to taste. It is served chilled as a refreshing energy drink considered good for the kidneys. Machica is toasted barley flour, labeled as harina de cebada tostado. It looks like fine white sand and is used in baking breads and as a thickener in soups, stews, sauces, and gravies. Amazonas brand has all the barley grains in 12-ounce bags. Doña Isabel has the toasted flour and peeled barley in 15-ounce bags. Phoebe has the flour in 1-pound bags.

CREMA DE ARVEJA

Toasted pea flour. This is a soft, buff-colored powder made from ground, dried green peas. It gives bread a delicious, slightly sweet, nutty flavor and is used to thicken soups, sauces, and puddings. Look for Amazonas in 15-ounce bags and Doña Isabel in 12-ounce bags.

HARINA DE CAMOTE

Sweet potato flour. This is made from the starch of the potato and is used like cornstarch as a thickener in sauces, gravies, and puddings, and for dusting fish and other foods before frying, to form a crisp coating. Mixed with water, the starch is kneaded into doughs for fritters. The Peruvian version of Mexican buñuelos are picarones—deep-fried, anise-flavored pumpkin fritters. Flour and sweet potato starch are beaten into a puree of cooked and mashed pumpkin with a solution of yeast, warm water, and sugar. The smooth paste is left to rise and bits are pulled off and dropped into hot oil where they puff up. Sometimes they are formed into rings, making a doughnut-shaped fritter. They are served with sugar-flavored dried fig leaves. Amazonas, Doña Isabel, and Phoebe brands have it in 12-ounce bags and La Hacienda in 1-pound packages. Negritas brand has 9-ounce packets of picarones mix.

HARINA DE HABA

Fava flour. This pale, tan flour is made from skinned, dried, and ground fava beans. It's used to enrich breads, tamale dough, and homemade noodle and dumpling doughs. There is also a toasted version called harina de habas tostada, used to add a rich, nutty, flavor to doughs, batters, and sauces and to make thick beverages flavored with spices and sweetened with brown sugar. The toasted type is offered by Phoebe brand in 14-ounce bags. Amazonas has regular fava flour in 12-ounce bags.

KIWICHA

Also called quihuicha. This grain is related to quinoa but has even teenier grains. It needs to be rinsed before using. Place the seeds in a large bowl of cold water and rub gently to remove the bitter layer on the seed coats. Strain and rinse well. Kiwicha cooks quickly—simmer about 10 to 15 minutes until tender, then drain, and add to soups and stews, use in salads, side dishes, and savory or sweet porridges. Use cooked kiwicha as a bed for pan-roasted fish, vegetable stir-fries, or grilled meats. Toss with oil and vinegar and chopped vegetables with shrimp or other seafood as a salad, served on leafy greens. The tiny grain is also ground into flour,

kiwicha pop

pressed into flakes, and used to enrich flours for breads, tamales, and pasta dough. Kiwicha is also sold popped into tiny, crunchy puffs that taste like nutty popcorn. These are munched as a snack; eaten as cereal with fruit, milk, and honey; or used as a breading for fried fish and chicken. Turrones de kiwicha are nougats—small, thick, round, and sticky sweets made from popped kiwicha, finely ground peanuts, and dried fruit paste mixed with sugar syrup. These

kiwicha cookies

are made by the Gino brand. Piemco Inca's Food has the whole grain in small bags. Amazonas, La Ollita, and Inca Sun brands have popped kiwicha in 8- and 12-ounce packages.

QUINOA

Pronounced keen-WAH. This versatile grain has become very popular with the health food crowd, who value it as a complete protein and appreciate its flavor and slightly chewy texture. It tastes like couscous infused with essence of wild rice. The tiny yellow, white, or pinkish seeds are threshed and winnowed to remove the husks and processed in an alkaline solution to remove the bitter sapoin compounds on the seed coats. Nonetheless, it is wise to always rinse and wash quinoa because not all brands pre-process the seeds. To do this, place in a mesh sieve and rinse thoroughly under cold water. To cook, combine 2 cups of washed quinoa with 8½ cups water in a saucepan and bring to a boil, reduce heat, and simmer 10 to 20 minutes or until the grains are tender and somewhat translucent. Remove from heat and drain. The quinoa can now be seasoned to serve or added to other dishes. Never add salt or sugar to the cooking water or the seeds may toughen. Add the cooked seeds to soups, meat stews, or mix with chopped cucumbers, tomatoes, scallions, parsley, mint, salt and pepper, and chill. Serve on leafy greens with a squeeze of lemon juice. The grain also enriches breads, biscuits, and tamale dough and is ground into flour for baked goods. It can also be sprouted and used like alfalfa sprouts. In Peru quinoa is fermented to make a type of chicha (beer). It is also sold popped, which looks like miniature popcorn with a crunchy, nutty taste sprinkled over foods, added to breads, or enjoyed as a breakfast cereal. Most quinoa sold in this country is the pale yellow to beige type. Amazonas and La Ollita brands sell the grain in 12-ounce bags and quinoa for popping in 4-ounce packets. Inca Sun brand also has the popped grain in 4-ounce bags and Phoebe brand has the whole grain in 14-ounce bags.

TRIGO PELADO ENTERO

Whole, hulled wheat kernels. Trigo partido tostada is toasted, split wheat kernels. Both types need to be soaked overnight, then drained before adding to hearty beef and vegetable soups and stews. An example is sopa de trigo, a richly flavored soup of beef chunks and whole wheat kernels simmered in stock with seasonings, chopped leeks, carrots, potatoes, and pumpkin, garnished with oregano and fresh mint, cilantro, and parsley. Sopa chambar is another stew-like soup based on whole or split wheat kernels simmered with fava beans, navy beans, garbanzos, chopped smoked ham and onions, garlic, chili powder, and oregano. Traditionalists add a pig's ear as well. Split wheat is good for porridges and cooked pilaf-style. Soaked wheat kernels take about 45 minutes or more to cook and have an earthy flavor and chewy texture. Split wheat takes a little less time. Always season with salt after the grains are tender. Amazonas and Doña Isabel brands have whole and split wheat in 15-ounce bags. Pheobe brand has the whole kernels in 14-ounce bags.

Beans

In Peru, beans are known as menestras and many types are used, especially the native canary and Lima beans. Black-eyed peas, called castillas, are also popular as well as white beans, lentils, garbanzos, and favas (habas). These are all discussed in chapter 2. Some unique, native types found in Peruvian groceries are listed below. Beans are added to soups and stews and are mixed with rice to make tacu-tacu, a side dish served with meats or a vegetarian main course. Bean brands that offer a wide variety, including the ones described here, are Amazonas, La Ollita, Doña Isabel, and La Hacienda in 15- to 16-ounce bags.

FAVA BEANS PACAE

A type of fava, these beans are dark olive green with wrinkled skins and resemble large Lima beans in shape. Fava beans pacae should be soaked at least 24 hours and the skins removed as they have a slightly bitter taste. Rub the skins off or squeeze firmly to pop the beans out of their skins. Skinless fava are pale yellowish and when cooked have a nutty flavor and creamy texture, but they hold up well in simmered dishes. They can also be cooked and pureed for dips or thickening soups. The beans take about 2½ hours to cook. They are often added to chupe, milk-based chowders made with shrimp, corn, carrots, cabbage, squash, and a handful of rice, seasoned with paprika, cumin, and allspice. Cubes of queso blanco are added just before serving. Fava pacae are also simmered in milk with chopped mushrooms, onions, cumin, and pepper, with beaten eggs and crumbled cheese added at the end. Ground, dried fava beans are used as a caffeine-free coffee substitute.

NUÑAS

These are Peruvian popping beans, the bean counterpart of popcorn. They are a common type of bean which, when heated in a little oil in a covered pan, burst out of their seed coats. Nuñas are similar to cancha (toasted corn), crunchy on the outside and soft within, and taste a bit like roasted peanuts. Nuñas supply all the protein and fiber of ordinary beans but pop quickly, rendering them edible in minutes. They resemble common beans but are hard-shelled and come in eye-catching colors and patterns—such as white-, red-, and black-spotted. Besides being popped, they are added to soups and stews, but are much tastier—and more fun—popped. They make a delicious, healthy snack sprinkled with a little salt and chili powder. Amazonas has them in 15-ounce bags.

PALLARES

Giant white Lima beans. Also called alubias pallares, judia Lima beans, and potato beans. Native to Peru, these were a staple of pre-Hispanic civilizations in South America, providing protein and fiber. The dried beans are large, flat, and white. They should be soaked overnight and take longer to cook than other Lima beans—about 1 to 2 hours. Pallares have a mild, nutty flavor and creamy, starchy texture. Good cooked and seasoned with fried onions, hot sauce, and chopped fresh herbs as a side dish or added to salads, soups, stews, and vegetable dishes. A very similar type called gigantes are sold canned in Greek stores.

Chilies, Chili Sauces & Chili Pastes

In Peru every market has piles of chilies, called ají, usually separated by color and laid out on brightly colored woven cloths. There are numerous types, including small, round red, yellow, and orange ají limo, tiny berry-like round red ají cereza, wild ají charapa, aji montana (long, red, and very hot), and ají pinguita de mono, inch-long red screamers, which are a variety of monkey chilies grown in the jungle. A few of these may be found pickled in Peruvian markets. The more common Peruvian ají are listed below. Most are sold canned or in jars of brine and some are found dried, ground, or as pastes.

AJÍ AMARILLO

Yellow chili. These are 4- to 6-inch long banana-shaped peppers, which turn a deep sunset orange color when fully ripe. Ají amarillo are moderately hot, aromatic, and flavorful. They are combined with potatoes, corn, and quinoa in stews and add depth along with a golden hue to meat, chicken, fish, potatoes, pasta, and rice dishes as well as creamy milk chowders and creamy cheese sauces. Yellow chilies are sold whole in

ají amarillo

brine (escabeche) and frozen. Dried whole ones are called cuzqueño and may also be just labeled as ají amarillo seco. This chili is sold as salsa,

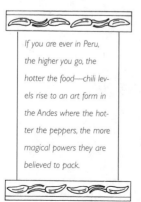

If you are ever in Peru, the higher you go, the hotter the food—chili levels rise to an art form in the Andes where the hotter the peppers, the more magical powers they are believed to pack.

blended with passion fruit, pineapple, or black mint (huacatay), hot sauce (called tabasco), and as a pureed paste. The pastes are handy for flavoring stir-fries, rice, pasta, and sauces. Yellow chili paste is essential for authentic salsa de Arequipa, a hot sauce from the city of Arequipa in southern Peru famous for its fiery food. The sauce is made by pureeing the yellow chili paste with crushed saltines, walnuts, grated cheese, a little vegetable oil, chopped onion, and garlic, hard-boiled eggs, cooked shrimp, and milk in a blender. The sauce is traditionally served over boiled and sliced potatoes but is also good poured over fried fish or grilled jumbo shrimp. Dried yellow chilies are packaged by Amazonas, La Hacienda, Huascaran, and Phoebe brands in 1.5- to 2-ounce bags. To use them, remove stems and seeds, soak in warm water to soften, and puree in a blender with a little liquid. Amazonas also has the fruity salsas and ají amarillo-black mint sauce in 7-ounce jars as well as hot yellow pepper tabasco sauce in 7-ounce bottles. Doña Isabel, La Casita, La Hacienda, and Tambo de Oro brands have the paste in 7.5-ounce jars and Doña Isabel also sells a yellow chili and black mint paste in 6-ounce jars. Andes Foods offers yellow chili salsa and whole peppers in 8- and 13-ounce jars. Tambo de Oro has 12-ounce bags of whole frozen yellow chilies. They should be blanched in boiling water 1 to 2 minutes to soften, and can then be drained, cut in strips, or stuffed.

AJÍ PANCA

This is a 5-inch long shiny pepper that changes from green to yellow, then red, and finally eggplant purple when fully ripe. Panca chilies are so popular in Peru that they are nicknamed the "princess of the kitchen." Dried ají panca are dark maroon, glossy, and wrinkled with a mild, sweet flavor. To use, remove the stems, slit and scrape out the seeds and soak until soft in warm water. Dried ones can just be broken into pieces and added to soups, stews, and chili con carne. Panca chilies' rich red color and flavor enhance chicken, meat, pasta, potato, and bean dishes. Try sautéing finely chopped dried panca with onions and garlic in olive oil, then add tomato paste and blend the mixture into beans cooked with pork—quick and tasty when canned beans are used. The dried chilies may also be called ají rojo seca. This chili is also found in pastes, barbecue sauce, and ground into powder. All forms are used in marinades for grilled fish and meats and as table condiments. Spread the paste and sauce

or sprinkle the powder on burgers, scrambled or fried eggs, and sandwiches; or mix into soups and stews for color and mild kick. To make a marinade for meat or chicken, mix some of the paste with vinegar, crushed garlic, oregano, and lemon juice with salt and pepper and use to marinate. Amazonas has the barbecue sauce, labeled "ají panca especial" in 7-ounce jars, panca tabasco hot sauce in 7-ounce bottles, and whole dried ají panca in 1.5-ounce packets. Huascaran brand sells the paste in 6.5-ounce jars and whole chilies in 1.5-ounce packets. Phoebe brand offers dried panca in 1.5-ounce packets and powdered panca in 6.5-ounce jars. Andes Foods has panca paste in 8- and 13-ounce jars and La Casita has the paste in 7.5-ounce jars.

dried panca chili

ROCOTO

Also called manzano, or chili apple, due to its shape. This pungent pepper is the only pepper in the world with black seeds and its fire engine red color is a warning of its five-alarm heat. Even diehard chili heads should proceed with caution when using this chili. In Peruvian groceries they are sold whole in jars and cans or frozen and as a paste. Rocoto are bell pepper–shaped,

rocoto pepper-peach salsa

Ceviche rivalry is hot between neighboring Peru and Ecuador. Both types are addictive and some folks get their first fix as early as 11:00 A.M. from street vendors who sell it freshly prepared from hot dog carts. Ceviche is fresh fish and other seafoods including scallops, shrimp, clams, octopus, squid, and langostas "cooked" in lemon or lime juice. Ecuadorian ceviche comes in a bowl, the seafood swimming in citrus liquid, spices, and chilies, served with boiled corn, beans, patacones (fried plantain patties), and toasted corn kernels. Peruvian ceviche is spread out on a plate in just a nice splash of marinade, enlivened with minced garlic, chilies, sliced onions, and chopped herbs, served with boiled corn, yuca slices, and rounds of sweet potato, often garnished with wisps of seaweed.

about the size of a plum tomato with shiny red skins. For a real mouth sizzler try them Peruvian-style as rocoto rellenos. Cut half an inch from the tops, scrape out the seeds, rinse and stuff with cheese or a ground meat filling, and bake. Rocoto adds flavor and fire to everything from stews and grilled meats to potato dishes and creamy sauces—the best known of these is the cheese and chili sauce for papas Huancaína. This very picante pepper is also toned down in sauces, blended with peaches, pineapple, or tamarind. Roasted chicken is delicious smeared with rocoto-peach sauce. Look for Amazonas' plain or fruit-flavored rocoto salsas and tabasco in 7-ounce bottles and whole peppers in 13-ounce jars, 20-ounce cans, or frozen in 1-pound bags. Tambo de Oro brand has whole frozen rocoto in 12-ounce bags and the paste in 8.5-ounce jars. Doña Isabel, Huascaran, and Phoebe brands have 6.5-ounce jars of rocoto paste and Huascaran also offers whole rocoto in 13-ounce jars as well as pickled montana (monkey chilies) in 13-ounce jars. Andes Food has rocoto mitades, halved peppers in 8- and 13-ounce jars, and rocoto salsa, chutney, and pickles in 6.5- and 13-ounce jars. All the major exporters sell mixed chilies, good for sampling several varieties. These are often labeled "ceviche mezcla de ajices," or mixed peppers for ceviche. They're cut into thin rings and added to ceviche citrus marinades for flavor and heat, a contrast to the cool seafood. They are also used in cooking and to garnish salads and sandwiches. For a ceviche recipe, see page 248.

Sauces & Mixes

From Peru we get a selection of ready-to-use sauces, powdered instant mixes and ready-made creamy chili and peanut sauces for pouring over rice or boiled, sliced potatoes. There are also mixes for cream of artichoke and pea soup and alfredo and pesto pasta mixes.

AJÍ DE GALLINA

Instant mix for making chili chicken with walnuts. A blend of powdered chili, milk powder, ground crackers, garlic powder, and walnuts. To use, mix with milk and a teaspoon of oil and heat gently, stirring until smooth, then add cooked and shredded chicken. This is offered by Doña Isabel and Provenzal brands in small packets, with directions and recipe suggestions on the back. A recipe for ají de gallina is on page 252.

ALBAHACA

Basil sauce. This is a puree of fresh basil, used to tint and flavor rice, pasta, and stews. Use like pesto, with added minced garlic and ground nuts, or spoon directly out of the jar as is, and use in place of the fresh herb. Blenderize with walnuts, chopped spinach, milk, garlic, onion, and cottage cheese to make a creamy salsa verde for tallarines (the South American term for spaghetti). A little basil sauce adds fragrance and flavor to meat and vegetable soups, white bean dishes, salad dressings, stir-fries, steamed fish or mussels, and chowders. Look for Amazonas in 7.5-ounce jars and Andes Food and Phoebe brands in 8-ounce jars. Also Rosilima basil paste in 8-ounce jars.

CILANTRO SAUCE

Salsa de cilantro. A puree of cilantro, handy to use in place of the fresh herb. Cilantro flavors potatoes, rice, soups, stews, and sauces. To make salsa verde picante, a bright green hot table sauce, blenderize some cilantro sauce with a little oil and water with chopped garlic, onions, and jalapeño or serrano chilies. The sauce adds flavor and pep to most any food. It is especially good with fried fish and grilled or roasted chicken and makes great dip for chips, empanadas, fritters, and starchy vegetables such as yuca and green plantains. Look for Andes Food and Phoebe brands in 8-ounce jars labeled "paste de cilantro" (pasta in this case means paste) and Doña Isabel in 7.5-ounce jars.

HUACATAY

Black mint or Peruvian black marigold. A type of wild marigold with dark green, serrated leaves with a sharp, sweetish-anise flavor. The leaves are ground into a paste with a little salt and preservatives. Use the paste thinned with water to season seafood, soups, and stews or blend into chili sauces. Salsa huacatay is made by whirling some of the paste with oil, cottage cheese, chilies, garlic, and salt. It is great over boiled and sliced potatoes, corn, eggs, steak, roasted chicken, and fried fish or as a dip for garlic bread or chips. Another famous herb and chili sauce using huacatay is ocopa, a creamy blend of shrimp, peanuts, and cottage cheese. Mix huacatay sauce into cooked rice and use in pasta sauces. It is also sold frozen in large balls, two to a bag. These are best ground in a blender with some water into a paste and stored in a jar, refrigerated. Fresh huacatay is available by mail order; see appendix 4. For frozen, look for Inca's

frozen huacatay sauce

Food in 12-ounce bags. Amazonas, Andes Food, La Casita, and Phoebe brands are in 7.5- and 8-ounce jars.

HUANCAÍNA

This is a ready-made sauce or instant mix for making papas a la Huancaína, boiled and sliced potatoes smothered in a creamy chili-cheese sauce. Huancaína sauce is also good over rice, roasted meat, grilled or fried chicken, shrimp, pasta, and salads or used as a sandwich spread. Also makes a delicious dip for chips, crackers, and garlic bread and thickens soups and stews. The sauce is a blend of yellow chili, crushed crackers, half-and-half, cottage cheese, and a tiny amount of olive oil. Some cooks add hard-boiled eggs, a pinch of sugar and turmeric, chopped onion, and lemon juice. The ingredients are processed in a blender until smooth and poured over warm potato slices piled on lettuce leaves and deco-rated with sliced hard-boiled eggs and olives. This is usually served with boiled corn on the cob and hot sauce. Every Peruvian restaurant serves a version of papas a la Huancaína, each with its own twist. For the ready-made sauce, look for Amazonas and La Casita brand in 7.5-ounce jars, while Doña Isabel and Provenzal have small packets of instant mix—just add 1 cup milk and stir until smooth.

huancaína

OCOPA

A shrimp and chili sauce for potatoes. Ocopa con papas is a variation of papas a la Huancaína. Yellow chilies are pureed with peeled, cooked shrimp, a little olive oil, roasted peanuts or walnuts, chopped onion and garlic, cottage cheese, huacatay (black mint), and salt. The sauce is poured over small, whole boiled potatoes or mashed potato balls and garnished with sliced hard-boiled eggs, sprigs of cilantro, and strips of red pepper. Ocopa sauce is also used as a dip, as a sandwich spread, and over rice, roasted meats, pasta, burgers, kebabs, and salads. Most com-mercial ocopa sauces do not contain shrimp or nuts and are a puree of yellow chili, black mint, cheese, crackers, salt, oil, and spices. For this type look for Amazonas in 7.5-ounce jars and Tambo de Oro brand in 8.5-ounce jars. Doña Isabel and Provenzal have powdered mixes in small packets—add milk or cream and blend until smooth.

ocopa sauce

PAPAS CON MANÍ

A powdered mix for making a spicy, creamy peanut (maní) sauce for potatoes. Toasted peanuts are pureed with cream, milk, chili powder, chopped onion, a little peanut oil, cottage cheese, salt, and pepper and the mixture heated gently over low heat, about 5 minutes, and poured over hot cooked potatoes. The sauce is also mixed with rice, tossed with pasta, and used as a dip for crackers, chips, and garlic bread. Provenzal brand has instant mix in small packets.

PASTA DE AJOS

Garlic paste. This is simply pureed garlic with salt, a little oil, and preservatives. Use in place of fresh garlic in any recipe. Store refrigerated once open. A delicious, garlic-infused dish is papa a la diabla, or deviled potatoes. Grate the equivalent of 4 cloves of garlic (about 4 teaspoons of paste) with 2 canned yellow chilies, some turmeric, and chopped onions. Process in a blender with cottage cheese and evaporated milk until smooth, then heat over low heat a few minutes and set aside. Line a plate with lettuce leaves topped with boiled sliced potatoes, pour the sauce over them, and garnish with sliced hard-boiled eggs and olives. Garlic paste is also mashed with roasted rocoto chilies and mixed with salt to make a hot table condiment, good with meat and fish dishes. Look for Amazonas in 7.5-ounce jars, Andes Foods in 6.5- and 8-ounce jars, and Productos Orezzoli in 8-ounce jars.

Frozen Goods

The freezer cases of Peruvian groceries are packed with bags of vegetables; chilies; herbs; tubers such as ollocos, potatoes, and yuca in chunks; corvina (sea bass); banana leaf–wrapped tamales; snacks; and other delicacies mentioned below. Not to be missed is the lucuma ice cream!

CAIGUA

Also spelled cayhua. Twisted, pale green hollow gourds, pointed at each end and with soft skins. They are often mislabeled as "hollow chayote," as they resemble hollowed-out, halved chayote squash. The mushy, thawed gourds are crumpled looking and have been cut in half with the seeds removed. They are mild, bordering on bland, and are

frozen caigua

best pickled, stewed, or stuffed—think of them as vegetable pita bread pockets for putting tasty things inside such as dips and sliced radishes, rice and bean mixtures, or whatever you are eating. They are good stuffed with cheese, mashed potatoes, and flaked fish or shredded chicken mixtures, seasoned with spices, olives, and chopped onion, bound with breadcrumbs and eggs. The gourds should be loosely stuffed and steamed or baked about 15 minutes and served with rice, salad, and hot sauce. Look for Tambo de Oro brand with 6 to a bag.

FISH ROE

Huevera. Compact, egg-filled sacs of various fish—usually flounder, mackerel, or corvina (sea bass). Considered a delicacy, they're rinsed, sprinkled with salt and lime juice, dredged in flour, and fried in hot oil 3 to 4 minutes until crispy to make hueveras fritas. Fried fish roe is often served as a part of mixed fried seafood platters with a zesty hot, dipping sauce, or zarza, such as thinly sliced onions and diced tomatoes mixed with lemon juice, salt, and pepper. As roe tends to splatter and pop when frying, it is best to partially cover the frying pan and use the lid as a shield. Fish roe is found in small, plastic-wrapped packaging, usually unlabeled.

LUCUMA ICE CREAM

Pronounced "lu-KA-ma." Lucuma are large, tennis ball–sized round fruits related to canistel, which are also called eggfruit. The thin, green skins turn yellowish green when ripe and begin to burst, revealing flesh that is dry and starchy with a few brown seeds. As fresh lucuma are not available (and not very palatable), you can try it as ice cream. The peachy-orange ice cream tastes like very rich, intense butterscotch with date undertones and is sold in single serving cups and larger tubs. Amazonas has it in pints and 1½ gallon containers. In some stores, the containers are just labeled "lucuma." This frozen treat is so incredibly good, it's worth finding a Peruvian market just to try some. Many stores also have lucuma powder made from ground and dehydrated pulp, sold in 1-pound plastic bags. The powder is used to flavor ice cream, yogurt, mousse, custard, cakes, and candies.

PAPA RELLENO

Stuffed potato. A frozen, pale yellow, football-shaped snack the size of a large sweet potato. Boiled and mashed potato is shaped into a cup and a spoonful of ground beef seasoned with sautéed chopped onion, cumin, raisins, olives, and bits of chopped, hard-boiled egg are placed in the hollow. The potato mash is squeezed up and around the filling to encase it, forming a small torpedo. This is brushed with beaten egg and fried in hot oil until golden. The outside is crispy and inside soft. Defrost 1 to 2 hours, reheat, and serve with hot sauce. Most are homemade, sold in sealed plastic bags by the piece.

TAMALE

Peruvian tamales are large rectangles wrapped in banana leaves and tied with string like a birthday package. They are made from maza, a mixture of masa harina, chopped yellow chili, salt, annatto, corn oil, and hot water. Tamale dough can be stuffed with any number of fillings, but the most common is chicken. Bits of meat are cooked with garlic, scallions, chili powder, pepper, and cumin. A thick layer of maza is spread on a piece of leaf, a depression made and the filling pressed in with an olive and piece of hard-boiled egg. The leaf is folded, sealing in the filling, and steamed in a pot of boiling water. There might also be smaller tamalitos verdes tinted green with cilantro

frozen peruvian tamales

133

sauce mixed into the cornmeal and stuffed with bits of pork. Thaw the frozen tamales 1 to 2 hours and place in 2 inches of boiling water and cook, covered, for 10 minutes and serve with hot sauce.

YELLOW POTATOES

Papas amarillo. Also called limeña. These are pre-cooked small yellow potatoes, also grown in Colombia, where they are known as papa criolla; see page 111. The skins are thin and smooth and the flesh golden and buttery flavored, good boiled and mashed. Use these spuds to make cuasa, stuffed mashed potato cakes served chilled. This is party fare, often served at weddings and other festive occasions. To make a basic variety, mash peeled and boiled potatoes with some yellow chili powder, turmeric, salt, and corn oil. Make a filling from chopped, cooked chicken blended with diced celery, parsley, and mayonnaise. Spread half the potato mixture in an oiled dish, spread the filling over it, and cover with the rest of the potato mixture. Cover with plastic wrap and refrigerate several hours and serve cold, cut into slices. Yellow potatoes can also be roasted, fried, and added to soups and stews. They are packaged by Amazonas and Tambo de Oro brands in 1-pound bags. Thaw and drop into boiling water and cook about 5 minutes or bake in the oven 10 minutes. Amazonas brand also has the potatoes in 20-ounce cans and a puree in 8-ounce cans.

Odds & Ends

A potpourri of goods still awaits exploration in the Peruvian grocery. There are packets of medicinal herbs, jars of olives, bottles of Pisco, dried fruits, a turmeric-like yellow powder, sweets, sodas, and both soy sauce and spaghetti, called tallerines. Spaghetti reflects one of Peru's many ethnic influences, brought by Italian immigrants. Spaghetti is baked, al horno, with cheese, tomatoes, and eggs; tossed in pesto; mixed with creamy cheese and chili sauces, and used to make sopa secas (dried soups where all the sauce or broth is absorbed). Because many Chinese and Japanese people came to Peru in the mid-1800's, the cuisine has a strong Asian influence—any Peruvian menu includes some Asian-inspired saltados, or quick sautés based on the stir-fry method, as well as steamed seafoods drizzled in soy-based sauces.

In addition to Japanese-style ceviche, specialties from the Japanese community in Lima include sopa kun fun, noodles in fish broth with garlic, clams, chicken, beef, Napa cabbage, and onions, thickened egg drop–style with beaten eggs; whole steamed fish in soy sauce; and a tomato-based seafood soup seasoned with garlic, ginger, oregano, and bay leaf. Of course there are vegetable tempura dumplings, more like fritters made from battered and deep-fried chopped lettuce, carrots, peas, and scallions served in a ginger, lime, and soy dipping sauce.

There are interesting Peruvian-Chinese chifa dishes, a unique amalgamation of Chinese ingredients such as soy sauce, ginger, tausi (black bean sauce), and lo mein noodles and Peruvian hot peppers, potatoes, spices, and seafood, leavened with Spanish influences. You might find chop suey on a chifa menu, but it would be a shame to not try arroz chaufa mixto, a mix of fried rice tossed with oyster sauce, onions, eggs, nuggets of roast pork, hunks of chicken and shrimp, or cam lu wantan, pork-stuffed, deep-fried wontons in a tangy tamarind sauce. Another specialty is sazimi Peruvana, a version of ceviche served with grated daikon radish, a gingery lime juice, and wasabi-infused soy dipping sauce; and tiradito, a type of ceviche with the fish cut sashimi style and marinated in spicy citrus juice. You can use any type of noodle and soy sauce to create Italian-Asian-fusion dishes, but you need to visit a Peruvian grocery store for the following assortments of goods.

GUINDAS

Dried cherries. Cherries with glossy purple skins and meaty green flesh. They taste like a tart raisin and contain a rather large brown seed. As they are impossible to pit, use with caution in desserts or baked goods. Another dried fruit in the same vein are guindones, dried plums—also known as prunes. Both are eaten as snacks or added to mazamorra, the purple corn jelly-like pudding. The prunes are easier to pit and go into

guindas

bread pudding (budín) and the purple corn gelatin dessert or can be chopped and added to empanada fillings and meat stews. Chocoteja de guindone are caramel-and-chocolate–covered prune sweets, sold by the piece, wrapped in foil and white paper. Amazonas and Doña Isabel brands have the cherries in small 2.5- to 3-ounce jars and Amazonas also has 4-ounce packages of the prunes. Helena Company sells the prune candies.

INKA COLA

A sparkling yellow soda with a sweet, creamy bubble gum flavor. You either love it or loath it, but most Peruvians drink more of this than any other soda. Inka Cola was invented in Peru in 1935; the soda's formula is top secret, but is thought to be a combination of sweetened and carbonated essences and fragrances, flavored with lemongrass and several fruits. Inka Cola is sold in soda cans and 2-litre plastic bottles. There is also Kola Inglesa, which is a sweet strawberry-flavored soda.

MACA NECTAR & POWDER

Maca nectar is a thick, pale, creamy juice made from maca pulp, water, and sugar. It should be chilled and shaken before drinking. The flavor is a weird combination of raw potato, celery, cabbage, cherry, butterscotch, and toasted corn. At first it tastes sweet, then sour. Maca is high in proteins, carbohydrates, vitamins, and minerals and is taken for almost everything—to stimulate the immune sytem and treat anemia, menopause, stomach disorders, chronic

maca nectar

fatigue syndrome, sexual problems, and to boost energy and enhance memory. Inca's Food brand has the juice in 10-ounce bottles with a wool-capped Inca child on the label. You might also find Maca Inka's instant powder in 150 g (about 5-ounce) plastic jars. To use the ochre powder, dissolve one spoonful in a cup of water or hot milk.

OLIVES

Aceituna. Aceituna de botija are large, dark purple, meaty olives with a mild flavor. The juicy pulp is also made into pastes, sold in jars. Spread the paste on crackers, bread, and fried snacks or whirl in a blender with grated mozzarella or cottage cheese, yogurt, chopped walnuts or pecans, and a chili paste to make a delicious dip. Hollowed-out, small cooked potatoes are stuffed with the mixture and topped with a boiled shrimp as an appetizer. Whole olives garnish salads, potatoes smothered in sauces, and mashed, stuffed potato cakes. The dark olives are sold in jars of brine and dry-cured, called seca. Aceituna verde Peruvana are smaller green olives, also sold in brine. These are used in salads and meat stews or as a garnish and are chopped for various stuffings. Amazonas has the black olives, both dried and brine-packed, and green olives in 8- and 16-ounce jars. La Cholia and Del Viejo Olivar brands sell the black Yauca Valley olives in 1-pound jars. Andes Food, Doña Isabel, and Phoebe brands have black olive paste in 6.5-ounce jars.

PALILLO

Also called raiz de color, or "coloring root." This is a yellowish-orange powder made from the dried, ground rhizome of a South American herb. The turmeric-like powder is virtually tasteless and used only for tinting rice and other foods. You may also find small packets of sazondor, a bright red-orange powder made from ground panca chilies, annatto, salt, and spices. It clearly states on the label "sin picante," meaning "not hot." This basically adds color and a slight bite to dishes—use like paprika. The Sibarila brand offers it in tiny packets. Palillo tints tamale dough, breads, and pastries as well as mashed potatoes, soups, and stews. Amazonas brand has palillo in 2.5-ounce jars and Doña Isabel in 1.5-ounce ones.

The chifa restaurants of Peru are known for their excellent Peruvian-Chinese food. The term "chifa" is derived from the Chinese expression "chi fan seck," literally meaning "preparing to eat rice." Meals might start off with asparagus soup, which is egg flower soup with white asparagus, and move on to pollo con yuyo, chicken with cloud ear mushrooms. Lomo saltado is a popular choice. This consists of strips of beef stir-fried with chopped onions and tomatoes with crispy French fries folded in just before serving. Other dishes include lay chi ti, battered fish in a sesame sauce, and tangy pork in gingery tamarind sauce, all washed down with tea or a Cusquena or Cristal beer.

PHYSALIS

Also called aguaymanito, alkekengi, cape gooseberry, and golden berry. In Hawaii it is known as poha. These golden-hued berries have a bittersweet taste with a lingering pleasant aftertaste. They are not found fresh in Peruvian groceries, but as preserves. Tierras Atlas "Inca Conserve" brand offers physalis in several forms: regular and bitter-sweet conserve, jelly, and preserved whole in light or medium syrup, all in 8- and 13-ounce jars. Use the conserves as a spread or like chut-ney to accompany meat or fish. The syrupy conserves are good spooned over ice cream and stirred into yogurt or drained and used as a pie or tart filling.

PISCO

The national drink of Peru, pisco is a clear brandy distilled from green, ripe muscat or mission grapes with a high alcohol content. There are several different kinds, but Ocucaje Pisco is considered the best. A pisco sour is made by blending or shaking together 3 ounces of pisco, a teaspoon of sugar, 2 teaspoons lime juice, ½ cup of crushed ice and egg white beaten with a drop or two of Angostera bitters. The egg white forms a thin layer of foam on top of the cocktail glass. Pisco sours taste like sweet lemon juice but are quite powerful.

Sweet Endings

ALFAJORES

Pastry discs sandwiched with dulce de leche (caramel). They vary in size from about 1- to 3-inch cookies to cake size. The dough can be made from chuño flour (ground freeze-fried potatoes) or wheat flour, mixed with butter or shortening, sugar, and lemon zest. The cookies are soft, pale, and crumbly and not overly sweet, but the caramel and dusting of powdered sugar compensate. Alfajores are sold nestled in ruffled paper cups or in plastic-wrapped packs of about six.

CHOCOTEJAS

tejas de pecanas

Chocolate bon-bons with various fillings, wrapped in foil, then white paper, twisted at the top with the ends cut in strips. In addition to the chocolate and caramel covered prunes (chocotejas guindones), there are tejas de pecanas (pecans and caramel coated in a lemony white icing), chocotejas passas borraches (rum-soaked raisin filling coated in chocolate, the name means "drunk raisins"), and naranjas (orange marmalade and caramel covered in chocolate). All are made by the Helena Company and are sold by the piece from candy jars or boxes.

SWEET BEAN PASTE

Frijol colado. A sweet puree of black or red beans cooked until thick with evaporated milk, brown sugar, and ground cinnamon, cloves, and sesame seeds. It is usually served with cookies or crackers. The paste is also rolled up in crêpes or pancakes and used as a pastry filling.

Look for Doña Isabel brand in 6.5-ounce jars. Some stores make their own and sell it in small tubs near the register.

TEJAS IQUENAS

Tejas de Ica. These soft candies are made by boiling halved lemons in six or seven changes of salted water to remove the bitterness, and then in sugar syrup until the mixture is very thick and honey-like. When cool enough to handle, the substance is rolled into balls and stuffed with caramel, whole pecans, raisins, chopped prunes, or marmalade. The candies are then dipped in a lemon-infused white icing, wrapped in foil, and tied with white paper twists. These are made by the Helena brand and are sold by the piece in candy jars or boxes.

TURRÓN DE DOÑA PEPA

Cured of her paralysis through her faith, Doña Pepa first made these lucious sweets in honor of God. The recipe was revealed to her in a

dream. Three thick, yellow slabs of shortbread stuck together with syrup. The tops are covered in the syrup and sprinkled with colorful little candies. The dough is made from a mixture of flour, egg yolks, shortening, and anise. The tops are decorated with multi-hued candy hearts, stars, and little balls—a dentist's delight!

turrón de doña pepa

S t o c k i n g   U p

To create the flavors of Peru in your kitchen, you will want a stash of potatoes, yuca or other tubers; corn, including cancha for pan-frying and snacking on or serving with beer and ceviche; kiwicha or quinoa for healthy grain dishes and salads (the popped type is great as cereal); beans; ají pastes and huacatay sauce for an exotic and authentic touch. You might also want some of the quick cheese sauce mixes, black olives, purple corn cider or dessert mix, and delicious lucuma ice cream. Meats, seafood, and produce from the supermarket round out your ingredients. Keep in mind that ceviche is not really cooked in the citrus marinade, so use only sushi quality fish or poach just until cooked through, then marinate and chill. Pisco or Cristal beer are perfect lubricants for a pre-meal gathering or party.

· 11 ·

Sabores Chilenos:
A Taste of Chile

Chilean cuisine, called comida criolla, is a fusion of European influences and ingredients with those of the native Mapuches Indians. It is a celebration of the simple pleasures of life and bounty from the land. When it comes to food, the name Chile is a bit of a misnomer, as it is not a super hot cuisine. It is subtly spiced with sweet paprika, cumin, and oregano and hot salsas are served on the side for heat control.

Asados are Chilean-style cookouts, a fiesta of meats marinated in adobos and grilled on parillas—often just racks set over oil drums fueled by wood coals. El Curantos are clambakes, similar to those of New England, prepared along the watery coasts of Chile's southern islands. Basic staples are corn, tomatoes, pumpkins, beans, peppers, rice, and bread. Signature dishes include marine soups and chowders, meat casseroles topped with creamed corn, and bean soups called porotos granados. They are all improvised variations on immigrant specialties using native ingredients. With Chile's string bean–like shape, regional dishes change with the local crops and climate as one travels north and south. Empanadas, crescent-shaped pastry turnovers stuffed with mixtures of minced meats, onions, cheese, and seafood, are popular throughout the country. This snack may have Spanish roots, but the onion-filled type known as el pequén is uniquely Chilean. Another popular portable bite is the humita, similar to a tamale but made with fresh corn steamed in green corn husks.

Flours & Grains

CHUCHOCA

Similar to polenta, this is cooked and dried ground corn resembling fine yellow cornmeal with a strong corn flavor. It is often difficult to find in America, but you can substitute instant polenta if necessary.

COCHO

Harina tostada. Toasted, very fine, powdery semolina flour. It is used to thicken sauces, soups, and stews and is mixed with hot water or milk and sugar and eaten as a hot breakfast cereal, called ulpo. The watermelon-like alcayota are cut open and the juice and fruit mixed with the toasted semolina as a refreshing sweet dish. Look for the Alhue brand in 1-pound bags.

MOTE DE TRIGO

Whole wheat kernels prepared the same way as corn mote: boiled with wood ashes (lye) until the husks loosen and the kernels turn golden and swell. The mote is then washed, boiled, and dried. Mote de trigo is also found in health food stores and some specialty shops labeled "puffed wheat"—not to be confused with airy puffed cereals. The kernels need to be soaked overnight before cooking. The mote is added to meat and vegatable stews, used in salads and side dishes, and to make mote con huesillo, a dried peach and wheat berry beverage. Look for the Campo Lindo brand in 1-kilo (2-pound) bags.

S'EMOLA

Semolina. A cream-colored, coarse powder with a bland flavor and grainy texture. Semolina is made from hard durum wheat and is used to thicken soups and stews, is added to baked goods, and made into sweet puddings. Look for the Semola de Frigo Candeal Carozzi brand in 550 g (19-ounce) yellow paper bags.

Chilean Breads

Breads are basic and simple, eaten with almost every meal to sop up juices or smear with creamy mashed avocado. Some Chilean breads, as well as Chilean pastries and empanadas, can be found in South American panaderías with a mix of baked goods from Argentina, Colombia, and Venezuela.

AMASADO

Flattish, rustic bread rolls made from whole wheat flour (trigo), salt, water, and yeast. The most basic of Chilean breads, amasado goes well with hearty soups and stews. The tops are usually pricked with a fork, creating tiny steam vents.

amasado bread

COLISA

Flat, shiny, slightly curved slabs of bread with brown flecks. This is basic bread dough mixed with finely chopped chicharrónes (pork cracklings), baked in sheets and cut into rectangles. It is rather chewy with a subtle bacon flavor. Eat as a snack or with spreads.

DOBLADITAS

Double breads. Bread dough enriched with shortening and rolled into a flat round, folded in half, then in half again, forming a flaky triangle when baked (it puffs slightly). Good with butter or jam and for tearing into pieces to soak up juices or enfold pieces of grilled meat.

EMPANADAS

More like a sandwich than a bread, there are two main types of empanadas. Empanada frito are deep-fried, slightly smaller ones, with a lightly textured, bubbly surface. Empanada de horno are baked, larger pastry turnovers. They are smooth and shiny from an egg glaze. A variety of the baked version are empanadas mil hojas, in which the dough used is mille feuille (thousand leaves), meaning buttery, layered puff pastry. Fillings include locos, a mixture of minced Chilean abalone and hard-boiled egg with spices, chopped olives, and raisins. Mariscos is a filling of chopped clams, fish, and mussels with spices and olives. De pinu, also called carne (meat), is a mixture of ground beef, onions, and spices. Espinaca ricotta is a spicy spinach and ricotta cheese filling; queso is a filling of crumbled queso blanco cheese.

HALLULLAS

Pan especial. Flat, small, everyday bread rolls made by extensive kneading of basic dough. Usually made from white flour, hallullas are light with a crusty, smooth surface. They are a little like biscuits, good with cheese or jam and also with meals.

MARRAQUETAS

Small, golden baguettes, also called pan frances and similar to French bread. This is another common bread, crusty on top and soft inside. It is mainly used for sandwiches.

MILCAO

Small flatbreads made from potatoes and flour, a specialty bread based on a traditional Mapuche Indian recipe.

PAN CANDEAL

Bakery-style, fluffy loaves of white yeast bread, whole or sliced.

PAN DE PASCUA

Christmas fruit bread. This rich, cake-like bread is packed with candied fruits, raisins, nuts, and spices. The batter is made from flour, baking powder, sugar, milk, and eggs and baked in a round springform pan. A must for the Navidad festivities, pan de pascua appears in bakeries in early December.

Grocery Items

ACEITUNAS AZAPA

Large, black, meaty olives, cured in a vinegar brine, similar to Kalamata olives but less pungent and softer. Used to garnish bean and green salads, are added to fillings for empanadas and are served with cubes of cheese, ham, pickled onions, and hard boiled-egg pieces as an appetizer. Look for Don Juan brand in 200 g (7-ounce) brine-filled sealed pouches.

AJÍ CACHO DE CABRA

A fiery red chili, sold dried or powdered in small packets, often unlabeled. Dried ones are soaked and pureed for sauces, soups, stews, and meat marinades. The powder can just be sprinkled over food for added heat.

AJÍ CHILENOS SALSA

Chilean hot sauce. Chunky puree of hot red chilies, often the cacho de cabra, with the seeds. Used as a table condiment, sandwich spread, or dip for empanadas and fried snacks. Made by Don Juan brand, sold in 200 g (7-ounce) sealed pouches and JB in 240 g (9-ounce) plastic squeeze bottles.

AJÍ CREMA

A mild, brick-red chili sauce made of a smooth puree of seedless red chilies, salt, and vinegar. Used like ketchup as a table condiment on sausages, grilled meats, burgers, and fried foods, or squirted in sandwiches. It can also be used in cooking. Look for JB brand in 240 g (9-ounce) squeeze bottles.

ají crema

AJÍ DE COLOR

Paprika, made from dried and ground sweet red peppers. A staple of Chilean cuisine, added to almost every savory dish or sprinkled over food just before serving. A popular spice mixture is made from a blend of paprika, hot chili powder, dried oregano, crushed coriander seeds, and salt.

BEANS

Both fresh and dried beans are a staple in the cuisine of Chile. White beans, cranberry beans, lentils, and chick beans are the most commonly used. Less well-known varieties are the mendez bean, also called coscron, a small white bean similar to cannellini, and tortola el burrito, a small gray turtle bean. These are occasionally available in Chilean and South American specialty stores.

CALLAMPAS

Chilean wild mushrooms, sold dried in small packets. Similar to porcini with a deep, earthy flavor. Callampas should be soaked in a little warm water about 20 minutes, drained and chopped—be sure to save the soaking liquid for sauces or soup. They are good in red wine sauces for meats, added to risottos and other rice dishes, fried in olive oil and added to mashed potatoes, or served as a garnish for roasted vegetables and bean dishes.

CEBOLLITOS

Small pearl onions pickled in vinegar brine, served with olives and cheese as an appetizer, chopped and added to empanada fillings, and used to garnish salads. Look for Don Juan brand in 200 g (7-ounce) sealed pouches.

COCHAYUYO

Dried seaweed. The roots (ulte) and leafy fronds (luche) are sold fresh and are steamed in white wine with shallots, chopped, and added to soups and salads. Chilean markets here sell the dried, long, tubular rust-colored stems, cut diagonally into small pieces. They resemble miniature loofah sponges. To use, soak 15 minutes and drain. Finely chopped cochayuyo is used as a ground meat substitute in many dishes. It is cooked like pasta and served in light herb-infused sauces and mixed with grated carrot, cooked corn kernels, and peas as a salad,

cochayuyo

dressed with mayonnaise thinned with lemon juice and seasoned with salt and pepper. Cochayuyo has a pleasant briny taste and chewy texture. Look for the Delmar brand in 80 g (3-ounce) plastic bags.

CRÈMES

Purees of nuts or fruits used to spread between cakes or pastry layers, roll-up in crêpes, smear on toast, or flavor ice cream. Puree de castanas is a thick, chestnut crème; duranzo crème is a jam-like puree of peaches, the golden paste is especially good in layer cakes and to fill pastries. Lucuma crème is a thick, golden puree of lucuma fruit that tastes like butterscotch and is used to make torta de lucuma meringue—a layer cake encased in egg white meringue. Look for the Mel brand in 300 g (11-ounce) plastic tubs.

DULCE DE MEMBRILLO

Quince paste. Rosy-red jelly paste sold in plastic sealed blocks. This is sliced and served with cheese (usually queso blanco or cream cheese) and used in pastry filling. Chilean quince paste is offered by the Antuco brand in various-sized slabs. For more on the paste see Latin Basics, page 78–79.

LOCOS

Chilean abalone. The limpet-like mollusks are considered a great delicacy, eaten mariscal (raw), steamed, fried, or grilled. Locos are also added to minced seafood mixtures for empanada fillings or pastel de choclo. The pale, thin slices are sold canned, mostly under Chinese labels and are expensive, about $15 a can. The ones I tried were in a 15-ounce can labeled with Chinese characters and the Chilean name. In addition to the Asian imports, look for the Don Pio brand in 213 g cans (about 7 ounces). The flavor and texture (somewhat rubbery) are similar to Asian abalone and should not be overcooked or you will have a costly piece of rubber! In a filling any type of abalone can be used.

MACHAS

Also called almejas rosadas (pink clams) and razor clams. These pink, meaty, plump clams are sold canned in their juices and a light brine. Chill and serve in the brine with chopped onion, lemon juice, and cilantro; add to seafood soups and chowders; or bake in white wine topped with a mixture of melted butter and grated Parmesan cheese. Look for (or ask for, as they are often behind the counter) Robinson Crusoe brand in 6-ounce cans packaged in a box. The same brand also offers caracoles, a type of Chilean sea snail. You'll also find tins of assorted shellfish in brine, a mix of clams, pink clams, and mussels. All are good served with a squeeze of lemon as an appetizer.

machas

The curato, or Chilean clambake, began in ancient times along the seacoast of southern Chile and appears to have Polynesian roots. When summer ended and the water became too cold for diving, fishermen collected huge quantities of shellfish from shallow waters, dug a hole in the ground, and lit a fire. The glowing coals were covered with rocks, then a layer of large leaves and seaweed. Seafood was piled on and a briny soup developed as the shellfish was smoked for future use in the cold months—the soup was eaten right away. Today the curato is a social affair and meats and sausages are added to the smoking shellfish along with ears of corn, potatoes, and vegetables.

MARMELADA

A thin, syrupy jam made from a variety of fruits sold in foil-lined plastic

alcayota jam

pouches. Snip off a corner and squeeze into a plastic container or glass jar for storage. Some also come in plastic boxes. These jams are used as spreads, in sweets and pastry, or are spooned over ice cream and other desserts. Choose from cherry (guinda), plum (ciruela), peach (duranzo), blackberry (morro), papaya, and alcayota, a type of melon with pale green, crisp flesh that tastes like very sweet winter melon. Dos Caballos and Witts are two popular brands in 9-ounce pouches.

PAPAYAS AL JUGO

Poached papaya. Chilean papayas are fragrant, yellow, and ridged, similar to the Babacao hybrid from Ecuador (see page 46). They resemble large golden starfruit

and are poached over low heat in a sugar syrup and packed into jars. They are tender, sweet, and still firm enough to slice. Poached papaya is a favorite end to meals, often served with whipped cream. They are also chopped and added to fruit salad and meat stews. Brands to look for are Aiken International in 900 g (35-ounce) jars and Olivier and Saturne in 450 g (about 14-ounce) and 35-ounce jars. Also Dos Caballos in 590 g (17-ounce) cans.

papayas al jugo

PEACHES

Duranzo. There are both canned peaches and dried ones called hue-sillos that means "little bones." The canned type are chopped and mixed with sliced strawberries and white wine as a sort of wine cooler–fruit punch and are added to ground meat stuffings. The dried ones are made from peeled, sun-dried peaches and resemble large, shriveled apricots. Their main use is in a refreshing but unusual drink called mote con huesillos. This is made by soaking the dried peaches overnight and poaching them in spiced sugar and water syrup with soaked wheat berries (mote). The chilled mixture is served in tall glasses with a long spoon. Huesillos are packaged by the Ekono brand in 300 g (11-ounce) bags. Most stores sell the pre-made drink in cov-ered plastic cups in the beverage case along with sodas and beers.

TRUCHA AHUMADA

Smoked lake trout in oil with peppercorns. The pinkish-orange fillets are about 4 inches long and 1 inch across and have a salty, smoky flavor. Good as an appetizer on bread or crackers with olives and cheese, or flake and mix with lemon juice and mayonnaise and stuff into halved avocados. Also good with rice or potatoes and added to fish soups and chowders. Look for the Quillem brand in 1-pound jars.

trucha ahumada

The Deli Case

ARROLLASDO DE HUASO

Roulade. A large, flat cut of flank steak rubbed with a spice paste made of crushed garlic, salt, ground cumin, black pepper, and oregano, rolled up jellyroll-style with hard-boiled egg and strips of carrot and bell pepper. The whole roll is tightly tied at intervals with string and simmered 2 to 3 hours, then cooled in the broth and refrig-erated overnight. The roll is cut into slices and served as an appetizer, used in sandwiches with hot sauce, or served warm. A similar roll called arrollasdo de Malay is made with skin-on pork rolled up with a spice paste and simmered.

PÂTÉ DE AVE/CERDO

Ave means chicken liver pâté; cerdo is pork liver pâté. Both are a pale, creamy beige color and are sold in small vacuum-sealed tubes that resemble sausages. Use as a spread on bread or crackers or in sandwiches. Look for the Winter brand.

PRIETAS

Chilean blood sausages based on the Spanish original. Stubby, blackish-maroon links made from beef blood mixed with chopped onions, spices, and rice. They have a coarse texture and rather spicy, rich flavor. Slice as an appetizer with cheese, pickles, and bread or throw on the grill with other meats, pan-fry, or chop and add to soups and stews.

QUESO FRESCO DE CABRA

Fresh goat cheese. Tangier and more robust than cow's milk cheese, but since it is not aged, it is soft with only a mild tang. A drier type called maduro, or matured, is harder and sharper in flavor. The best

queso seleccion

quality is queso seleccion, a special selected aged cheese. Sold in irregular slabs or thick rounds, goat cheese is served as part of an appetizer spread or used in baked casseroles, added to bean stews, salads, sandwiches, and omelettes. The soft type is good whipped with fresh herbs for spreads or dips. Both types are made under a French license in Chile from pasteurized goat's milk under the Chevrita label.

Seafood

Some of the more interesting Chilean seafoods follow. A few types are now becoming available in New York, imported by Chilean native Patricio Osses and his company Pacifica International. For more information see appendix 4.

CENTOLLA

Patagonian king crab, a red monster from the deep, cold waters of the southernmost tip of Chile. It looks like a gigantic snow crab.

CHOROS ZAPATOS

Mussels the size of a man's shoe (zapato means shoe in Spanish).

ERIZOS

Giant sea urchins, eaten raw with a squeeze of lemon juice.

GRENADIER FISH

Also known as rat tail, this is a squat, large-headed deepwater fish with enormous bulging eyes and a long, skinny tail like a whip.

PICOROCO

Large-beaked barnacles with sweet, white flesh, sort of like a cross between crab and lobster. When baked or added to soup they give off a delicious juice. The foot-long barnacles resemble a little volcano with two small claws that emerge from the crater when provoked.

PIURES

Strangest of all, these soft sea squirts resemble a mossy potato. When opened, they are like an egg with a roundish red yolk. The bright red meat has a strong iodine taste and is eaten in small amounts raw or in ceviche.

REINETA

A large, silvery fish similar to pompano. It is extremely popular in Chile.

ROBALO

Like salmon, this fish lives in both fresh and saltwater but has white somewhat oily flesh, similar in flavor to black sea bass.

Chilean Sandwiches

In the typical Chilean café, there are usually two menus: one for sandwiches (to eat in or to go), and another for dishes served in the dining area. The deli case has cured meats, cheeses, stuffed flank rolls, and prepared salads. Sandwiches are made with the small, freshly baked baguettes called marraquetas. Following are typical offerings to choose from.

The agregados is a vegetarian's delight, made from mashed avocado, sliced onions, and mayonnaise. For an arrollado, slices of cold roasted pork or beef are layered in a crusty roll with salsa, sliced hard-boiled egg with mayo, lettuce, tomato, and onion slices. The ave palta sandwich is seasoned, shredded chicken with mashed avocado on a roll. A barros jarpa means a melted cheese and ham sandwich, while a barros luco is a grilled steak and cheese sandwich. The chacarero is a steak and vegetable sandwich, usually made with porotos verdes (blanched green beans), tomato slices, and mayo. The completos is a hot dog on a freshly baked bun with the works—tomatoes, chucrut (sauerkraut), mashed avocado, sliced onions, pickles, mustard, and mayo. Jamón y queso is a good old ham and cheese (usually queso blanco) sandwich. A lomito is sliced pork tenderloin on a roll with mashed avocado, mayo, onions, and tomatoes. Pan con pernil means sliced roasted leg of pork with chili sauce, mashed avocado, and mayo.

Hot Menu Features

Here is a mix of popular Chilean bocadillos (appetizers) and entrees. A la pichanga may also be offered—this is a platter of cured meats, grilled sausages, cheeses, assorted pickles, and fresh fruit cut in small pieces and served on a tabula, or wooden board. The mix of hot, cold, savory, and sweet flavors awaken the taste buds for the meal to come. All of the following may be served with pil-pil, a table condiment of chopped, hot red chilies, minced garlic and olive oil, and salsa de pebre, a Chilean hot sauce served separately in little bowls. Pebre is a mixture of minced chilies, garlic, onion, cilantro, and fresh oregano blended with salt, olive oil, and red wine vinegar.

ANTICUCHO

Small skewers of marinated and grilled baby beef heart pieces, chicken gizzards, beef liver and little bits of cow udder, sort of like a kebab. Many places just offer the bits of beef heart.

CAZUELA DE VACUNO

A hearty winter dish, often served as a special. There are many variations, some with rice on the bottom or top, others thickened with chuchoca (cornmeal polenta), but most are based on beef broth in which lots of vegetables, including calabaza pumpkin, potatoes, and fresh beans or green peas, are simmered with a veal shank or other meat on the bone. The meat is then shredded and served with the broth and vegetables accompanied with hot sauce and a lemon wedge.

CALDILLO DE CONGRIO

This is a famous, fragrant, fisherman's soup made with cusk eel (not conger), potatoes, onion, and garlic. The celebrated Nobel poet of Chile, Pablo Neruda, waxed poetic on the virtues of the cusk eel in one of his best-known poems, *Ode to Fish Chowder.* Cusk eel, also known as golden kingclip and congrio dorado, has a delicate, white flesh with a sublime, scallop-like taste and is considered the king of all fish in Chile. Stateside versions of this soup are made with sea bass, red snapper, monkfish, halibut, or grouper or a mix of several fishes. Shellfish are often added to the creamy broth, infused with white wine and sweet paprika, and enriched with cream and egg yolk.

HUMITAS

Tamales wrapped in fresh green corn husks, tied with string and boiled. The unique feature of Chilean tamales is that they're made from fresh, creamed corn kernels mixed with chopped onion, basil, and salt. Humitas are often eaten warm, sprinkled with a little sugar as a snack or side dish. Cold ones are in the deli case to reheat at home.

LOMO A LO POBRE

A smallish, pan-fried or grilled steak served on a plate with spaghetti, fried eggs and onions, hot sauce, and French fries—with the idea that there is so much other food that you'll forget the steak is on the skimpy side.

MACHAS AL MATICO

Pink razor clams cooked in their juices and mixed with chopped onion and cilantro. Cafés here use canned clams or substitute almejas (other clams such as cherry stones). Machas a la Parmesana is a dish of pink razor clams in white wine

A salad eaten with most meals in Chile, made from sliced onions soaked first in cold water to eliminate the sharpness, mixed with sliced ripe tomatoes, dressed in oil and vinegar with a sprinkle of salt and pepper. Minced chilies and cilantro are also sometimes added. For a recipe, see page 238.

or sherry, broiled under a layer of Parmesan cheese and served bubbling hot with bread.

MERLUZA

Antartic queen fish. Seasoned fried, grilled, or broiled fish with flaky, mild, white flesh similar to hake, usually served with rice and salad. Pejerreyes, small fish similar to smelts and whiting fillets, are frequently served.

PALTA RELLENA

Stuffed avocado. Halved avocados are filled with canned tuna mixed with chopped onion and cilantro, shrimp salad, or seasoned shredded chicken with diced red peppers.

PASTEL DE CHOCLO

Chopped chicken or ground beef casserole with a crispy corn topping. This is the national dish of Chile and is traditionally baked and served in a brown glazed shallow dish from Pomaire, a village of potters east of Santiago. The casserole, based on shepherd's pie, is made from pinu, the mixture of ground beef, raisins, onions, and spices also used to stuff empanadas or chopped cooked chicken mixed with spices, chopped hard-boiled egg, raisins, and olives topped with a layer of creamed corn (choclo). Before baking the top is often sprinkled with sweet paprika and salt (salado) or sugar (dulce) to create a brittle carmelized crust. Pre-baked, cold pies are sold in the deli case. Pastel de papas is the same, but topped with mashed potato. For a chicken pastel de choclo recipe, see page 253.

TORTILLAS DE VERDURA

Thick wedges of Spanish-style egg frittata made with any variety of vegetables, including shredded romaine lettuce, grated carrots or zucchini, asparagus, cauliflower and cheese, or spinach. The tortilla slices are usually served as an appetizer with drinks or as a light meal with salad and hot sauce on the side.

Pastries & Sweets (Postres)

Typical Chilean pastries are made from puff pastry or shortbread and embellished with swirls of meringue or a snow of powdered sugar and filled with caramel or jams. Chileans of German ancestry have added rich kuchens, tarts, cheesecakes, and fruit breads to the national diet along with cured hams, pâtés, cheeses, and sausages. The Spanish influence is apparent in the desserts once made by Catholic nuns, such as wine-flavored meringues, puddings, fritters in syrup, and rosquillas (braided anise rings).

BERLINE

German-style cream puffs filled with jelly or custard cream and dusted in powdered sugar.

BORRACHITOS

Little "drunken" liqueur-filled pastries.

CALZONES ROTOS

Literally meaning "old ripped under-pants," these are bow tie–shaped lemon flavored, crispy fried pastries sprinkled with powdered sugar. They are delicious with poached fruit and a scoop of ice cream.

CARAMEL CONFECTIONS

Caramel is a favorite with Chileans. Look for alfajores, cookies sandwiched with caramel and coated in shredded coconut or dipped in chocolate; empolvados, large alfajores sandwiched with caramel and covered in powdered sugar; and tortitas, alfajores with three layers. Brazo de reina are swirled slices of spongy jellyroll cake with caramel replacing the jelly. Cachos are pastry horns filled with caramel, and cachitos are smaller tubes, also filled with caramel but dusted in powdered sugar. Cuchufli are tubular pastries filled with caramel. Panqueque Celestino, or Celestino crêpes, are thin crêpes rolled up with caramel and dusted in powdered sugar; when folded into quarters they are called trozo de queque.

Chileans often enjoy a pastry with a cup of coffee or tea at onces, between 5 and 7 P.M. Onces means elevenses (once is 11 in Spanish) and is derived from a British custom turned topsy turvy. It originally meant a tea break at 11 A.M. It is believed the Chilean version of the tradition came from a customary (and surreptitious) happy hour featuring the local beverage aguardiente, which not so coincidently contains eleven letters. Today, onces refers to a pick-me-up before dinner, which may not begin until 11 P.M. in Chile.

CHILENITOS

Also called dulces chilenos, these are pastry rounds sandwiched with various fillings and encased in a shell of baked meringue. Fillings include caramel mixed with chopped nuts with orange zest, dulce de alcayote (a preserve made from a crisp, pale green fleshed melon with dark and light green stripes like a watermelon), candied egg yolk (huevos mol), and lucuma fruit puree.

chilenito

EMPANADAS DE ALCAYOTA

Small pastry turnovers filled with melon preserves. The light green translucent jam is sweet with small shreds of the melon-like flesh.

KUCHEN

Coffee cakes and tarts with a German accent. The most common type is kuchen de manzana, or German apple cake. Kuchen de nueces is a walnut tart in a buttery pastry crust served with whipped cream.

Kuchen de guindas is lemon-flavored coffee cake topped with cherries preserved in syrup with a dash of kirsch or other cherry liqueur. Kuchen de quesillo is a type of cheesecake tart with a filling of smooth ricotta pureed with eggs and sugar, flavored with lemon zest and rum-soaked raisins, baked in a buttery crust.

MIL HOJAS

Also may be called torta mil hojas, these are square tarts of multi-layered sheets of thin pastry filled with caramel or jam.

SOPAIPILLAS SECAS

Crispy pumpkin fritters soaked in brown sugar syrup, traditionally made on rainy days.

TURRÓN DE VINO

Wine-flavored soft meringue. Thick sugar syrup flavored with red wine, lemon zest, and spices is folded into stiffly beaten egg whites. The soft swirled mounds are served in a pool of crème anglaise (vanilla custard sauce).

A Word on Wine

Chilean wines are the only South American wines to gain worldwide recognition and if you can't make it to Chile, you can sample the wines sold in Chilean grocery stores and fine wine shops. Some of the best labels to look for are Miguel Torres, Concha y Toro, Vina Undurraga, Cousino Macul, Santa Rita, and Los Vascos. The very best are reserve Cabernets, with a concentrated fruit flavor without being overly tannic or hard. Most are under $12 a bottle and are drinkable sooner than other Cabernet types. Sauvignon Blancs are excellent, go well with both meats and seafood, and are dry, medium-bodied, and light. Chilean Reisling, a favorite of Chilean-Germans is a little on the sweet side, as are the bright and fruity Chardonnays. Reserve Chardonnays are briefly aged in new oak barrels, infusing them with a vanilla-spice accent. Chilean Merlots are gaining popularity and have a rich body with no hardness. Two of the best are Santa Carolina and Curvée Alexandre. Another red hot Chilean wine is Undurraga Cabernet Sauvignon. Good quality white wines are Caliterra Sauvignon blanc and Viña Calina Chardonnay.

Stocking Up

To get your Chilean kitchen in order, select some fresh bread rolls, baguettes, empanadas, and at least one pastry. Staples include beans (fresh and dried), polenta, rice, wheat berries, dried peaches, paprika, oregano, Chilenos salsa (hot sauce), and poached papayas for a sweet ending. Supplement your supplies with fresh seafood, meats, and produce (tomatoes, pumpkin, corn, and onions) from the supermarket. Round things out with a bottle or two of Chilean wine and some fat Azapa olives and goat cheese.

12

The Argentine
All-in-One

Like our own, the cuisine of Argentina is a coalescence of many foods and cultures. As the beef capital of the universe, the one true cuisine seems to be the parrillada, or mixed grill.

Beef, or bife as it is called in Argentina, is the staple of both the diet and politics—when beef prices rise, so does the level of unrest in the street. Overall, beef is inexpensive and enjoyed at least four times a week by the average citizen. Because Argentina's population includes people of European ancestry, there are several distinct food traditions—those of the "old country" reflected in dishes such as empanadas, pizza, pasta, polenta, and quiche, and those that were born from a merging of Spanish colonial and native Quechua Indian traditions. The latter include humitas (fresh corn tamales); lorco, a meat and bean stew thickened with hominy; beef stews sweetened with peaches and served in a hollowed-out pumpkin (carbonada criolla); and puchero, a beef and vegetable pot-au-feu, all washed down with red wine.

Beef & More Beef

Argentina is well known as beef country and the asado is a favorite Argentine repast. Huge quantities of salt-rubbed beef and sausages, innards, lamb, and chicken are slowly roasted over glowing embers—Argentines use quebracho leña, a native hardwood. Treated wood, briquettes, and lighter fluids are avoided as they taint the meats' flavor.

Asado participants go back and forth from the table (always outside) to the grill, taking a few small bits, then returning for more. The Argentine expression for this constant motion is "asado es un viaje de ida y vuelta," meaning "asado is a journey of going and coming." Asado accompaniments are chimichurri sauce for dipping, salads, fried potatoes, and a simple dessert. The meat is the main event. Beef also shows up in stews, empanada, and humita fillings, under a drift of mashed potatoes in pastel de papas, and thin steaks are breaded and fried à la Milanesa. Flank steak is also stuffed and rolled up, simmered and sliced to make matambre. Leftover, shredded beef is used to make into salpicón salads, tossed with diced potato, carrots, and tomatoes in a mayonnaise–lemon juice–red wine vinegar dressing.

The drink of choice for these meat orgies are full-flavored, bold red wines from the province in Mendoza, high in the Andean foothills. All the various cuts of beef popular with Argentines are listed below, with a reference to the corresponding equivalent American cut if there is one. Most are just sprinkled with ground salt and grilled or roasted. Argentine beef has been imported since 1997, but it may take some searching to find it—most Argentinean markets have U.S.-raised beef cut to Argentine specifics. You will also find homemade sausages laced with garlic, morcillas (blood sausages, some seasoned with fruit and cinnamon), and plump, paprika-spiced chorizo.

ACHURAS

This means variety meat, including bofe (lungs), chinchulines (small intestines, delicious grilled until crispy), mollejas (sweetbreads), mondongo (tripe), tripa gorda (large intestines), and ubre (the fatty part of a cow's udder). All of these are grilled and served as appetizers before the main beef cuts are thrown on the parilla.

AGUJA

Meaning "needle," this is a very thin cut of boneless chuck, cut close to the neck. Grill, roast, or pan-fry.

AZOTILLO

T-bone steak, or if boneless, strip steak, also known as churrasco. Marinate and grill, broil, or pan-fry.

BIFE ANCHO

Similar to boneless rib eye, a large piece of meat that lies along the outer side of the ribs. The cut can come from the delantero, or front section, or trasero, the back end of the ribs. This is an asado staple for grilling but can also be roasted.

BIFE DE CHORIZO

Unrelated to the sausage of the same name, this is a thickly cut shell steak, also called strip sirloin, and is about three times larger and thicker than U.S. cuts. It is considered one of the national dishes of Argentina when grilled and served with chimichurri sauce. Bife angosto is strip loin, also good tossed on the grill, roasted, or pan-fried.

BIFE DE COSTILLA

A bone-in sirloin or top butt. The cut comes from the part of the hindquarter just in front of the round. Grill, roast, or cube, and add to stews. It is very lean and is also sliced very thin and sun-dried to make charque (beef jerky). Colita de cuadril is a thin, boneless cut from sirloin or top butt and is best grilled, pan-fried, breaded and fried, or cut in strips for stir-fries.

BOLA DE LOMO

A round lump of sirloin tip cut from the hind part. Roast whole or ask to get it cut in thin steaks for sandwiches. Also called bife de lomo, this is known as knuckle in U.S. butchers' parlance.

CARNAZA

The U.S. equivalent is called scottie or chuck tender, and it is cut from the back shoulder portion. Another name for this is shoulder blade. Stew, broil, roast, or grill.

ENTRAÑA

Outer skirt steak. This comes from the diaphragm of a steer and has a rich taste, sort of a cross between steak and variety meat, and is always a part of an asado, sizzled on the grill.

FALDA

Flank steak. A thick cut from the flank muscle. The Argentine cut comes from the last part of the ribs and is quite fatty and cartilaginous. Perfect for grilling, roasting, broiling, or braising.

GARRÓN

Also called corte de la pata, this is beef tendon, the dense white cords of connective tissue that hold together the feet (pata) and shank (leg). Tendons are thrown on the grill for mixed asado and also added to simmered stews, creating a gelatinous texture. Brazuelo is whole front shank, good roasted, braised, or stewed. Tortuguita is the muscle between the hind shank and outside round, used mainly in soups and stews.

MARUCHA

Bone-in chuck steak, cut from the neck, parts of the shoulder blade, and the first three ribs. The slabs contain some cartilage and are good grilled or braised.

MATAMBRE

A type of flank steak cut from the steer's lower flank. Matambre is also the name of a preparation known as "hunger killer." Pounded flank is marinated overnight in a mixture of vinegar and minced garlic, then stuffed with strips of vegetables and hard-boiled eggs; seasoned with ground cumin, pepper, and red pepper flakes; rolled up; tied; and simmered in a pot of water, weighted down with a plate and tin cans. When cooled it is wrapped in plastic and refrigerated overnight for the flavors to develop, then served in thick slices at room temperature—a perfect make-ahead party food.

NALGA

Nalga is the general term for round, the cuts from the back hindquarter. Peceto is eye round, often simmered, then marinated overnight in a mixture of wine vinegar, corn oil, oregano, carrots, and onions and served cold, cut in slices with the vegetables. It's good party food as it is prepared in advance. Tapa de nalga is the "tapa" or "cap" of the back round muscle and is usually grilled or broiled.

PALOMITA

The U.S. name for this is clod or blade, cut from the muscle of the shoulder and backbone. Roast, stew, or broil, or ask for it cut into thin steaks to bread and pan-fry.

TIRAS DE COSTILLAR

Also known as asado de costillar or costillar, this is thin-cut short ribs. The rib section is cut crosswise into narrow strips of meat and bone. Also called asado a seca, this is a quintessential cut for the asado grill.

Tapa de asado is cap meat, meaning the sirloin tip end, also always a part of an asado mixta. Tapa means cap and costillar is short rib. When the cap is attached to the ribs it is known as tiras de asado.

tiras de costillar

VACÍO

Flat meat. A thin piece of muscle from the hindquarter covered by membrane. It comes from the large internal muscle of the loin on each side of the vertebral column and ribs, near the flank. Only filet mignon is leaner. Marinate and grill, broil, or pan-fry.

Grocery Items

CHEESES

Various imported cheeses may be offered in the deli case. There is always mozzarella used in Italian-Argentine dishes, empanada fillings, salads, and sandwiches. And there is provolone parillero, two round slabs of provolone smeared in adobo spices, found in vacuum-sealed packs. This is used to make provoletta, campfire cheese melted on the grill and served with bread and barbecued meats. There are also big, round waxed balls of sardo (Argentine Parmesan), wedges of Gruyère and pategras (similiar to Edam) offered by the Veronica brand. Look also for Argentine-made wheels of sheeps' milk cheese.

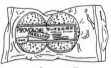
provolone parillero

CHIMICHURRI

This is the indispensible spicy parsley sauce found on every Argentine's table, served with grilled and roasted meats, chicken, and seafood. Look for the house-made; it's much tastier than the commercial blends, which use dried and dehydrated herbs and spices.

There is the 151 and Layco brands in 500 g (about 16-ounce) squirt bottles and Chef Cesar's in 12-ounce bottles.

It's easy to make your own chimichurri—just blend together about 10 minced cloves of garlic, a bunch of chopped parsley, a few teaspoons dried oregano, and a tablespoon of red pepper flakes with a cup of olive oil and ¼ cup red wine vinegar. Season with salt and pepper and set aside a few hours so the flavors can mingle and develop. Store in a jar, refrigerated, up to a week.

chimichurri sauce

COOKIES & CRACKERS

A section of shelf space is stocked with packages of chocolate-covered alfajores (cookies sandwiched with caramel), biscotti, crispy almond cookies, and Roquefort cheese crackers. There's also Kremakoa (rich, bite-sized cookies topped with caramel and covered in milk chocolate). Express cereal (dense hearty whole wheat crackers), crisp, sweet champagne wafers sandwiched with lemon or strawberry fillings, desayuno doble buttery crackers (water crackers enriched with butter), and cocadas (coconut macaroons). Popular brands are Caneli, Terrabusi, and El Gallito. All are good with a cortado, a short measure (shot) of strong coffee, served in glasses in Argentine cafés.

GARBANZO FLOUR

This is a pale, nutty-flavored, powdery flour made from dried and ground chickpeas. The main use is in pizza dough; it is also used as a batter for deep-fried foods. Look for Faina brand in 200 g (7-ounce) bags.

GOLF SAUCE

Also called salsa golf anacoa. This strangely named sauce is a tangy combination of lemony mayonnaise and ketchup. It is used as a dipping sauce for French fries and other fried snacks such as empanadas, fritters, and tostones (green plantain fritters) and as a salad dressing or sandwich spread. Look for Fanacoa brand in 290 g (8-ounce) jars. RI-K brand has extra lemony mayo in 500 g (16-ounce) jars, good to jazz up pasta salads, egg or tuna salad, seafood dips, and dressings. Mayoliva is mayonnaise made with extra virgin olive oil, sold in 475 g (17-ounce) plastic jars.

HONGOS SECOS

Dried mushrooms. Dark brown, curled pieces of a wild mushroom known as porcini. They have an intense, aromatic woodsy perfume and need to be soaked 15 to 20 minutes before draining and using. Sauté with button mushrooms (hongos silvestras), add to sauces for meats, pasta, or soups (try corn), and meat stews. Store in a tightly sealed dry jar. Layco offers them in small packets.

MOSTAZA

Thin, deep yellow, slightly spicy mustard. A shot of vinegar and spices enhance this familiar condiment. Trimmings and off cuts of grilled meat are served as fiambres (cold cuts) with the mustard, olives, bread, and butter as an appetizer or snack. It is also good with grilled sausages, in dipping sauces, dressings, marinades, and as a sandwich spread. Look for Savora brand in 200 g (7-ounce) jars with a red and yellow label.

OILS

Good labels of Argentine olive oil are Cocinero, Lira, Marilen, Resolio, and Tittarelli. Some of these companies also make delicate sunflower oil that is low in saturated fat but has a low smoking point—best for sautéing and salad dressings, not deep-frying. Olive oil has a high smoking point and can be used for deep-frying, but don't waste extra virgin oils this way. Lira brand has a sunflower-olive oil blend, 85 percent sunflower and 15 percent olive oil, good for both deep-frying and sautéing. Most oils are in 1 litre (32-ounce) or 500 cc bottles (about 16 ounces). And note: Argentine olive oil is high quality and less expensive than Italian imports.

PEANUT HALVAH

Small foil-wrapped bars made from powdered peanuts and sugar. Crumble bits off and enjoy with coffee or milk. It has a smooth nutty flavor, sort of like condensed dehydrated peanut butter. Made by Mantecol brand in black-and-white striped packets.

POLENTA INSTANTANEA

Also called presto pronto or instant polenta. This is a fine, pale yellow, quick-cooking cornmeal for making polenta. To use, simply stir one cup of the meal into 3 cups of boiling water, stock, or milk, and stir one minute to prevent lumps. Serve plain or with butter and grated cheese as an accompaniment to grilled meats and sausages or vegetable dishes. Polenta also comes flavored with dried mushrooms, ham and cheese, and chicken and vegetables. Aecor brand has all these types as well as plain in various-sized bags. Quaker offers polenta agica, another instant type in 500 g (about 16-ounce) packages.

*polenta
instantanea*

REBOZADOR

Ultra fine breadcrumbs used as a coating for baked and fried foods. It creates an extra crispy crust on fried chicken, breaded steaks, and fried fish. Look for Preferido brand in 500 g (16-ounce) bags. Coarser breadcrumbs are called harina de trigo and are used for thickening stews and breading foods for frying and baking. Mix with dried parsley flakes and dust a thin steak in the mixture to make pan-fried steak Milanesa.

YERBA MATÉ

Yerba maté is a most interesting tea popular in Argentina, Brazil, and Uruguay. The maté is actually the gourd the tea is served in, sucked up through a bombilla (a metal straw fitted with a filter at one end to prevent particles of tea leaf from being drawn up the tube into the mouth). Maté tastes a little like percolated tobacco and alfalfa with an acrid, bittersweet, and seemingly addicting flavor. Yerba maté is sold loose leaf and in cello-wrapped boxes of tea bags. Two high-quality brands from Uruguay are Armino in blue bags and Canarias in yellow bags.

yerba maté

ZAPALLO EN ALIMBAR

Pumpkin in syrup. Chunks of calabaza pumpkin preserved in a thick, dark amber syrup until it becomes a soft, sugar-saturated glacé. Pour

zapallo en alimbar

out of the jar and serve plain or with whipped cream or ice cream. It can also be pureed and used in cake, tart, and pastry fillings; rolled up in crêpes; and as a base for pumpkin pie or custard. Look for Fru Glace and Jorgito brands in 6- to 7-ounce jars. Also Orienta in 22-ounce jars and Achad Hnos in 450 g (15-ounce) jars.

Herbs & Spices

Salt plays a large role in Argentinean cooking, and it is often the only seasoning most meats get before grilling or roasting. Finely ground salt is called salfina or barbecue salt and is sold in large plastic shakers. Meats for the grill are rubbed all over with the salt, which keeps the meat juicy under a flame-licked crispy crust. Most Argentines like their meat well-done—in Argentine parrilla restaurants ask for jugoso if you want rare. Coarse salt crystals, called sal gruesa, similar to kosher salt, is used to season corn on the cob, vegetables, soups, stews, and some meats. Look for the Dos Anclas brand for both types.

Aromatic spice and herb blends, chili powder, and dried herbs are sold in small 1-ounce packets under the Layco label. Ají molido is a mild chili powder used to add heat and color to empanada fillings, tomato sauces, soups, roasted chicken, fried fish, and pickles, and is sprinkled over everything from fried eggs and beans to meat and seafood. Pimenton, better known as paprika, has a mild, sweet flavor and is widely used in Argentine cooking and to add a dash of color to many dishes. There is also pimenta blana molida (ground white pepper), ajo en polvo (sandy lumps of powdered garlic), albahaca (dried basil), perejil (parsley flakes), oregano, and ground cumin. Adobo para pizza is a blend of crushed oregano, hot pepper flakes, and paprika. Sprinkle over pizza, add to tomato-based sauces, season beef

especias surtidas molidas

flank for arrollados (stuffed meat rolls), and season soups and stews with the blend. It can also be mixed with water, vinegar, oil, and minced parsley to make chimichurri sauce. Especias surtidas molidas is a mixture of various ground spices, cascara (orange peel), and chilies used to flavor soups and stews.

The Freezer Case

The Italian influence on Argentine cuisine is prominent in the freezer case where you will find pasta, dumplings, and sheets of pastry dough. The small, round ones are used to make empanadas. Tapas para pastilitos are small squares of pastry dough used to make little pies, cannelloni, and capellitos (belly button–shaped stuffed pasta). You'll also find packages with 2 sheets of round or rectangular puff pastry for baking pies and tarts. Brands that offer all of the above are La Salteña and Tapetti. More products are listed below.

MASA DE PANQUEQUE

Literally "crêpe dough," a package of a dozen 5-inch wide paper-thin pre-cooked crêpes. To use, heat them one at a time in a frying pan with dabs of butter, a few seconds on just one side—they become soft and limp and are like Swedish pancakes. Serve rolled up with jam, powdered sugar, or dulce de leche. They are also stuffed with savory fillings such as crab or shrimp in cream sauce, spicy shredded chicken, or cheese sauce. Made by La Salteña brand in 200 g (7-ounce) plastic packages. Once defrosted, use within a day or two, and store in the fridge.

Italian immigrants to the Mendoza province of Argentina have contributed many ingredients and dishes to the country's cuisine. Pastas, sun-dried tomatoes, olives, olive oil, and fresh mozzarella cheese are produced here. Plump homemade ñoquis, potato dumplings similar to gnocchi, are a favorite, always served in restaurants with a 2 peso note tucked under the plate, a reminder of their humble origins as an end-of-the-month staple when family finances were low.

PASTA

Both Italian and Argentine pastas are available. Choose from frozen ravioli with ricotta and other fillings, tortellini, capelleti, spinach and cheese filled angolotti (Piedmont-style ravioli), gnocchi, and fideos (nests of angel hair). Manjar and La Salteña brands have most in 1-pound bags or cardboard boxes.

TARTA

Large, thin, flat rounds of dough and rolled-up square sheets of pastry dough. The defrosted dough is used to make pies, tarts, and pastries. In Argentina the dough is often brought on camping trips and filled with fresh seaweed and baked over the coals of a campfire. To use at home, place one in a greased pan the same size as the pastry and layer with a mixture of spinach, cheese, and beaten egg; cover with another sheet and bake. To make tableton, a sweet dessert, bake 8 round sheets until browned and layer with dulce de leche, stack one pastry crisp on another, and dust the top with powdered sugar. Look for Tapetti brand in 400 g (14-ounce) packets or 12 round sheets. The rolled-up square sheets are in plain plastic bags, made by the local pasta provider.

Hot Snacks & Baked Goods

ALFAJORES ROGEL

Meringue cake layered with dulce de leche, found in the pastry case near the cream puffs and glazed fruit tarts. It is sticky, gooey, and chewy. Alfajores danubio are flour and ground almond cookies sandwiched with jam, chocolate, or caramel.

CACHITOS

Ham and cheese sandwiched between layers of flaky puff pastry, kept warm in the hot box on the counter so the cheese is melting. Tequenos are slender cheese fingers made from puff pastry, rolled up with melted cheese, also sold warm.

EMPANADAS ARGENTINE

Round, plump baked pastries resembling large Chinese dumplings with the dough pinched and twisted at the top like a little bag. Fillings include shredded chicken, minced seafood, and cheese.

empanada argentine

There are also crescent-shaped, baked empanadas and smooth, shiny, fried half moons, both with beef, chicken, or ham and cheese fillings. They are sold by the piece, still warm from the counter hot box.

FRACTURAS

Small croissants filled with dulce de leche, jam, chocolate, or guava paste, also called media lunas. Fracturas is also the general term for sweet baked snacks such as cras sucias, or "dirty faces," little pastries encrusted with melted brown sugar and pastries stuffed with caramel or jam.

HUMITAS DE ACHIOTE

Argentine tamales tinted a rich yellow with annatto (also called achiote). Tender, fresh corn kernels are pureed with milk, chilies, annatto oil, sautéed garlic and onions, eggs, grated Parmesan cheese, and salt and pepper. The mixture is simmered until thickened, spread on corn husks, the ends tucked in and tied with string and the parcels steamed.

PASCULINA

Also called pastel el espinaca. In Genoa, Italy, where it originated, it is known as torta pasqualina, meaning Easter tart, and traditionally made with 33 layers of paper-thin pastry, one for each year of Christ's life. The Argentine version is a sort of pie with a soufflé-like filling of chopped spinach, grated cheese or ricotta, eggs, and cream layered between two crispy sheets of thin pastry. The pies are baked in rectangular pans and cut into squares, sold by the piece. You might also find pastel de ricotta, the same thing but with savory ricotta filling.

Stocking Up

To get your pantry supplied for Argentinean fare, you'll want to buy beef—and lots of it—fine salt for seasoning meats for grilling, chimichurri sauce, pasta, polenta, tomato sauce, pastry dough for savory pies and desserts, mozzarella and ricotta cheeses, paprika or mild chili powder, and dulce de leche. You may want to add some yerba maté. If there is no Argentine market nearby, this is one cuisine you can easily cook using meats and Italian basics available in most super-markets.

13

The Brazilian Padaria

Brazil's extraordinary cuisine is made up of three main cooking heritages: the native Indians, the conquering Portuguese, and the West African slaves brought to work the sugarcane fields and coffee plantations. Later immigrants from Eastern Europe, Germany, Italy, Japan, Lebanon, and Syria added their culinary stamps. The African impact is the strongest—with the slaves came palm oil, peanuts, hot peppers, okra, yams, plantains, and coconuts, all now integral parts of the Brazilian palate. Other staples are rice, beans, dried salt cod, shrimp, and beef. The native Amazon Indians contributed yuca meal, hearts of palm, sweet potatoes, dried and smoked fish, and corn porridges. Brazilian dishes range from fiery hot to mild, with optional hot pepper sauces served on the side. Brazil is huge and has many regional cuisines, but despite the differences, feijoãda (pronounced fish-wada), the national dish of beans and pork parts, unites food-loving Brazilians everywhere. All the ingredients necessary to make the dish can be found in Brazilian markets. Most are padarias, or bakeries, which, as in Brazil, sell much more than just baked goods.

Flours, Grains & Starches

Before bread, there was manioc in Brazil. This native tuber, also called aipim in Brazil, was first processed by Amazon Indians and remains a staple, both as a starchy vegetable and as a toasted flour. The extracted juice is also made into starch and tapioca. Manioc is better known as yuca or cassava in other parts of Latin America. Corn, rice, and wheat are other staple grains, made into polenta, flours, and breads.

BEANS

Feijoãdas. Most Brazilian markets will have both black beans (feijoãda negro) and white beans (feijoãda branco). Some might also have brown beans, known as feijoãda mulatinha, or mulatto beans (cranberry and pinto beans can be substituted for brown beans if they are not to be found). Beans are the foil for all the salted, smoked, and simmered meats served in feijoãda (also the name of Brazil's traditional pork and beans dish). Beans are pureed with coconut milk for creamy soups and are mashed and blended with toasted manioc flour for use in salads. Beans also accompany roasted chicken, grilled meats, and sausages with hot sauce. Beans and rice are a meatless staple of the country. Black, pinto, and white beans are packaged by the Combrasil, Chinezinho Vitalis, and Yoki brand in 1-pound and 1 kg (32-ounce) bags. Black beans are often labeled Carioca beans, referring to the people of Rio who prefer this type for feijoãda.

CANJIQUINHA

Dried corn. This is Brazilian mote (hominy). There are also crushed corn bits. Both are added to soups and stews or are cooked until tender, about one hour, then added to sautéed onions, garlic, bell peppers, and lingüiça sausages, served with rice and a side of kale or mustard greens. Julia and Yoki brands have both types in 1-pound bags.

FARINHA DE ARROZ

Rice flour. A soft, white powder made from finely milled rice. Used to make a thin batter for pancakes and various puddings and sweets and as a thickener for sauces. Acaçá is a steamed rice flour pudding served with seafood soups, grilled shrimp, and bobó de camarão, a spicy Bahian shrimp and coconut milk dish. It is like white polenta, soaking up the bobó sauce or soupy liquids. In Brazil the pudding is steamed in banana leaves and sold by street vendors. Goya has rice flour in 1- and 2-pound bags.

FARINHA DE MANDIOCA

Farofa pronto milho. Also called manioc or cassava flour. Blended with other flours, manioc flour goes into bread and puddings. It also coats meats and fish for frying. Manioc flour is used to make beijus, flat, tortilla-like cakes stuffed with grated coconut and pirão, a creamy puree of fish, broth, chili oil, and palm oil, blended with the flour and served as a condiment with fish or meat dishes. Bolo de aipim is a sweet breakfast bread made with manioc flour, flour, sugar, eggs, coconut milk, and butter, and is like a rich, golden cornbread. Biscoitos de polivilho are light puffy biscuits made from powdered manioc flour, salt, eggs, and coconut oil, sold in snack-sized bags.

When toasted, manioc flour is called farofa, the powdered condiment found on every Brazilian table. The texture and taste are similar to breadcrumbs, and it is sprinkled over everything from rice and beans to grilled meats, seafood, fried foods, eggs, and salads. Farofa can be plain or seasoned. Farofa is also made from farinha de milho, pale yellow crumbly corn flakes. Julia, Vitoria, and Yoki brands are in 1-pound bags and have both coarse and fine manioc flours.

FARINHA DE MILHO

Corn flour flakes. There are two types: amarela, made from yellow corn flour, and branca, made from white corn flour. Unlike cereal cornflakes, these are not thin and crisp but are soft, light, and crumbly. They're used to make cuscuz Paulista, the Brazilian take on couscous and a specialty of São Paulo. Corn flour flakes can also be used to

farinha de milho

make stiff, steamed sweet or salty-spicy puddings, mixed with manioc flour, shredded coconut, and coconut milk with sugar or salt, hot peppers, and spices. The flakes are toasted in melted butter or olive oil to make farofa. The yellow corn flakes are made by Nova Herd and Yoki brands in 1- and 2-pound bags. Dataps has white corn flour flakes in 1-pound bags. Paladar brand has both types in 1-pound bags.

FARINHA DE ROSCA

Fine flour-like breadcrumbs, used for breading foods, such as thin steaks, fish fillets, and sliced rounds of eggplant, before frying. Ideal for thickening soups and stews and adding texture to ground beef for meatloaf and hamburgers. Look for Yoki brand in 1-pound bags.

FAROFA PRONTA

Farinha de mandioca temperada. This is ready-to-use farofa, the ubiquitous toasted manioc flour table condiment that has been toasted in soybean oil with garlic, scallions, onion powder, spices, ground red pepper, and black pepper with annatto coloring and smoked bacon flavoring. The golden brown meal has a rich, smoky, and spicy flavor. Look for the Yoki brand in 1-pound foil bags.

farofa pronta

MAIZENA

Cornstarch. The well-known white starch extracted from corn, used to thicken sauces and to dust foods for deep-frying. In Brazil, sequilos (also called biscoitos de maizena) are a popular cornstarch cookie, which are sold in giant bags by the kilo. Here they are freshly baked and sold in small plastic bags. They are thick, small squares with crosshatched tops and have a soft, melting texture and sweet pastry taste. Some have coconut added. Commercially made

sequilo

maizena cookies are flat; they are good dipped in melted chocolate or dulce de leche or smeared with jam. Nestle offers them in 7-ounce packages. Sortidos brand has cornstarch in 1-pound bags.

POLENTA PRONTO

Ready-to-use, pre-cooked cornmeal, packaged in vacuum-sealed boxes. Simply open, slide out, slice, and pan-fry in butter or olive oil. Serve topped with tomato sauce or as a side with bean dishes, grilled meats, soups, and stews. Yoki brand offers polenta pronto in 2-pound, 3-ounce boxes and also has 1-pound bags of corn "pudding" (polenta)—just mix with boiled water, cover, and it is ready in 5 minutes. Yoki has 1-pound bags of polenta pre-cozico. This is pre-cooked, fine cornmeal for making quick polenta and tamales. For a Brazilian polenta and fresh corn recipe, see page 246.

POLIVILHO AZEDO

Slightly fermented, sour-smelling, gritty white manioc flour. This is blended with sweet manioc flour (see following entry) in cheese breads and other baked goods, adding a tangy flavor. It is also used as a thickener in soups and stews. Made by Julia and Vitoria brands in 1-pound bags.

POLIVILHO DOCE

Amido de mandioca. A fine, powdery white starch, similar to cornstarch, also called tapioca starch or sweet manioc flour. It is made from the starch extracted from manioc and is used in puddings and as a thickener in soups, sauces, glazes, and fruit fillings for pies and tarts. It is also used to make a batter for thin, crispy crêpes. Made by Julia, Vitoria, and Yoki brands in 1-pound bags.

SAGU DE MANDIOCA

Pearl tapioca. Pearl tapioca has to be soaked in double its volume of water until all the water has been absorbed. When cooked in puddings with coconut milk, cream, eggs, sugar, cinnamon, and vanilla, the pearls become translucent and jelly-like. Tapioca is also added to savory stews and is cooked with salt and spices and served as a starch with meals. Look for Dataps and Julia in 1-pound bags.

TRIGO PARA KIBBE

Bulghur or cracked wheat. Sold in coarse and medium grinds, when cooked it has a tender, but chewy texture and delicate nutty taste. To use, soak 3 hours, drain, and squeeze dry. It can be used to make pilafs, tabouli salad, or added to hearty meat and vegetable stews. Cracked wheat is also combined with ground lamb and seasoning to make kibbeh, shaped into logs or patties and eaten raw, grilled, or fried as croquettes. If served raw, only very fresh meat is used. Look for the Bronzeli Nogueria and Yoki brands in 1-pound bags.

trigo para kibbe

Baking Mixes

CORN BROINHA

A blend of corn and wheat flours used to make little biscuits. Mix packet with 2 eggs and 3 cups of water, shape into small balls, flatten, and bake until crispy. Offered by Yoki brand in 250 g (6.5-ounce) packets.

NHOQUE DE BATATA

Bread stick mix. A blend of flaked dehydrated potato (batata), flour, sweet tapioca starch, powdered milk, salt, and pepper. Mix with water and 2 eggs into a soft dough, roll into ropes, cut, flatten, and bake. Yoki has this mix and potato flakes for instant mashed potatoes in 6.5-ounce packets.

PÃO DE QUIJO

Cheese bread mix. A blend of sweet tapioca starch, vegetable shortening, powdered cheese, milk, and salt. Mix with ½ cup water and 2 eggs, forming a thick dough. Knead and roll into small balls and bake about 25 minutes. The rolls have a chewy consistency and delicious cheesy flavor. Freshly baked pão de quijo are sold in the bakery area, while frozen cheese dough balls can be found in the freezer case. Yoki brand has the mix in 6.5-ounce packets and Tropical Flavor brand has the frozen dough in 26.5-ounce bags. Uai! has 1-pound bags of frozen bake-and-serve rolls.

pão de quijo

Produce

In Brazil, jumbled masses of brilliant, exotic fruits and fresh vegetables vie for attention in the feiras, or open-air street markets. Sadly, what you will find in Brazilian markets here seems paltry in comparison, and you'll most likely find only basics like garlic, onions, potatoes, corn, plantains, cabbage, and a few tropical fruits. But look for the following items in larger markets.

CARURU

Okra. Also known as quiabo in some regions of Brazil. (In Bahia, quiabo is also the name of a dish made with dried shrimp, okra, and cashews cooked in palm oil.) The slender, ridged, tapered pods have an unctuous texture when cooked that can be reduced by pan-frying sliced rounds in a little oil, stirring constantly to burn off the sticky goop. The resulting slightly crunchy slices are then added to dishes near the end of cooking. In São Paulo, chopped tomatoes are stewed with sautéed onions, minced garlic, and hot peppers with prepared, sliced rounds of okra. In the Amazon region frango com quiabe is a favorite. This is sautéed chicken simmered in stock

okra

with pre-cooked slices of okra, served with polenta and hot pepper sauce. Choose small, crisp, bright green pods. Store in a loose paper or plastic bag, refrigerated, and use within 4 days.

COUVE

Kale. Also known as collards. This hardy relative to cabbage was introduced by the Portuguese and has become the favorite green of Brazil. The large leaves are dark blue-green, fibrous, and ruffled at the edges. Couve has a strong, faintly bitter flavor and is good in soups and long-simmered stews. To reduce the bitterness, blanch a few minutes in salted boiling water before cooking. The tough-ribbed stem running down the center should be removed by cutting it away. In Brazil, the leaves are usually cut into ribbons,  quickly sautéed, and served as an accompaniment to

couve

feijoãda (beans with pork parts) and slices of orange. Sautéed kale strips are also served with tutú a Mineiera, a bean mash mixed with toasted farofa, chopped scallions, and hard-boiled eggs with grilled sausages, fried pork chops, pork cracklings, and roasted meats. Store kale up to a week, refrigerated.

JABUTICABA

Brazilian tree grapes. Small, round grape-like berries with thick, glossy bluish-purple skins and translucent, sweet juicy pulp. Jabuticaba taste like a cross between muscadine grapes and huckleberries. Here, tree grapes are grown in central Florida and California and can occasionally be found at farmers' markets. They are delicious eaten out of hand or made into jellies, jams, or wine. Some Brazilian markets and specialty stores sell jabuticaba jam, usually labeled "Brazilian grape jelly."

JILÓ

Pronounced gee-loh, these adorable baby eggplants are the size of a plum tomato with shiny, lime green skins and pale, spongy flesh containing a ring of small white seeds. If allowed to ripen they turn beautiful hues—from yellow-orange to bright tomato red—and lose some of their characteristic bitterness. They can be cooked like any eggplant. First slice, sprinkle with salt, let stand 10 minutes, and rinse. (Scraping out the seeds also reduces bitterness as does peeling, but then you lose the color.) Dice and sauté with

jiló

onions, garlic, cumin, and ground meat, or dip slices in beaten egg, then coat with flour or breadcrumbs, and fry. Jiló are also good boiled and chopped, tossed with onions and tomatoes, and drizzled with olive oil as a salad. To make a Brazilian-Italian caponata, sauté some chopped celery and onion in olive oil, then add diced jiló and cook until soft. Stir in a pinch of sugar, a teaspoon of grated bittersweet chocolate, a splash of vinegar, some capers and green olives, and serve warm with rice and fish or meat, or chilled as a spread for crusty bread. The only grower outside of Brazil is Pedro Maia, based in South Florida. He distributes the green jiló to Brazilian markets all along the East Coast and is willing to ship green or ripe colored ones any-where—for more information, see page 260. Jiló are in season from November to late June. Store up to 2 weeks, refrigerated in a loose paper or plastic bag.

The Açougue (Meat Counter)

At the Brazilian market's meat counter, you will find a variety of salt meats and pork parts, including snouts, ears, tails, and feet. There's also salted pork ribs, slab bacon, pork butt, smoked beef tongue, salted beef, paio (fatty, spicy, smoked pork sausages) and spicy lingüiça sausage, all components of fei-joãda. You will also find whole chick-ens, pork chops, salami, ham, cheeses, and salt cod. Some cuts of beef to ask for are contrafilé, which is beef for steaks, maminha for roasts, picanha for barbecue meat, and alcatra for ham-burger—to get it ground, say "passar na manquina." Below the meat counter are large bags of natural charcoal (no chemicals) imported from Brazil for grilling your meat.

Variations of feijoãda, using different kinds of beans and meat, can be found all over Brazil. A typical version includes salted and smoked meats, sausages, bacon, pork loin, and ribs, and most likely some juilenned pig ear or small slices of tail. Meats are usually served on a separate platter from the beans, with sides of rice, kale, orange slices, farofa, and hot sauce.

LINGÜIÇA

Portuguese-style fresh pork sausage. It can be mild or spicy with hot chilies added to the ground meat mixture. Calabreze is the firm, smoked version. Lingüiça is similar to sweet or hot Ital-ian sausage and it can be grilled, boiled, or pan-fried and served with beans or polenta. Lingüiça is added to codizo, a Portuguese-Brazilian pot-au-feu. Salted and fresh meats, sausages, and vegetables are boiled together, then sliced and served with hot sauce, pickled peppers, and farofa. Sliced sausages are added to cooked, mote corn melanges and hearty bean dishes. (You may also find fat, slightly greasy, smoked pork sausages called paio.) Locally made lingüiça sausages should be available. You can also buy Ki Delicia brand's packages of 4 links of smoked paio and calabreze sausages.

CHEESES

Large Brazilian markets have several types of cheese. The most com-monly found type is requijao, a buttery rich cream cheese sold in jars and used as a spread, in dips, and mixed into bread dough. Look for Puck brand in 8.5-ounce jars with Arabic lettering and Pocos de Caldas brand in 8.8-ounce jars. Another popular cheese is Catupiry, named after a Brazilian Indian chief and sold in round plastic containers with a bright blue and red label. This is a high-fat cream cheese, sort of like Brie, made from pasteurized cows' milk. Slice the round into slices or thick wedges and serve with fruit, cold cuts, olives, and bread as an appetizer, or cut into small bits and use in creamy casseroles with shrimp, tomato sauce, and hearts of palm. Be sure to check the label for a freshness date. Qeuijo de Minas is a fresh white curd cheese. The Brazilian queso blanco is slightly tangy and dense, and it is often paired with slices of guava or quince paste to make the dessert Romeu e Julieta. Look for Queijo Fresca D'Minas brand in 1-pound rounds and Quata brand Queso Minas in 2-pound rounds or 1-pound half rounds.

catupiry cheese

Sweet Stuff

COCONUT PRODUCTS

The versatile coconut is found in many guises in Brazilian markets. There is refreshing leite de coco, or coconut juice—the clear liquid inside the coconut shell. Two popular brands are Menina and Soco-cio in 200 ml (7-ounce) bottles in the fridge case. You'll also find coconut milk, both regular and "lite," made from the second or third squeezing of fresh coconut meat mixed with water. It is thinner and lighter than regular coconut milk. Either type is used extensively in Afro-Bahian cuisine, balancing hot and pungent ingredients with a creamy, slight sweetness. Coconut milk is used in soups, stews, sauces, rice dishes, drinks, and numerous desserts from puddings and custard to mousse. Look for the Sococo brand in 200 ml (7-ounce) bottles. Don't get coconut milk mixed up with the cans of sweet blends for cocktails such as piña coladas. Lastly, there is coco ralado—grated, unsweetened coconut also called desiccated coconut. The fine shreds are ready to use in a wide range of sweet and savory dishes. Add to fruit salads, sprinkle over chocolate puddings and cakes, and add to black beans and rice. Quindão is a coconut torte, a sort of large baked pie made from a mixture of egg yolks, sugar, and grated coconut. Quindim are small individual tarts of the same mixture, available in the bakery section of the market. Coco queimando are popular Bahian sweets, little patties of grated coconut, caramelized brown sugar, and egg white flavored with cinnamon and cloves. Beijos de coco com chocolate are chocolate-dipped coconut kisses with raisins. Brasileiras are coconut cookies flavored with vanilla. Look for the Ducoco and Sococo brands in 100 g (3-ounce) pouches. Desiccated coconut can also be found in supermarkets. A recipe for rice cooked in coconut milk is on page 245 and a Brazilian shrimp and coconut milk recipe is on page 249.

DOCES

Sweets. Brazilian markets have at least one aisle stocked with a wide array of biscuits, sandwich crème cookies, chocolate and strawberry wafers called tostines, and all types of chocolate in bags and boxes in colorful wrappers. Garoto is the best chocolate brand—try the bombones suridos (assorted chocolates) in 14-ounce yellow boxes—you can sample banana paste–filled chocolates, caramel and coconut, coconut, raisin-cashew, and hazelnut creams. Others in the mix include torrones (cashew chocolates), rum-flavored white chocolate, and white chocolates with cashew nut and coconut fillings. The small match-size boxes labeled "rapadurinha" contain paper-wrapped cubes of dark brown sugar, good carried in pockets for a quick energy rush. There are also plastic-wrapped trays of sugared black banana sweets, mixed fruit gummies, heart-shaped maroon doce de batata (sweet potato paste), and pe de molque, little squares of peanut fudge. You might also find different and delicious banana and cinnamon cookies.

chocolate bon-bon

rum and chocolate bon-bon

GOIABA CALDA

Guava halves in light syrup. The rosy-red fruits are great as a dessert—plain, stuffed with cream cheese, or drizzled with thick, sweet cream. They're also sliced and used as a cake filling and added to fruit salads. Look for ETTI brand in 400 g (14-ounce) cans.

Spreads

AROBORA COM COCO

Calabaza pumpkin and coconut paste. A dense paste made from pureed pumpkin and coconut with sugar, eaten as is, spread on crackers, cookies, or slices of cheese. It tastes a bit like intense coconut-pumpkin pie. Look for ETTI brand in large round tins. This brand also has white sweet potato paste.

BANANADA

Banana butter. A mixture of ripe bananas, sugar, and cinnamon with a thick consistency and sweet grainy flavor. It is used as a spread on toast, crackers, cookies, or muffins and in desserts and sauces for cakes and custards. Delicious served with whipped cream or spread on queso blanco cheese. Look for the ETTI brand in red and yellow 700 g (25-ounce) round tins.

BUTTER & OILS

Manteiga is butter, azeite is oil. Butter is used for sautéing, toasting manioc flour to make farofa, in baking, and as a spread. Fresh, lightly salted Brazilian butter is found in the fridge case—look for the Itambe brand in 1-pound tubs. There are also long-life tins of butter in small

dendê

Afro-Bahian cuisine evolved from plantation slave cooks improvising on African, Indian, and traditional Portuguese dishes, using locally available ingredients. Examples, all using dendê oil, are bobo de camarão (shrimp in a coconut milk-manioc root puree, seasoned with dendê oil, cilantro, onion, and garlic); moqueca (fish stew in coconut milk with dende oil); and xin xin (chicken and shrimp stew thickened with ground cashews and peanuts in a spicy coconut milk base flavored and tinted with dendê oil). All of these are served with white rice, farofa (toasted manioc flour), and hot sauce.

orange cans. Olive oil has a high smoking point and is used for deep-frying as well as sautéing and in salad dressings and marinades. Gallo brand is one of Brazil's best virgin olive oils, and there is also Saloio Portuguese olive oil in 1-quart bottles.

Rich, orange dendê, also called palm oil, is the oil of choice in Bahia and African dishes. There are two types— unrefined, yellow-orange oil and pale, refined oil. The type used in Brazil is the thick orange oil, which is high in vitamin E and beta-carotene, but is also high in saturated fat. The flavor is heightened by heating and, as it has a high smoking point, is used to deep-fry snacks such as black bean fritters and battered whitebait. Dendê oil is also added near the end of cooking in many dishes for color and flavor and to sauté chicken, seafood, okra, and other vegetables. Brands to look for are Central in 200 ml (7-ounce) glass bottles, Cepera and Tallisca brands in various-sized bottles.

Beverages

AÇAI CONCENTRATE

A violet-colored concentrate sold in jars in the fridge case, made from the pulp of blackish-purple berries. Mix two parts water to one part concentrate. It can also be mixed with cooked tapioca pearls and sugar or used to flavor ice cream, sherbet, and popsicles. The taste is similar to slightly tart grape juice. Look for the Caneco brand imported by Supre Stock Co. in 580 ml (22-ounce) jars.

COFFEE

Brazilians drink a lot of coffee. Cafezinhos, meaning "little coffees" appear in tiny glasses or demitasse cups wherever you go. (Never decline an offer of a cup of coffee, it is considered rude.) Brazilian coffee is roasted dark and finely ground and is drunk strong and black with lots of sugar. It has an intense aroma and rich flavor. To brew cafezinho, add one

brazilian coffee

heaping tablespoon of coffee powder to each cup of water, add sugar to taste, bring to a boil, stir well, and remove from heat. Pour mixture through a cloth strainer (available in Brazilian and Latin markets) or a paper coffee filter, and serve. Coffee is sold in vacuum-sealed bags. Brands to look for are Café Bom Jesus, Café Do Pronto, Minas extra forte, Milita, Pilao, and Vascafe. "Extra forte" on the label means extra strong.

FRUIT CONCENTRATES

Suco de fruta parcha. Thick, strained liquids made from various fruits and berries. As they are very concentrated, dilute with water to make juice, generally about five parts water to one part concentrate, plus some crushed ice. Can be used undiluted in milk shakes, sorbets, and mousse or in reductions for fruity sauces and glazes with cream, butter, rum, or citrus juice and seasonings. A rainbow of concentrates is sold in 500 ml to 1,000 ml (16- and 24-ounce) bottles. Flavors include acerola (Barbados sour cherry); cashew apple (suco caju) with a musty, sourish taste; guava; grape; passion fruit; Suriname cherry (suco de pitanga, with a tangy tomato-sour cherry flavor); pineapple; and mixed berry

pitanga fruit concentrate (boituva xarope groselha). Add sugar to the tart varieties, such as cashew apple, Suriname cherry, and acerola. Brands to look for are Dafruta, Jandaia, Palmeiron, and Serigy.

GUARANÁ SODA

Pronounced wa-RAN-na. A popular Brazilian soft drink made from guaraná, a tropical vine with small red berries. The soft drink is made from carbonated water, corn syrup, guaraná extract, and caramel coloring. It provides a jolt similar to that of a cup of coffee and is also sold in powdered form in some Brazilian markets and health food stores. This is mixed with water or fruit juice and sugar to make a drink. Guaraná soda tastes like sparkling

guaraná soda

cherry or apple-tinged cream soda and is quaffed to combat heat exhaustion and headaches. It is very refreshing and is added to alcoholic punches, blended with grape juice, and pineapple chunks and champagne. Look for Antarctica and Golly brands in 12-ounce cans.

TEA

Cha. Tea is popular in Brazil—especially lemon-spiked yerba maté. Green maté is called chimarrao and sipped through a silver straw with a strainer at one end, a gaucho tradition from southern Brazil. Black maté is sipped iced with sugar and lemon and is sold in soda-type cans called cha maté or beba bem gelado, made from maté extract, water, and sugar. Green maté is available in 1 kilo (2-pound) and 500 g (16-ounce) bags. There are also boxes of black maté with 25 bags, labeled "matte leao limão" (with lemon). Other teas you may find are apple, made from dehydrated apples and steeped as a fruity warming tea; peppermint tea; and chapreto, Chinese black tea that brews into a deep reddish liquor and is good served hot or iced with lemon. All are offered by the Leao brand in boxes of 10 to 20 bags.

In-Store Snacks

One of the joys of visiting a Latin grocery is the chance to sample typical snacks, sweets, and beverages on the spot. Most Brazilian padarias have a snack counter where salinginhos—finger foods—such as breaded fried shrimp, meat croquettes, and pão de quiejo are kept warm in hot boxes. Many also have juice and batido bars and offer cafezinho, little coffees served black in demitasse cups. Batidos are fruit shakes whirled with condensed milk. Suco de fruita means fruit juice and milk, and fruit shakes are called vitaminas. Mista means mixed fruit and banana com aveia is a banana and oatmeal blender drink. Caldo de cana is fresh pressed sugarcane juice. If there is no juice bar, grab a soda or bottled fruit drink from the fridge case to go with any of the following salgados (snacks).

ACARAJÉ FRITTERS

Black-eyed pea fritters made from a puree of the cooked, skinned beans mixed with hot pepper sauce, salt, and pepper; shaped into patties; topped with dried shrimp; and deep-fried. The crispy treats are either served with vatapá (seafood coconut cream) or malagueta pepper sauce.

AIPIM FRITES

Deep-fried pieces of manioc root like thick French fries. Sprinkle with salt and dip into hot sauce.

BOLINHO DE BACALHAU

Salt cod fritters. A favorite tira-gosto (appetizer) or snack in Brazil. Soaked, drained, and flaked salt cod is mixed with mashed potatoes, beaten eggs, chopped onion, salt, and pepper, formed into little balls, and deep-fried. Delicious with a batido or ice cold beer. A salt cod fritter recipe is on page 236.

CROQUETTES DE QUIJO

Cheese croquettes. Little balls are formed from a mixture of flour, grated Parmesan cheese, butter, and egg yolks, dipped in fluffy beaten egg whites, rolled in breadcrumbs, baked until golden, and served with hot sauce.

EMPADAS

Also called empadinha, or little pastry. These are Brazilian empanadas, baked turnovers stuffed with various fillings such as minced heart of palm, olives, and shrimp; chicken; cheese; or vegetables. The pastries are brushed with egg yolk before going into the oven, giving them a golden sheen. Pastels are fried empadas.

PAMONHA

Sweet cinnamon-laced corn pudding, steamed like tamales in corn husks. Served with hot sauce to counter the sweetness.

Odds & Ends

BRAZIL NUTS

brazil nuts

Castanhas. Also called cream nuts and Para nuts as most of the crop comes from Para State in the Amazon basin. The outer shell of the Brazil nut's fruit (resembling a coconut) is called an ourico and is burned as fuel or made into cups and bowls. Inside, a dozen or more nuts rattle around. The shell is cracked open with a machete and the nuts dumped into running water—they get both washed and sorted, as good nuts sink and bad nuts float away. The nuts are sold both shelled and unshelled, but the shelled are preferable, as Brazil nuts are very tough to crack open. Shelled nuts, however, have a shorter shelf life and can quickly turn rancid. Stores that sell the shelled nuts usually store them in the fridge case for this reason. The nuts have a rich texture and mild creamy flavor. They're used as candy fillings, cake fillings, and dipped in chocolate. In cooking, the nuts are oven-roasted, the brown skins rubbed off and finely ground, then pureed with broth into a smooth paste. This is blended into a butter and flour roux with cream and seasonings to make creamy soups. The nuts are also available in specialty stores and whole food and health food stores.

DRIED SHRIMP

Camarão seco. Used whole in some stews, and acarajé fritters made from pureed black-eyed peas and some stews, but are mainly ground and the gritty powder used in the cooking of Bahia for flavor and as a thickener. Some types are salted and are best soaked in warm water 20 to 30 minutes before using. They can also be quite old, tough and oily. It is much better to make your own. All you need is about a pound of unshelled small shrimp, with heads intact, if possible (most Asian markets have these) and half a cup of dendê. Toss the shrimp in the oil, place in a baking pan, and bake about 20 minutes in a preheated oven set at 500 degrees. Turn the shrimp several times so they cook evenly. Once the shells start to get crunchy, preheat the broiler, place the pan under the broiler, and crisp the shrimp 1 to 2 minutes, watching carefully to avoid charring them. They should be a reddish-golden color and dried out. Remove from the pan and season with salt. When completely cool, store in a tightly sealed container up to one week—longer if refrigerated. Grind the shrimp in a blender with a little stale bread to make the powder. Many Bahian seafood stews start with a base of dried shrimp ground with cracker crumbs or stale bread, milk, and roasted cashews and peanuts, forming a creamy sauce.

GELÉIA DE MOCOTO

Mocoto jelly. Also called animal protein gel. This strange but popular substance is dark brown and gelatin-like, sold in small glass jars. It is an animal protein extract made by boiling cows' feet blended with agar-agar (a seaweed extract that thickens and gels), caramel coloring, and drop or two of carnation oil. It has a mild, sweetish taste with a floral aroma.

Mocoto tutti frutti is flavored with fruit concentrates. It is also used as a spread for toast, crackers, and cookies and as a delicate and unusual cake filling. Made by Arisco and Colombo brands in 3-ounce jars.

HOT SAUCE & SEASONINGS

Brazilian food gets its fire from pimenta malagueta, a small red chili. It is blended with vinegar to make salsa de picante, a thin, pungent sauce that is bright red-orange and very hot. Môlho de pimenta verde is a similar hot sauce made with unripe, green malagueta chilies. Some versions have lime juice added and are labeled "con limão." Whole red malagueta chilies are pickled and used as a table condiment, as are the tiny round red baina chili and small, oval green comari pickled peppers, both of which are extremely hot and sold in small bottles.

Dried or pickled peppers are added to bean dishes, salsas, and stir-fries. Môlho de acarajé is a delicious chili-shrimp sauce served over black-eyed pea fritters, rice, or potatoes. A paste is made by combining cooked shrimp, minced onion, fresh or pickled malagueta chilies (or hot sauce), and salt, then sautéed in palm oil over low heat, about 10 minutes to meld the flavors. Tempero completo is a marinade for seasoning meat, poultry, and seafood before roasting or grilling. It is a blend of vinegar, olive oil, minced parsley and garlic, red pepper flakes, and spices. Brands that offer most of these sauces and pickled chilies are Arisco, Cepera, ETTI, and Vitoria in various-sized bottles and jars. The Arisco brand also sells a powdered blend of salt, garlic, chives, parsley, basil, onion, bay leaf, and rosemary. Use this as a dry rub to season meats and seafood and to flavor rice dishes, soups, and stews. Mix with oil and vinegar as a marinade. McMace brand sells bags of garlic and oil seasoning, good for sprinkling over pasta, pizza, salads, baked potatoes, beans, and rice.

ROCK SALT

Sal Grosso. Also called grosso especial para churrasco. Coarse salt, similar to kosher salt, is sprinkled on meats 1 to 2 hours before grilling— shake off any excess over the grill. Look for Arisco and Cisne brands in large plastic bags of 1 to 2 pounds and Vit sal sea salt in 2.2-pound bags. These brands also offer fine salt used in the same way and dissolved in water as pickling brines for meats.

Stocking Up

Brazilian staples you will need to cook authentic dishes include manioc flour for farofa or instant farofa; rice; black or white beans; polenta; tapioca; and fresh baked breads, frozen dough, or a mix. Add some okra, eggplant, kale or other green, palm oil, coconut milk, cream cheese, and fresh or smoked sausages. Other items to consider are the exotic fruit concentrates, pastes and preserves, guaraná soda, chocolates, and coffee. Supplement your supplies with fresh produce, meats, and seafood, including shrimp to make your own dried shrimp. Some ingredients can also be found in Caribbean markets.

14

The Venezuelan
Marketcito

Venezuelan markets are small and compact, and many double as a café and bakery with a few limited grocery items. Cooked foods are kept warm in steam pans, cafeteria-style, behind glass. Cakes, pastries, and breads are laid out in glass cases. You can eat at the few small tables or order take-out. Many marketcitos also offer catering. The cuisine of Venezuela is a blend of Spanish colonial adaptations of dishes from neighboring countries and Caribbean islands. In the last century, an influx of Italian immigrants have added their culinary touch, putting pizza, pasta, and lasagne on the menu. Germans contributed excellent cheeses and beer. Staples include corn, bananas, yuca, black beans, coconut, rice, and avocados. Popular seasonings are annatto, black pepper, capers, oregano, and paprika. Both corn and wheat breads are served with most meals that consist of vegetable, meat, seafood, and rice dishes, soups and stews, and tropical fruits.

Cornmeal
CACHAPAS MIX

Mezca para hacer cachapas. Corn pancake mix for making mildly sweet pancakes. Mix with water and eggs to make a smooth batter and cook on a buttered griddle or in a skillet. Look for the Misia Juana brand in 8.8-ounce bags.

PRE-COOKED WHITE CORNMEAL

The most used cornmeal in Venezuela and throughout South America, sold in many Latin markets. It is mixed with lukewarm water and salt, kneaded into a smooth dough, and used to make arepas and gorditas. To make arepas, roll the dough into balls and flatten into 1-inch thick rounds. Fry in a greased skillet until a crust forms on both sides, then bake until done in a preheated oven, about 10 to 15 minutes. (See Café Items, page 179, for more on arepas.) For gorditas, make a little hollow in the ball and stuff with a ground meat mixture, seal, and fry. With a little sugar added, the dough is used to make empanadas. Mixed with broth, a pinch of cinnamon, and a little corn oil and steamed in banana leaves, the dough is used to make tamales. The ubiquitous P.A.N. brand cornmeal is sold in 1 kg (2-pound) yellow bags. Ricarina brand has harina de maiz amarillo, or yellow cornmeal, in 24-ounce bags.

white cornmeal

Sacripantina cake is Italian in origin and is basically a sponge cake, sliced thinly and layered with zabaglione. Zabaglione is a dessert sauce made by whisking together egg yolks, sugar, and Marsala (although other wines or liqueurs can be used) cooked over a double-boiler until light and foamy, with the consistency of whipped cream. The sauce is sometimes topped with a tiny dice of sponge cake, but traditionally is covered with crushed amaretti cookies. The name of the cake is derived from a character called Sacripante ("swashbuckler") in a poem by Lodovico Ariosto.

Baked Goods

BREADS

A wide range of breads is offered including sandwich rolls, hot dog buns, cheese-filled dinner loaves, salty breakfast loaves, Italian loaves, small round baguettes, sweet anise bread, flat cracker-like yuca meal bread, and pan de naranja, a sweet orange bread with marmalade and nuts. A favorite is pan de locha, a torpedo-shaped roll known as "penny bread" after the price it used to be sold for. There are also larger, crusty baguettes called pan de ariel (50 cents bread), and you may find long, flattish, airy ciabatta, perfect for sandwiches and spreads or toasted with melted cheese under the broiler.

CAKES & PASTRIES

Cakes are sold whole in various sizes or by the slice. There are sacripantina (Italian wine cake), coconut cake, mocha cream cake, strawberry shortcake, caramel meringue cake, dark chocolate opera cake, torta guanabana (soursop layer cake), and black forest chocolate cake. You'll also find jellyroll sponge cakes with strawberry jam or chocolate cream and tiramisu. There are also small fruit tarts, charlottes (bavarois custard chilled in a ladyfinger-lined mold), napoleons, suspiros (meringue kisses), vanilla and chocolate cream-filled eclairs, and profiterols. Another treat is the bien me sabe de coco (tastes good to me coconut custard) and flan. All of these are good with a café con leche, espresso, or cappuccino. Or wash the cake down with a cocado— coconut milk whirled in a blender with milk, sugar, vanilla, and ice—or merengada, a fruit milkshake.

bien me sabe

Dairy Products

Some markets may have queso llano, a hard, white salty cheese in 1-pound blocks, and queso paisa, similar to queso blanco. Both are used as arepa fillings and are crumbled or grated over black beans, vegetables, salads, and stews. Salted cream nata, also called crema de leche salada, is a thin, salty sour cream for topping arepas and cachapas (small corn pancakes) and used as a salad dressing. Look for the Barquisimeto brand in 1-pound plastic bottles.

Grocery Items

ALIÑO CRIOLLO

Creole-style seasoning powder. A mixture of ground herbs and spices used in many Venezuelan dishes. Store-bought blends are labeled "alino preparado" (prepared seasoning) and contain ground cumin, annatto, oregano, garlic salt, and paprika.

GUASACACA

Venezuelan barbecue sauce. This unusual sauce is best made from scratch as it contains fresh avocado and should be used immediately, although some cafés make their own and sell it in tubs from the fridge case. Used to marinate or baste grilled meats, chicken pieces, pork chops, fish, or shrimp. To make it, finely chop a jalapeño, an onion, and a red bell pepper and toss with a diced avocado and tomato and blend in some olive oil, red wine vinegar, or lime juice and salt to taste. Some cooks add chopped parsley or cilantro, hard-boiled egg, and a bit of mustard. Serve with steaks, rice and beans, and fried seafood.

PICANTE CASERO

House hot sauce. A blend of pureed onions, garlic, and yellow chilies made in-house. Use as a side sauce and smeared on arepas.

Beverages

Much of the little shelf space in a Venezuelan market is taken up with cans and bags of Venezuelan coffee and of powdered milk. El Penon is an espresso blend of finely ground Venezuelan-grown coffee in 14-ounce brown cans. Fama de America is another quality Venezuelan coffee in 8-ounce bags. Cerelac and Nido are brands of powdered malt drink mixes in cans. Leche en polvo completa La Sampina is a

1 kg bag of powdered milk enriched with vitamins A and D. Pamalat of Venezuela is another powdered milk—all should be mixed with water to use. Toddy is a popular kids' drink made from a blend of malt, sugar, cocoa, dried milk, vanilla, and caramel flavors, enriched with vitamins, good hot or cold and sold in 2 kilo and 200 g (7-ounce) cans. Fresca chicha is strawberry-flavored powdered drink mix.

venezuelan coffee

Café Items

Enter a Venezuelan café and you will be enveloped in the tropical Latin scents coming from the kitchen. Order an espresso and piece of caramel meringue cake or a full meal starting with a breakfast combination plate. Following are some typical menu items.

AREPAS

Round, thick corn cakes made from pre-cooked, processed white or yellow cornmeal mixed with water and salt into a soft dough. Richer versions have egg yolks, grated cheese, and butter added. The insides are soft and doughy with a rich corn taste, and the outsides are crisp, sort of like a large toasted English muffin. Plain arepa are split open and the soft part pulled out to sop up juices and the crisp shells buttered or spread with cream cheese. Arepas can be filled with almost anything. Breakfast fillings include perico (scrambled eggs with tomatoes and onions), fried eggs, or ham and cheese. Other fillings for anytime include black beans, reina (avocado and chicken salad), shrimp, shredded stewed beef or chicken, asado negro (pot roast slices in a dark spicy sauce), cheese, flaked fish, and even fried strips of baby shark. Any combination of available fillings can be requested such as dominó (black beans and white cheese), scrambled eggs and cheese, or shredded beef and beans. Arepitas are small arepas, served like bread to accompany meals. Arepas fritas infladas are deep-fried corn patty puffs with grated cheese, anise, and brown sugar added to the dough.

CACHAPAS

Mini sweet corn pancakes. These are made from a thick, smooth, pureed batter of corn, cream, egg, and a little flour, sugar, and salt, cooked in melted butter on a griddle. They are slightly sweet and are served with a fresh mozzarella-like cheese called queso guyanesa or cottage cheese. Cachapas de hojas are made from the same batter, but wrapped in banana leaf packets.

CACHITOS

Bread horns. These are hot croissants or half-moon puff pastries filled with chopped ham or cheese.

CORBULLÓN MANTUANO

Striped bass in sweet pepper and tomato sauce. Sautéed slices of fish are added to a simmering sauce made from sliced onions, green and red bell peppers, chopped tomatoes, cayenne pepper, red wine, olive oil, capers, and olives, and served with boiled potatoes.

EGGPLANT WITH GREEN BEANS

Berenjenas con vainitas. A mixture of sliced eggplant sautéed with chopped onions, salt, sugar, pepper, tomatoes, and olives until soft. The mixture is heaped in the center of a dish surrounded by boiled green beans tossed in butter or olive oil and garnished with chopped parsley. Delicious with grilled or roasted meats, chicken, or fish and can be served chilled as a salad if the beans are dressed in vinaigrette.

EMPANADAS

Baked pastry turnovers filled with chicken or tuna are called empanadas gallega, or Spanish style. Deep-fried cornmeal dough empanadas can be stuffed with shredded chicken, chopped ham, cheese, ground meat, flaked fish, or baby shark. There are also combo fillings such as chicken and cheese or black beans and cheese.

ESPINACAS CON ANCHOS

Spinach with anchovies. Cooked spinach or Swiss chard is chopped and sautéed in olive oil with mashed, canned anchovies. Served as a side dish with meat or roasted chicken or as a main dish topped with fried eggs and served with rice.

HALLACAS

Christmas tamales. A traditional yuletime treat, they are enjoyed at other times too. Most Venezuelan and some Caribbean markets make them fresh or they can be found frozen during the holiday season. A masa dough is made from cornmeal mixed with water, a pinch of brown sugar and salt, and shortening, tinted yellow with annatto and paprika. The dough is rolled out, stuffed, and folded up in a banana leaf parcel, tied with string and boiled. The filling is a mixture of chopped beef, chicken, and pork simmered with minced onions, garlic, tomatoes, hot peppers, olives, raisins, almonds, and seasonings. Small tamales are called bollitos (mouth bites). Hallaquitos are small tamales made from fresh creamed corn, either plain or stuffed with ground pork or red pepper.

HERVIDO

Hen pot-au-feu. Also called sancocho de gallina. Chunks of yam, yuca, potato, pumpkin, potatoes, corn, carrots, cabbage, and tomatoes are stewed in stock with pieces of hen (or chicken) seasoned with chopped cilantro, salt, and pepper. Usually served with guasacaca (avocado sauce) and hot sauce for punch. Also made with lean chuck.

MONDONGO

Tripe stew. A popular dish said to cure hangovers. The tripe is simmered in water with a calf's foot, root vegetables, seasonings, salt, and tomato sauce and served with a lemon or lime wedge on the side.

PABELLÓN CRIOLLO

The national dish of Venezuela, this is also called pabellón Caraqueño. Pabellón means "flag," which the dish resembles with all its different colors. It is a combination plate consisting of shredded beef sautéed with onions, garlic, and tomatoes served on top of steamed rice with fried eggs, caraotas negras (black beans) and strips of fried plantain with hot sauce on the side. Sometimes flaked fish replaces the beef.

PASTELITOS

Small stuffed pastries, rolled up with a filling before baking. They are made from buttery pastry dough or puff pastry. Popular fillings are spinach and ricotta; ground pork with onion, garlic, capers, olives, and raisins; ground, seasoned beef; and shredded spiced chicken.

PASTICHOS

Also called lasañas or baked pasta. Slices of eggplant or ground beef and tomato sauce are layered with lasagne noodles, béchamel sauce, and cheese and baked.

REPELLO RELLENO

Whole stuffed cabbage. The heart of a cabbage is cut out and the space is filled with a pork picadillo (ground meat) and diced potato mixture and simmered in stock. When tender, it is drained and topped with tomato sauce, cut into wedges, and served with crusty bread.

SANDUCHON

A large sandwich cake. Slices of bread are alternated with cheese and deli meats, then frosted with softened cream cheese. Tuna salad or egg salad are alternative fillings. The cake is then cut into slices and served as an appetizer.

TEQUENOS

Cheese fingers. Strips of pastry dough are wound around a strip of cheese, completely sealing it, and deep-fried.

Odds & Ends

In the Venezuelan market, you may also find chistorras, skinny, spicy cured sausages made by the La Vasca brand in 8-ounce sealed packs, which are good for snacking or used in cooking, sliced and scrambled with eggs, and added to stews. Other possible finds are fruit pulps and concentrates, slabs or cones of papelón (unrefined brown sugar), coconut milk, and toasted coconut macaroons. Knorr has 2-ounce packets of bases for seasoning black beans and carne mechada (beef stew). Casabe Fortitude brand makes crackers from cassava meal called rainforest bread, either plain or flavored with wild onion, garlic, or hot and sweet peppers.

rainforest bread

Stocking Up

Pre-cooked white cornmeal is a mandatory item, Venezuelan coffee is excellent, and the strawberry soda is an interesting change. Be sure to pick up some rainforest crackers: they're fat free, full of fiber, and a percentage of the proceeds goes to saving the rainforest. Finally, select some take-out foods, arepas, tamales, breads, cakes, or pastries.

15

The Caribbean Marketplace

Caribbean markets offer a lively and colorful mosaic of island goods, reflecting the mix of people from many places. The Caribbean encompasses a wide swath of turquoise sea, stretching like a chain of green jewels from Bermuda and the Bahamas off the east shore of Florida all the way down to Trinidad and Tobago, nudging the coast of Venezuela as far west as Aruba. Generally, each country has a similar legacy: European conquest, slavery, indentured labor, and, eventually, independence. The Spanish, Dutch, Danish, British, French, and Portuguese came first, followed in their wake by West Africans, East Indians, and Chinese. The cuisine of each country evolved uniquely, but with much borrowing and blending of foods and cooking styles. Similarly, the products and produce found in Caribbean markets overlap and criss-cross the islands. All Caribbean markets have a section of Afro-Caribbean goods, many imported from West Africa. Latin markets are also a source for Caribbean goods, as many ingredients are common to both cuisines.

Flours & Starches

ARROWROOT

Also called St. Vincent arrowroot. Arrowroot starch is fine and powdery and extremely digestible. When mixed with water it makes a light textured, almost transparent paste. In cooking, it is used in baked goods and as a thickening agent in soups, stews, glazes, and sauces. Arrowroot drops are little cupcakes made from creamed butter, sugar, and eggs mixed with milk and arrowroot starch, topped with a candied cherry, and baked. The starch may be sold in plain plastic bags, or look for West Indian Caribbean brand in 6-ounce jars. Ocho Rios has small packets good for when you want just a little as a thickener.

CASSAVA FLOUR

Also called yuca meal, this is a coarse, grainy meal made from grated yuca from which all the liquid is squeezed out, very similar to Brazilian farofa. It is used to make breads and can be toasted in butter or oil with spices and seasonings and sprinkled over cooked foods. Gari is a similar, coarse-grained flour, also called cassava grits. It is used in Afro-Caribbean cooking as a staple starch, in breads, biscuits, fu fu (thick pastes), and the popular dish gari foto. To make this, gari is stirred into a mixture of onions and tomatoes sautéed in palm oil with chopped vegetables, broth, and hot pepper sauce until all the liquid has been absorbed. Scrambled eggs are often served on top of gari foto. Gari is also used as a cereal, in stuffings, and mixed with water to make dumplings to float in stews. Tropiway brand has both cassava flour and gari in 24-ounce boxes. ACC African Caribbean brand sells cassava flour in 1-pound yellow boxes with green letters. Nina and Sands brands have gari in 3-pound bags, and WALA brand is in 5-pound bags.

CASSAVA STARCH

Similar to arrowroot starch, but made from the liquid starch extracted from cassava roots. It is used in the Caribbean to make a type of fu fu. Mix 1 cup of water with 2 cups of the starch and stir into a smooth paste; add a little palm oil and seasonings and heat over low flame until thick. Look for Ola-Ola brand in 4-pound bags. For more about fu fu, see pages 216–217.

CORNMEAL

Also called masa harina in the Spanish islands, this is finely ground yellow or white dried corn. It is used in baked goods and to make pancakes, dumplings, fritters, steamed puddings wrapped in banana leaves, and fungi, also called funchi and coo coo. This is a cornmeal mush made, like polenta, by slowly stirring cornmeal into boiling water, broth, or coconut milk with a wooden spoon; cooking for 3 to 4 minutes until creamy; adding butter, salt, and pepper; and serving. Fungi can also be poured into a shallow pan, cooled, cut into squares, and pan-fried until crispy on both sides. Another popular island preparation is to stir in sliced rounds of dry-fried okra with the cornmeal.

See Latin Basics, pages 28–29 for more on cornmeal.

DAL FLOUR

Also spelled dahl or dahll. A pale, soft, powdery flour made from ground split peas. It is mainly used in East Indian island cuisine to make breads, porridges, sweets, and snacks like sev (deep-fried squiggly noodles) and salt saye, spicy fried snack sticks flavored with salt, hot pepper, garlic, and cumin sold in small bags in the snack section. Bara bread is a specialty from Trinidad used to make doubles. A crispy piece of the deep-fried bread made from a dal flour and flour dough is topped with doubles channa, a mixture of boiled, spiced chickpeas, folded over, and served with hot sauce. Sahina is another snack, made by spreading dasheen (taro) leaves with a dal flour, flour, and turmeric batter and stacking them, rolling the leaves up, and slicing off half-inch long pieces. These are then fried in a little oil until crisp and served with hot pepper sauce or chutney. You will also find pholourie mix to make crispy fritter balls called phulouri. This is a mixture of flour, dal flour, cornstarch, salt, powdered garlic, and cumin. To use, add 1 packet to 1 cup of water and mix well to form a paste. Drop by the teaspoon into hot oil until they float to the surface and are golden all over. Drain and serve with green mango or tamarind chutney and hot sauce as a dip. This is made by Lion brand in 10-ounce red and yellow packets. There is also urdi dahll, a pale, grayish flour made from ground urad dal (black lentils). It is used as a thickener in creamy sauces, for dusting foods for frying, and in batter for pancakes, steamed cakes, breads, and fritters. Chief and Chatak brands have this in 8-ounce bags. Split pea dal flour is offered by Chief brand in 200 g (7-ounce) bags, Seeta in 1-pound bags, and Guyanese Pride in 28-ounce bags.

FESTIVAL MIX

Jamaican-style fritter mix. Festival is always served with fried fish and is also popular with jerk. The mix contains flour, baking soda, and sugar. To make festival, blend with water to make a paste, cover and let the mixture stand 40 minutes, then drop by the tablespoon into hot oil. You can also add soaked, shredded salt cod, chopped scallions, minced garlic, and hot peppers, thyme, and black pepper to the batter. One box of mix yields about 4 dozen fritters. Look for the J. F. Mills brand in a 1-pound box.

OATS PORRIDGE MIX

Island oatmeal. Little packets of quick-cooking breakfast porridge. Rolled oats are combined with a soy protein powder called supro, no milk is needed. Just boil water, stir in contents of 1 packet, cook 2 to 3 minutes, and sweeten with honey or sugar. Comes in plain, banana, and cinnamon flavors, made by the Lasco brand in one or three serving foil packets. Foska has instant oats in 7- and 14-ounce boxes. Oatmeal is also added to blender drinks, milkshakes, and root energy drinks made from various steeped herbs or bottled tonics. One popular one is oatmeal blended with milk, ginger wine, and nutmeg.

PLANTAIN FLOUR

Farine de banane. This is a speckled flour made from dried, ground green plantains, which was developed as a way to preserve excess crops. The flour is used in baked goods, spice-flavored drinks, and to make porridges, fungi (a type of polenta), and fu fu, a thick paste that is rolled into balls and served with stews and to batter food for frying. To make a bland, sweet porridge, dissolve 4 tablespoons of plantain flour in 6 cups of milk, add sugar to taste, and boil about 7 minutes, stirring to prevent lumps. Use a deep pan as the mixture bubbles and foams furiously as it thickens. Look for the Saint Marc brand in 14- and 24-ounce boxes and the Royal brand in 12-ounce bags. Tropiway and Ghana Fresh instant plantain flour are in 24-ounce boxes.

plantain flour

Breads

Depending on the size of the store and the owner's ethnic background, you will find several types of breads, rolls, and buns. Many packaged breads are offered by Carib and Jamaican Country Style brands in 14- to 28-ounce bags. Check also for locally made products.

BAMMY BREAD

Also spelled bammie. Pale, round, flat breads made from grated cassava (yuca) with a sandy-looking texture. They range in size from wafer thin to 1-inch thick. They have a bland taste and can be eaten hot or cold. Thick, commercially made bammy should be soaked in milk, coconut milk, or warm water before being pan-fried in a little oil, dry toasted, or grilled, about 3 minutes per side. Bammy can also be steamed without soaking and are often placed on top of a steaming fish when there is about 5 minutes cooking time left and served with the fish and yams. Bammies accompany fried fish and ackee and saltfish scrambles, topped with avocado. Once toasted, bammy will stay crisp and fresh up to a month if stored refrigerated in an airtight container. Look for Juliana, Ocho Rios, and Twickenham brands in packages of two 5-inch rounds.

bammy

CASSAVA BREAD

Also called casabe or yuca bread, this is like very thin bammy. The wafers resemble Styrofoam, but are dense and hard. It is sold in plastic bags of broken pieces and paper-wrapped large flat rounds or quarters, tied with string. Eat like a cracker with soups, stews, rice and beans, grilled meats, and vegetable curries. Crispy, bland, and absorbent, just break pieces off and dip into sauces or whatever you are eating. Made by Estrella brand in 17-ounce packages of rounds and quarters from the Dominican Republic. Broken pieces are in plain, unlabeled bags.

In the past, most island homes didn't have ovens, so recipes were adapted for the stovetop, such as Johnnycake, cornbread, bammy bread, and rotis. Commercial bakeries now supply standard loaves of white bread but bammy and other stovetop breads are still made and much loved.

COCO BREAD

Large, folded, yeasty bread rolls, baked with a pan of hot water set on the bottom rack to produce their soft, steamy texture. The rolls resemble coconut when baked, thus the name. Jamaican beef patties are often folded up in coco bread, making a substantial snack.

HARDOUGH BREAD

Also called "hardo" bread. This is a dense, slightly sweet loaf of Jamaican white bread. The shiny, golden crust is made by brushing the bread with sugar water before baking.

ROTI

frozen roti

This is the general term for West Indian flat bread, brought by East Indian immigrants. Caribbean grocery stores may have fresh roti, but most likely it will be found frozen. Sada roti is similar to a chapati or flour tortilla, made from a flour, water, and salt dough, rolled out into thin circles, about 8 inches wide and cooked in a dry skillet until golden on each side. This is mainly a breakfast bread, eaten with choka, a mixture of roasted tomatoes, or eggplant mashed with minced onion, garlic, hot peppers, salt, and a little oil. Paratha roti, usually just called roti, are enriched with ghee (clarified butter) or oil added to the basic dough. They are rolled out, folded, spread with ghee, re-rolled, re-folded, spread with more ghee and re-rolled again, creating a multi-layered, flaky pastry-like bread. This is then fried in a small amount of oil on both sides until golden. Dahlpuri is made by rolling the basic dough into balls, poking a hole in the top and inserting a mixture of mashed and seasoned cooked split yellow peas (the dal), pinching the sides together to seal in the dal mixture and then rolling the bread out into thin rounds and cooking them on a hot oiled griddle on both sides. Dahlpuri are delicious folded up with chicken or shrimp curry, burrito style. Island Chef brand sells frozen dahlpuri, three to a 12-ounce package. Suddle brand also has 1-pound packages of dahlpuri.

Buss-up-shut roti is a very large, paper-thin roti made for weddings and festivals. It is cut into strips or clapped between the hands to break it into small pieces when removed from the griddle. The name means "burst up shirt" as the strips or broken bits look like torn pieces of cloth. This and other roti are often served with kucheela, a tangy condiment made of grated green mango pickled in mustard oil with spices, minced garlic, and hot peppers.

Produce

Caribbean markets in the U.S. offer exotic and familiar fruits and vegetables from tamarind pods, coconuts, taro, and yams to avocados, okra, cho-cho (chayote), chunks of pumpkin, and guava. Other island specialties to look for are listed below.

ACKEE

Also spelled akee, aki, and called vegetable brain. This is the fruit of a beautiful West African evergreen tree with small glossy leaves, introduced to the West Indies by Captain Bligh of HMS Bounty fame. Peach-colored pods ripen to bright red and burst open, exposing three shiny, black, round seeds surrounded by creamy yellow segments of aril (seed coat). They are only safe to eat when the capsule splits open. When closed, ackee contain the poisonous substance hypoglycine, but when exposed to light it is dispelled. Ackee are cooked as a vegetable, boiled, or sautéed in oil or butter. The flavor is slightly sweet and delicate, a little like scrambled eggs. The national dish of Jamaica is a sauté of soaked, flaked salt cod, ackee, onions, tomatoes, and scallions seasoned with salt and pepper. Canned ackee are cooked and just need gentle reheating—drain, rinse, and sauté with ground meat, chopped vegetables, eggs, or tofu. Ackoa is a sauté of canned ackee with chopped onion, garlic, sweet peppers, okra, and cinnamon. Canned ackee are usually at the front counter—or behind it. You may have to ask. A good brand is Country Choice Jamaican Ackee in 540 g (about 1-pound) cans.

ackee

BORA BEAN

Bodi bean, boonchi, or snake bean. Often sold in looped bunches, these are slender and rope-like, and when slit open reveal immature seeds that resemble tiny black-eyed peas. The beans are drier and crunchier than regular green beans. Chop into short, equal-sized pieces to use. The texture holds up to long cooking and the mild flavor blends well with spicy seasonings. Sauté with onions, garlic, chopped tomatoes, hot sauce, ground cumin, and black pepper and serve with roti or rice; add to curries, fried rice, and chow mein; or blanch and add to salads. In Aruba they are parboiled, wrapped around skewered cubes of lamb, and grilled. Then the beans are unwrapped and eaten with the succulent meat, dipped into a spicy peanut sauce. Choose flexible pods without any dark spots and store up to one week in an open bag, refrigerated.

bora bean

BREADFRUIT

This is a large, round, starchy green fruit cooked as a vegetable. The fruit is patterned with small hexagonal brain-like markings and can weigh up to 10 pounds. It is best to select underripe breadfruit, not soft or brown-tinged ones. The firm-textured, potato-like flesh will retain its color if boiled with a little vinegar—otherwise it rapidly darkens. The taste is bland and starchy. To use, cut into pieces, boil and mash; roast, fry, or thinly slice and deep-fry as chips.

In the Caribbean, breadfruit is usually roasted whole in the skin for about 45 minutes. The central core is removed, it is cut into chunks, and served as a starch with grilled meats and other foods. It can also be wrapped in aluminum foil and baked. Boiled and mashed breadfruit is also mixed with milk, eggs, and seasonings, shaped into patties, breaded and fried as croquettes, or made into

breadfruit

a soufflé with stiff egg whites folded into the mixture. Breadfruit can be used in any recipe calling for potatoes, yuca, taro, or yams. Dried slices are ground into flour for bread, an appropriate use for something named breadfruit. Yellow heart breadfruits from Portland parish in Jamaica are considered to be the best. Store any breadfruit up to 2 weeks, refrigerated. It is also sold canned in brine. To use, heat contents in a saucepan, drain, and serve with callaloo soup, meat stews, and salt cod dishes; or drain, pat dry, and deep-fry. Look for Grace and Jamaican Country Style brands in 19-ounce cans. Also sold roasted, sliced, and flash frozen, in 1-pound bags under the Ocho Rios label.

Another, smaller variety contains chestnut-like seeds, called châtaigne in the French islands and pan de pepita in the Spanish-speaking islands. The breadnuts, as they are called in English, are sometimes available canned and are delicious fried and sprinkled with salt or pureed for creamy soups. Slice the base off each nut and peel off the skin. The nuts are also added to curries and meat stews. Goya brand has breadnuts in 10-ounce cans, but it may take some searching to find them.

CALLALOO

Also called colocasia, dasheen, or patra leaves. These are huge, dark green, heart-shaped "elephant ears" of the taro tuber, used to make a staple soup of the Caribbean, also called callaloo. Young leaves are cooked like greens and have a delicate flavor. The large leaves found in markets here must be carefully cooked to destroy the tiny crystals of calcium oxalate in them. If under-cooked, your mouth will tingle with a pricking sensation. By simmering or steaming them at least 45 minutes all danger is eliminated. They have a strong chard flavor and soft texture when cooked. Callaloo soup is found in many variations, but most are a dark green puree of the leaves simmered in coconut milk with salt pork, beef or cod, crab meat, onions, garlic, okra, and seasonings. Callaloo leaves are also boiled, drained, chopped, and cooked with coconut milk, spices, and salt cod; simmered in curries; or steamed and rolled up with a split pea flour paste, sliced and deep-fried until crispy. Choose unwilted leaves and store refrigerated in a plastic bag. Use within 2 to 3 days. You will also find pre-cooked, chopped callaloo leaves and stems in cans. Heat the contents, drain, add butter and black pepper, and serve like spinach. Look for Carib brand in 10-ounce cans and Blue Mountain Country, Jamaican Country Style, and Ocho Rios in 19-ounce cans. For a recipe for callaloo soup, see page 243.

callaloo leaf

CARAILLA

Corilla, caraille, bitter cucumber, bitter melon, foo gwa, or bitter gourd. This is an Indian-Chinese vegetable that resembles a light green, pointy cucumber covered in warty bumps and deep crevices. The flesh is pale and firm, sometimes yellowish. When young, the whole gourd is eaten, including the pith and seeds. With older ones, scrape the seeds out. When yellow-tinted and very ripe, the seeds turn bright red and are sweet. The bitter taste is due to the presence of quinine. To reduce the bitterness, sprinkle the cleaned, halved-lengthwise gourds with salt to draw out the bitter juices and rinse. Thinly sliced pieces are sautéed with garlic and onions, added to curries, stir-fried, or can be deep-fried into crunchy chips. Look for small, young, yellow gourds and store refrigerated up to a week.

DJON DJON MUSHROOMS

Tiny dried Haitian mushrooms with small caps and skinny inedible stems. When cooked they release a dark liquid, giving dishes a caramel color and rich meaty flavor. The mushrooms give off an exquisite shiitake-like aroma. To use, soak in hot water 30 minutes, remove the stems, saving the water and caps. To make riz djon djon, sauté rice and chopped garlic in a little butter, add mushroom caps and soaking water, and steam, covered. The cooked rice is traditionally served with griots (marinated cubes of pork simmered in water, drained and fried until crispy and browned), bananas pesées (fried green plantain slices) and ti-malice, a scorching hot pepper sauce. The mushroom caps are also added to roasted pork with potatoes, and chickens are stuffed with a mixture of chopped rice bananas, breadcrumbs, mushroom caps, spices, and lime juice, roasted and served with spicy rum gravy.

djon djon mushrooms

GARDEN EGGS

garden eggs

West African eggplants. Cream-colored eggplants the size and shape of an egg packed in brine. Also called melon vegetable, they have a soft texture and mild eggplant taste. Chop and add to coconut milk soups, spicy stews made with smoked fish stock and meat and vegetables, or sauté with salt cod or fresh fish. Slice and sauté in peanut oil with chopped tomatoes and blend with creamy peanut butter and salt for use as a spread, often served with deep-fried yam or breadfruit chips. Look for Ghana Fresh brand in 28.2-ounce cans

GREEN BANANAS

Unripe bananas eaten and cooked as a vegetable. Islanders call them green figs. Similar in taste to green plantains, the bananas are boiled in their skins or peeled with a little oil added to the water. Boiled green bananas are served whole as a starchy side dish, mashed in a mortar with a pestle (or in a blender), sliced and "soused" in lime juice or with melted butter and hot sauce. Cooked green bananas can also be chopped and added to bean salads. Grated sweet potato, yuca, and green bananas are mixed with shredded coconut, sugar, butter, raisins, and spices to make a moist, sweet pudding. If planning to use when still green, refrigerate up to 2 weeks—the skins will darken, but the fruit will remain firm. If left at room temperature they will eventually ripen and turn yellow.

GUINEP

Anocillo, St. Lucia, or Barbados ackee, Jamaica lychee, chennet, or kanepa. This is a light green fruit that grows in grape-like clusters. They have woody stems and pale, translucent cantaloupe-colored flesh covering a large seed. Bite gently between your teeth to crack open the hard skin. The taste ranges from sour to tangy and sweet. Guinep appear in Caribbean and Latin markets from late May to August. Taste-test one to make sure you are buying sweet clusters and store unrefrigerated up to a week.

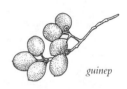

guinep

JACKFRUIT

This member of the fig family can grow up to 100 pounds, but most are a more modest 15 to 30 pounds. The greenish-yellow rind is covered in knobby spines with the texture of a leathery basketball. Inside, the fruit is divided into numerous segments encased in stringy white tissue. Each segment contains shiny white seeds. Ripe jackfruit has yellow-orange flesh and gives off a pungent, fermented smell. It tastes like a mix of ripe banana, mango, and pineapple. Because of its size, jackfruit is usually sold in chunks or segments. The flesh is firm and crisp or soft and stringy depending on the variety. Eat as is or add segments to fruit salad or leafy greens tossed with diced avocado in a honey-mustard dressing. It is also curried in the East Indian community and is a popular wedding and festival dish. The seeds are boiled or roasted and eaten as a snack. They have a soft, mealy texture and chestnut-like flavor, but have to be removed from their plastic-like seed case before eating. Jackfruit is also sold canned in brine or syrup. Jamaican Country Style has the syrup packed type in 20-ounce cans. Chakoh Thai brand has young green jackfruit (good for curries) and yellow ripe segments in 20-ounce cans.

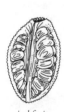

jackfruit

JINGY

Jinga, toray, ghisoda, or silk squash. A cylindrical squash in the cucumber family, anywhere from 6 to 12 inches long with spiny ridges running the entire length. To prepare for eating, peel off the sharp ridges and slice crosswise. If they are small and young, leave on some of the skin. If large and old, peel away the skin as it can be bitter. The buttery pale flesh is mild and delicate, tasting like a cross between zucchini and cucumber. This absorbent vegetable is good in stews and curries; diced, pan-fried, and folded up in omelettes; or thinly sliced and deep-fried into crisps and served with a spicy dip. Try sautéing jingy with chopped onion, garlic, and tomatoes with ground cumin, then toss with diced avocado and chopped cilantro with lemon juice, salt and pepper—good warm or chilled. Choose small squash with no dark spots and store, refrigerated, up to 3 days as it will toughen if left longer.

JUNE PLUM

Other island names for this fruit are Jamaica plum, golden apple, and pommecythere. It is also known elsewhere as ambarella, Tahitian quince, hog plum, and vi. The unripe, fairly thick skin is greenish-yellow, ripening to yellowish-orange. The fragrant orange, tangy flesh cushions a large, spiny seed that should be carefully nibbled around. When unripe, the green skin is peeled and the firm, pale, sour flesh is sprinkled with lime juice, salt, and chili powder as a snack. Half-ripe ones are used in tart-sweet chutneys. Ripe ones are stewed with sugar and spices or made into relishes and cooling drinks. When ripe, June plums taste like a tart crabapple and pineapple combination. They are in season from June through October.

ORTANIQUE

A natural hybrid of a tangerine and sweet orange, the name stands for ORange, TANgerine, and unIQUE. The hard, but easy-to-peel rind is a sort of mustardy-yellow color covered in brown specks. The aroma is reminiscent of a Seville orange and the pale golden flesh is tart and juicy. The zest and juice are used in cooking and they make good marmalade. Shredded ortanique peel and papaya puree are used to flavor custard and guava jelly. Ortanique juice is boiled down as a glaze for rum cake. Select large, heavy fruits with no soft spots or shriveled skins.

PEA EGGPLANT

Also called susumber. Clusters of small fruits from a tropical bush related to eggplant. Underripe, pale greenish or mottled ones are added to salt cod dishes, soups, stews, curries, and spicy hot dips for crudités. They have a slightly bitter, sour taste and are also pickled as a table condiment.

SCOTCH BONNET PEPPER

scotch bonnet pepper

These look like tiny, plump bell peppers and are found in a variety of colors (depending on the stage of ripeness) from green, yellow, orange, red, and brownish. They are fiery hot and have a spicy smell. Scotch bonnets are the prefered chili of the Caribbean, adding flavor and fearsome heat to almost all savory dishes and sauces with names like "Jamaican hell fire." Whole green ones are added to soups for special flavor, but are carefully removed before they burst. Picalese are Haitian-style pickled chilies made by thinly slicing Scotch bonnet peppers, onions, and carrots, and steeping them in vinegar for several weeks. The pickle is added to soups and stews and riz et pois (rice and peas). As with all chilies, handle with care as the volatile oils can inflame your eyes and irritate your skin—wearing rubber gloves helps.

SOUR REI

A small, crisp-fleshed, bright green fruit. The pale flesh is crunchy, juicy, and refreshingly tart-sour. Slice in half lengthwise and sprinkle with salt as a snack, or pickle whole. It is also chopped and added to hot pepper sauces.

TIPPY TAM-BO

Guinea arrowroot, topitambo, sweet corn root, tambu, cocurito. This is a tuberous root that resembles a small knobby new potato with thin, light brown skin covered in very fine short hairs. After cooking they remain crisp with the crunchy texture of a water chestnut. The flavor is a cross between Jerusalem artichoke and green corn. Boil from 20 minutes to an hour, peel, and mash into a coarse crumble with butter or olive oil, and season with salt and pepper and hot sauce. They can also be added to soups, stews, and salads with creamy dressings like potato salad. The white flower clusters are eaten in the West Indies and the leaves are used for wrapping tamales. The little tubers are sold loose in bins or in plastic bags. Store refrigerated up to 2 weeks.

UGLI

Also called hoogly, this is a Jamaican hybrid created by crossing a tangerine, Seville orange, and grapefruit. They are almost as big as a pomelo (known in the Caribbean as shaddock), but much of the girth is in the baggy, yellow-orange skin (like a Shar-Pei dog's), which is easy to peel. They give off a citron fragrance and taste like a mandarin orange with a hint of tartness with pineapple overtones. They are in season from January to May.

Forms of Fish

Refrigerated cases hold plastic bags of salt cod, pickled mackerel, salted and smoked herring and sprats, while a variety of fresh fish are on ice at the meat counter. There might be blue crabs for adding to callaloo soup, grey mullet, butter fish, king fish, tuna, snapper, haddock, marlin, or tilapia, and bags of frozen white belly shrimp. Less well-known fish finds are described on the following pages. Keep in mind that fatty fish have a stronger flavor than lean fish, and are best broiled or baked (frying makes them oily). Lean fish tend to become dry if overcooked and are best poached, added to soup, grilled, or pan-fried. Fresh fish are cleaned, rubbed with a cut lemon, and sprinkled with salt and pepper before cooking.

Drying, salting, and smoking fish were developed to preserve fish without refrigeration. The flavors are concentrated and need to be soaked in several changes of water to remove the salt.

CASCADURA

Also known as hassar and thorny catfish. The creamy flesh tastes like a mix of crab and tuna, but can have a muddy flavor if not carefully cleaned. They can be cooked in their scaly shells after cleaning or are steamed a few minutes, then shelled, cleaned again, seasoned with minced garlic, chopped onions, thyme, salt, and pepper and added to coconut milk curry thickened with cassava meal. To cook in the shell, slit open the belly with a sharp knife, clean, sprinkle with salt, and squeeze lemon juice into the cavity and all over the fish, cover with water and soak half an hour or overnight, refrigerated. Fry them in a little oil, then add to curries or stews or simply steam like lobster. To eat, break apart the scales and the flesh will fall out. Serve with a mayonnaise dip, hot sauce, or mixture of salt, pepper, and lime juice. Sold fresh or frozen in bags of about half a dozen.

cascadura

CONCH

Pronounced konk. Because it is an endangered species, conch are now being farm-raised in hatcheries to supply the demand for what are also called "sea snails." Conch tastes like slightly sweet abalone and is somewhat chewy. It has to be pounded with a meat tenderizer and marinated in lime juice to make it edible. Another method is to pound it, cut into strips, cover with water in a pan and simmer about one hour or until tender. The pieces can then be added to stews, chowders, salads, or used for fritters. The Bahamas are famous for cracked conch and conch fritters. To make cracked conch, the pieces are battered and deep-fried and served with a spicy dip. It is sold frozen on plastic-wrapped trays and resembles thick pieces of chicken.

FLYING FISH

Small, silvery-blue fish with slightly salty white flesh and lots of tiny bones. Barbados is known as "the land of flying fish" and Bajan fishermen can net up to several thousand on a good day. To prepare, clean the fish, remove the center and side bones, and flatten. Score the flesh by making several deep cuts. Grind parsley, thyme, garlic, paprika, and peppercorns with lemon juice in a mortar or blender, and rub the paste into the cuts. Dip fish in flour, then beaten egg, then breadcrumbs, and fry in hot oil until crispy on both sides or steam, unbreaded, in a little coconut milk with chopped onion in a covered pan over low heat. The fish can also be seasoned and pan-fried or broiled. Sold fresh from December to June and frozen during the off season.

GILLEYBAKA

Also called Guayana catfish. Whole fish and cut pieces are sold frozen. The flesh is similar in taste to catfish, but slightly salty. Add to soups, curries, and stews, or bread and pan-fry slices. You may also find the frozen roe in plastic bags. They resemble marble-sized egg yolks in a membrane sac. Boil them in the plastic bag, remove the membranes, and mash into potato curry cooked with a little tamarind for a typical Guayanese dish.

PICKLED MACKERAL AND SHAD

Sold in sealed plastic bags with a little pickling brine. Mackerel are bluish-silver with dark streaks and have somewhat oily flesh. Rub the fish with lemon juice and soak in hot water 2 to 3 hours, changing water several times to remove excess salt. While the fish soaks, boil down some coconut milk with crushed garlic, chopped onions, scallions, and tomatoes, a sprig of thyme, and hot pepper. When the mixture thickens (15 minutes), add the mackerel cut into pieces, season with salt and pepper, and simmer another 10 minutes to make a rundown. Shad is a silvery fish in the herring family and has many fine bones. It is boiled, skinned, boned, and shredded, then simmered with chopped onions, celery, green peppers, tomatoes, and a little butter, or is flaked, seasoned, wrapped in banana leaf parcels, tied, and boiled. Look for Ocean Joy brand whole pickled mackerel in 12-ounce bags and Ocho Rios and Sea Pro shad and split mackerel, sold by weight in sealed pouches.

Islanders enjoy eating many types of shark, including the rare whale shark. Divers hunting them sometimes hitch a ride on their backs! More common sharks caught for eating are the nurse shark, the silvery gray reef shark, and the tastiest of all, the blacktip. The tough, sandpaper-like skin is removed and the somewhat strong-flavored meat is soaked in water with lime and salt, then marinated in milk with hot peppers to mellow the flavor and soften it before cooking. It is battered and fried, braised in butter with garlic, added to curries, and minced into beaten eggs and baked in a pie crust. Shark can also be "cooked" in lime juice for ceviche.

SALT FISH

This can mean any dried, salted fish, but mostly refers to salt cod, called bacalao on islands where Spanish is spoken and morue on islands where the residents speak French. You may also find salted haddock, abadejo (pollack), herring, and mackerel.

Salt cod is soaked, flaked, and added to callaloo soup; and is sautéed with ackee and made into fritters, usually combined with mashed potato. "Pick up" salt fish is a type of ceviche, made from uncooked, soaked, and flaked salt cod mixed with vinegar, sliced onions, and minced hot peppers, served on crackers with slices of avocado or with hardough bread. Stamp and go are Jamaican salt cod fritters, a favorite snack of bus passengers. The name derives from the riders' habit of jumping off the bus, gobbling the fried patty from a vendor, then hopping back on before the bus pulls away. The national dish of Antigua is salt fish and ducana (sweet potato and coconut milk pudding steamed in banana leaf packets). Salt fish pie is another specialty, made with a "crust" of mashed yams. The yams are covered with layers of sliced onions, flaked salt fish, and tomatoes, topped with ketchup, minced hot peppers, mayonnaise, and sliced hard-boiled eggs and another layer of mashed yam. The baked pie is served on a bed of lettuce with hot sauce. Salted and smoked herring fillets are used to make soup stock or are soaked, boned, and cooked with black-eyed peas and greens. All types of salt fish are sold in sealed plastic bags or on Styrofoam trays wrapped in cellophane. Caribbean gourmet, Seastar Seafoods, and Ocho Rios brands have salt cod and pollack in 1-pound bags. Herring are sold unlabeled on trays, sold by weight.

STOCKFISH

Stiff, flattened, whole or cut-up pieces of dried cod. No salt or chemicals are used. To use, soak overnight with a little salt, then boil for several hours. It becomes chewy and the taste is much better than the smell. Prepared stockfish is used in soups and stews, and long simmered potages. Sold whole with the somewhat ferocious-looking heads on and skinned in curled, yellowish petrified slabs and chunks. You will also find bags of mealy looking ground stockfish. This is used in making fish stock and to thicken stews. Whole stockfish are sold loose. OAU and Sands brands have pieces and ground stockfish in 6- and 8-ounce bags.

TRAVALLI

Also called carvalli, carangue, crevalle jack, and google-eye jack. The flesh of this fish is dense and slightly oily, but remains firm during cooking, so is suitable for most preparations. Good in soups, broiled, steamed, grilled, or poached and flaked for salads. Add to coconut milk curries or serve in boiled-down coconut sauce. Available fresh and frozen.

Dairy

CHEESE

The three main types in Caribbean markets are red wax-covered balls or wedges of Gouda and Edam (a legacy of of the Dutch), and Jamaican cheddar-like cheese. The last is usually labeled "pasteurized processed Jamaican cheese," sold in big tins of Tastee brand or wedges. It tastes like bland cheddar. Grated cheddar is often added to spiced fruit buns, breads, and stuffings, and is sprinkled over casseroles and mixed with macaroni, milk, eggs, minced onion, mustard, and paprika to make Barbados macaroni pie, served as a side with stews. Edam or Gouda are used to make a specialty of Curaçao called keshy yena, a corruption of queso relleno, or stuffed cheese. This Dutch dish with a Caribbean twist is made using a hollowed-out rind of Edam or Gouda, stuffed with a savory mixture of ground beef, chicken, or fish. The meat or fish is sautéed separately, then mixed with chopped sautéed vegetables, tomato sauce, seasonings, beaten eggs, olives, capers, and raisins. It is stuffed into the cheese rind, covered with the sliced-off top of the cheese and baked in a shallow pan with water. Some cooks skip the cheese shell and line a buttered casserole with cheese slices, add the filling, and cover with more cheese. Tastee Cheddar is sold in 8.8-ounce pull-tab tins and 2.2- and 5-pound red tins. There is also Milkana vegetarian cheddar made without animal rennet.

YELLOW BUTTER

A yellow cooking fat, sort of like margarine and also called Mello-Kreem. It has a slightly sweet taste and adds flavor to boiled root vegetables, soups, stews, baked goods, coo coo (Caribbean polenta), and rice, and is also used as a spread. Made by Roberts Mello-Kreem and Glow Spread in large yellow tubs. There are also foil-wrapped slabs of Blue brand vegetable margarine and Anchor brand imported pure creamery butter.

Baked Goods

Caribbean markets carry cakes, cookies, tarts, such as pineapple and coconut, gingerbread, and other quick breads. They may also have sweet potato pudding, gingery coconut drops, and cornbread. Following are the most commonly found baked goods.

BAKES

Despite the name, bakes are deep-fried or grilled over coals. Bakes are made from a flour, salt, and brown sugar dough which is rolled into balls, dropped into hot oil, and fried until golden brown and puffed. Alternatively, the dough balls can be flattened and grilled over charcoal or cooked over low heat in a greased, covered pot, turned several times. Very similar to bakes are Jamaican johnnycakes. Johnnycakes have baking powder and butter, rather than sugar, added to the same basic dough, are formed into half-inch thick rounds and deep-fried. Shark-and-bake is a popular beach snack in Trinidad sold by vendors set up in colorful stalls. Freshly fried bakes are split open and filled with a battered and fried piece of shark. You add your own hot sauce, pickles, and salads at the stall.

BLACK CAKE

Also called Christmas cake as it is a holiday must, served with sorrel punch. The rich, dark cake is made from ground currants, raisins, and prunes, spices, rum, flour, eggs, butter, brown sugar, candied lemon peel or fruit, chopped nuts, and almond essence. It is sold year-round and is similar to fruitcake but is surprisingly light and springy in texture—no need to use this as a doorstop! Black cake is provided by local Caribbean bakeries and by talented home cooks.

BULLAS & TOTOES

Bullas are round, spicy cakes that look like large cookies. They are made from a thick syrup of reduced brown sugar and water mixed with flour, baking soda, and ground ginger, allspice, cinnamon, nutmeg, and melted butter to form a firm dough. They are sold individually wrapped in cellophane and keep for a long time. In Jamaica they are a popular snack with avocado slices.

Totoes are larger cakes, similar to gingerbread, but made with a cookie dough–like batter spread into round pans. Creamed butter and brown sugar is mixed with flour, eggs, vanilla, grated coconut, cinnamon, and nutmeg to make the batter. When cool, the cake is cut into squares. Totoes are lighter than bullas and are sold by the piece, wrapped in plastic. A recipe for Jamaican gingerbread is on page 259.

COCONUT BREAD

Cake-like, sweet, dense loaves of quick bread. The batter is made from fresh, finely grated coconut, flour, baking powder, butter, eggs, evaporated milk, sugar, cinnamon, nutmeg, and sometimes raisins. This is good sliced and spread with butter or jam for breakfast.

GIZZADAS

"Pinch-me-rounds." A mixture of grated coconut, brown sugar, and nutmeg is baked in small pinched pie dough crust shells. Most are tartlets, but some Caribbean bakeries have large pie-sized ones.

PONE

Chewy and spicy baked pudding. Pone can be made from cornmeal, gari (grated and toasted yuca meal), or freshly grated yuca—or a combination of grated yuca and coconut or mashed sweet potato or pumpkin yuca—mixed with brown sugar, melted butter, milk, vanilla, and spices. After baking, it is cut into fingers or wedges as a snack or into thick slices and served with cream as dessert.

ROCK CAKES

Popular in the West Indies, these are scone-like cakes made from a soft pastry dough studded with currants, candied peel, and sometimes grated coconut. They're called rock cakes because of their appearance, not because they are rock hard.

SALARA BREAD

Thick slices of sweet, spicy bread rolled up with a mixture of finely grated coconut, sugar, and cinnamon. After baking it is cut into thick slices and sold in packages of three.

Crescent-shaped spicy meat pies are sold by vendors everywhere as fast food in the Caribbean. Every island and every cook has a version, but in general, Jamaican patties are deemed the best— even though they originated in Haiti. The flaky pastry dough pockets enclose a spicy filling of ground beef (the most popular type), chicken, shrimp, fish, or vegetables. The fillings are liberally spiced with fresh ginger, onions, scallions, garlic, and hot peppers with cumin, chives, thyme, allspice, and often a splash of rum. Some cooks add chopped tomatoes, breadcrumbs, or curry powder. They are best hot out of the oven, and many stores sell them in warmer boxes near the front counter. They are also often available frozen.

SPICED FRUIT BUNS

Spicy, sweet cake-like buns with candied fruit and raisins made from whole wheat flour, golden syrup or honey, eggs, stout, and melted butter. It is baked in loaves and sold in thick slices. Some versions replace the stout with yeast and add grated cheddar cheese, milk, and caraway seeds.

S w e e t s

Coconut and tamarind sweets are found near the front counter, many made in the kitchens of home cooks who have a small cottage industry supplying the treats to homesick islanders.

BUSTA

Also called bustamonte backbone, these are hard sweets made from melted sugar and grated coconut. They are named after Sir Alexander Bustamonte, Jamaica's first prime minister, who was known for his firm character.

CHOCOLATE BALLS

In the Caribbean you will find fat cigar-shaped chocolate logs as well as the balls. Both are made from sun-dried cocoa beans. The outer layer is peeled off and the beans are ground. The mixture is soft and pliable and can be rolled into small balls or thick sticks. Sometimes cinnamon is added. To prepare cocoa from a ball, grate some off and boil with grated nutmeg and a dash of cinnamon in milk. (Or add to coconut milk to make what islanders call cocoa tea.)

chocolate balls

COCONUT DROPS

Chunky brown lumps made from pieces of fresh coconut and fresh ginger boiled in a brown sugar and water syrup until the mixture is thick and sticky and the sugar almost burned. Spoonfuls are dropped on a cookie sheet to harden and cool. They are delicious, chewy and gingery sweet. Sold freshly made in Caribbean bakeries and individually wrapped in groceries.

grater cake

GRATER CAKES

Large, lumpy, red and white coconut patties made from coarsely grated fresh coconut boiled in a sugar and water syrup until thick and sticky. Half the coconut mixture is tinted red and a tablespoon of each is pressed together to form the rounded patties. They're chewy with a sweet coconut flavor.

gum arabic

GUM ARABIC

Mastic. A tree resin, this is sold in packets of small, smooth, yellowish-tinted crystals and is used as a sweetener in root tonics. Gum arabic has a slightly sweet, resinous taste and should be crushed with a teaspoon of sugar just before using. You can also pop a lump in your mouth and chew it like gum.

TAMARIND BALLS

Tamarind pulp, sugar, salt, and pepper are kneaded together, shaped into into marble-size balls, and rolled in sugar. They are sold in little bags or packets and have a tangy, salty-sweet flavor.

TOOLOOM

Cones or balls made from a mixture of melted molasses and sugar, boiled with grated coconut, fresh ginger, and dried orange peel until stiff. When cool the mixture is rolled into balls or little cones. Sold in small bags.

Beverages

FISH TEA

A highly seasoned broth made by boiling fish heads and tails with vegetables. Jamaicans call all hot beverages "tea," including light soups. Use the soup mix packets if you like, but this is best made from scratch. To make your own, boil a whole cut-up fish in about two quarts of cold water with a sprig of thyme for about 30 to 40 minutes. Strain and remove fish, flake, and set aside. Add a chopped onion, clove of garlic, sliced carrots and celery, cubed potatoes, and a chili pepper. Simmer in the stock until the vegetables are tender, then add flaked fish, and serve with cornbread or dumplings. Good made with snapper, grouper, or black sea bass. Be sure to use a whole fish (not fillets), as the flavor comes from the boiled bones and head.

fish tea

IRISH MOSS

A beverage made with carrageen, the fan-shaped fronds of a red sea moss. The pale creamy drink is sold in cans and glass or plastic bottles. Cleaned and dried sea moss is boiled with cinnamon and nutmeg until it forms a thick gel, which is used as a base for drinks and puddings. The gel is blended with sweetened condensed milk and flavored with vanilla or pureed peanuts. It is considered an aphrodisiac and it is often added to rum cocktails. Best served chilled. Look for Big Bamboo brand in 12-ounce pull-tab cans in vanilla and peanut flavor. Also Acassan Mrs. French's AK-100 brand in 12-ounce cans, Caribbean International Juice in 12-ounce bottles and Lion of Judah and Jamaican Country Style brands in 10-ounce cans.

irish moss

MAGNUM

Another drink based on carrageen concentrate, blended with ground peanuts, oats, salt, and spices. Creamy and pale beige, it has a pleasant, sweet nutty taste. Look for Caribbean International Juice brand in 12-ounce bottles and Big Bamboo in 12-ounce cans.

PEANUT PUNCH

A creamy drink made from peanut butter blended with evaporated milk, honey, salt, and vanilla. Tastes like a peanut butter milkshake. Made by Caribbean International Juice brand in 12-ounce bottles.

PLANTAIN DRINK

Bouillie de banane. A thick, creamy drink made from plantain flour blended with water, sugar, evaporated milk, corn syrup, vanilla, and spices. Made by Big Bamboo brand in 9.5- and 12-ounce cans.

VANILLA CORN SHAKE

Batida de harina de maiz. A health-energy drink made from corn flour creamed with water, sugar, evaporated milk, soybean oil, corn syrup, carrageen, vanilla, and spices. Thick, sweet, and creamy. Look for Big Bamboo brand in 9.5-ounce cans and Acassan Mrs. French's AK-100 in 12-ounce cans.

MAUBY CONCENTRATE

Mawby or mabí. A dark brown liquid made from the bark of several small trees native to the Caribbean. Mix 1 part mauby concentrate with 3 parts water to make a refreshing licorice-anise flavored drink. Mauby is also considered a cancer preventative as well as an energizing drink. Best served over ice. Try mixing a little concentrate with lemonade or ginger beer. Made by Matouk's brand in 10- and 26-ounce bottles. Also Caribbean Natural's, Baron, Top Seed, and Mauby Fruti Fresh brands in 750 ml (26-ounce) bottles and Chief brand in 10-ounce bottles.

mauby concentrate

ROSELLA

Also called roselle, flor de Jamaica, bissap rouge, and red sorrel. A dark red concentrate made from red sepals of a small annual plant. Because the sepals are ready for picking in December, sorrel punch is a popular Christmas drink. The sepals are also used to make jelly and jam. Sorrel drink tastes a little like sweet, aromatic cranberry juice. Look for Caribbean Natural's in 26-ounce bottles. Some West Indian markets have unlabeled plastic bottles of sorrel concentrate. Mexican markets have powdered mixes to make Jamaican (sorrel) horchata. The fridge case has Tropik Fresh sorrel drink (not a concentrate) in 10-ounce bottles.

CORDIAL SYRUPS

Concentrated sweet syrups for diluting with water and ice for drinks—rum is optional. Flavors to choose from include ginger beer, kola champagne, orange punch, fruit punch, grape, guava, mango, papaya, and strawberry. Sky juice is a popular drink in Jamaica consisting of fruit syrup poured over crushed ice, sold by vendors in plastic bags with a straw. Brands to look for are Kelly's Jamaican, Baron, Caribbean Natural's, Buccaneer, Chief, and Jamaican Country Style in 10- and 26-ounce bottles.

ESSENCES

Liquid extracts used to flavor drinks, sweets, cakes, and puddings. You will find them in small 3- to 4-ounce bottles in flavors such as pear, almond, anise, pineapple, and artificial vanilla often labeled "coumain" and made from tonka beans. Brands that offer them are Benjamin's, Flavormate, Chief, Chinelles, and Jamaica Country Style.

ROOT TONICS

Root tonics are derived from root extracts and are used as both preventive medicine and as remedies for everything from anxiety to poor circulation. The tonics are made from various combinations of roots, barks, and herbal extracts and most are fairly bitter—Jamaicans believe the more bitter the medicine, the better the cure. Most are general tonics, some are geared toward specific problems—check the labels. Some popular tonics, sold in various-sized glass bottles, include Healthee Doctor Bird Bitters (general tonic), Healthee Woodroot Tonic (general), Atomic Roots Drink (with ginseng for energy and strength), Mount Zion Organic Roots Drink (for strength), Mount Teman Roots (energy and strength), and Sundial Wood and Root Tonic (colonic and intestinal cleanser). Any tonic can also be added to blender drinks with oats and milk or juice.

woodroot tonic

Most everyone knows that Rastafarians sport dreadlocks and smoke "holy weed" as part of their religion. What is less well-known is that true Rastafarians are vegetarians and eat only what is known as Ital foods— natural, organic, and full of vital energy, with no added salt. Ital foods are as pure as possible and no canned or processed foods are used. Kitchens and cooks must be clean and the food blessed. Typical dishes include rice and beans cooked in coconut milk (cows' milk is not Ital), vegetable stews with cornmeal dumplings, peanut soup, salads, chocolate brownies, and lots of fresh tropical fruits. Spices and seasonings add flavor and heat. Meals end with mint, aniseed, and basil tea sipped as a digestive.

Caribbean Chinese Noodles

Chinese-style noodle dishes are common throughout the Caribbean, a legacy of the Chinese workers who brought noodle-making know-how with them when they arrived in the mid-1800s. Most Caribbean markets stock Chinese noodles, soy sauce, fried rice seasoning mixes, a selection of fresh Asian vegetables, ginger, canned baby corn, water chestnuts, lychees, and dried sour plums. There might even be bags of purple taro-flavored mini-gels in tiny, sealed plastic cups.

CHOW MEIN

Also called low-mein, pronounced to rhyme with "cow." These are the long, thin, flat Chinese noodles made from wheat flour and water. The type found in Caribbean markets are tinted vivid yellow or light orange and may be labeled Guyanese style or vegetarian chow mein. They are sold in large coiled skeins or several small nests in 12- to 16-ounce bags. To use, plunge the noodles into boiling water for about 1 minute and drain under cold water or soak in a bowl of hot water until the coils are loosened. Do not overcook or soak. Mix the noodles in a little oil or butter to keep them from sticking together—they should remain slightly springy. To make island-style chicken, beef, pork, or shrimp chow mein, heat some peanut or corn oil in a pan or wok and stir-fry the meat or seafood pieces with minced garlic. Stir in soy sauce, chopped onions, hot peppers, celery, and other veggies with a little tomato paste and water, adding noodles at the very end. Stir to combine. Cassareep (boiled down cassava juice) can also be added for color and flavor. Lo mein is made by pouring a stir-fried mixture of meat or seafood and vegetables in an arrowroot-thickened sauce over a bed of prepared noodles. Caribbean brands include Bedesse, Diana's Guyana, and Lams. West Indian Queen brand has thin yellow broken bits of noodle, good tossed in the soup pot.

RICE VERMICELLI

Thin, semi-translucent noodles made from rice powder and water that become opaque after cooking. They are sold in long, looped skeins and must be soaked until softened, about 15 minutes in cold water before adding to stir-fries. For soup, drop them into boiling water for 1 to 2 minutes and rinse under cold water. In the Caribbean, rice noodles are popular in spicy coconut milk–based soups with shrimp or chicken, stir-fries, and bami, a fried noodle dish. To make this, blanched and drained rice vermicelli are fried with cubes of pork; soaked, dried shrimp; chopped onions, garlic, and vegetables such as cabbage, green beans, and bean sprouts with minced hot peppers, shrimp paste (trasi), and soy sauce; served garnished with chopped scallions. This is served with a wedge of lime and sambal, an Indonesian chili sauce, but any hot sauce would do. Most rice vermicelli brands are Chinese, labeled "mai fun"—look for Caravelle and Oriental Mascot. You will also find fine, pale, off-white wheat flour vermicelli, also called sawine and noorjehan, used the same as rice vermicelli and prepared the same way, plunged into boiling water, swirled around to prevent clumping, and rinsed under cold water. Muslim Indians use these in dessert puddings as well as stir-fries and in soups. West Indian brands include Auntie Lucky in 12-ounce bags; Indian Pride, Noorjehan, and Champion in 10-ounce bags; and Lam or Sheik Sawine in 7-ounce bags.

Seasonings & Condiments

Here you will find a bewildering array of sauces and tropical relishes—some are smooth, thick purees, others are thin and watery or chunky with seeds. There are East Indian–influenced chutneys and amchars (pickles), marinades, coconut cooking sauces, and a spicy fish pâté to choose from.

ALIÑO DE HIERBAS

Also called West Indian marmalade, garden seasoning, green seasoning, sazón de campo, and creole sauce. This is a green sauce made from a coarse puree of fresh herbs, scallions, spices, onions, garlic, salt, and vinegar. Some varieties have sweet peppers, celery, parsley, cilantro, thyme, chives, or long-leaf coriander (known as shado beni in the Caribbean), added. Green sauce is used like sofrito as a seasoning base for meats, poultry, fish, rice and beans, and in stuffings and casseroles, and is also used as a table condiment. Brands to look for are Matouk's for the West Indian type in 8.5-ounce jars, Caribbean Gourmet sazón campo in 5.5-ounce jars, Chief brand in 11- and 26-ounce bottles, and Calypso brand creole sauce in 14-ounce bottles. Other brands with various blends include Baron, Health Choice Gourmet Caribe, and Royal.

ANGOSTURA BITTERS

Bitters have a tart flavoring with a spicy bite. The formula (from over 40 plants, aromatics, and herbs) is top secret and even the label is vague. The bitters are a mainstay in mixed drinks such as rum punch, Manhattans, and old-fashioneds, and are 45 percent alcohol. A few dashes also add aroma and flavor to soups, chowders, salad dressings, gravies, fish dishes, stewed fruits, jellies, mince pie, applesauce, and, according to the label, ice cream. Though they originated in Angostura, Venezuela, they're now produced in Port of Spain, Trinidad, and come in 4-, 10-, and 14-ounce bottles.

angostura bitters

BROWNING

Also called burnt sugar. A thin black liquid, similar to molasses but not as sweet. Like molasses, browning is made from boiled-down juice left over from processing granulated sugar. Browning adds a rich caramel color and flavor to gravies, meats, stews, jerk sauce, cakes, puddings, and candies. Only a small amount does the trick, as it is very concentrated. You will also find molasses, the dark brown natural syrup that is separated from raw sugar in the manufacturing of white sugar. This is used

browning

in cookies, cakes, and gingerbread, is poured over ice cream and mixed with hot water as a drink—use about one tablespoon per cup. Blue Mountain Country brand has browning and molasses in 6- and 12-ounce jars. Carib, Uncle Panks, and Benjamin's brands have browning in 4.8-ounce jars. West Indian Pride and Sunrite have browning in 5-ounce bottles.

CANE VINEGAR

A clear vinegar made from distilled sugarcane juice, used in preserving and pickling, especially for escovetch (fried fish in a vinegar marinade).

Haitian cooks wash meats in a solution of vinegar and salt before cooking and add a splash of vinegar to meat stews. Look for the Shimu brand from Jamaica in 15-ounce bottles.

CASSAREEP

A dark, very thick and spicy syrup popular in Guyana and the southern Caribbean. First created as a preservative, cassareep is now used to add a distinctive flavor to pepperpot and stews and for seasoning meats, gravies, and vegetable dishes. It is made by squeezing the juice from grated cassava and boiling it to neutralize any toxins. The juice is then boiled down, mixed with salt, pepper, cloves, cinnamon, and dark brown sugar until thick like molasses. The flavor is sweet like treacle and spicy with a slight burnt-bitter undertone. For delicious roasted chicken, brush on before putting in the oven—it produces a wonderful rich color and carmelized flavor. When added to pepperpot or stews it acts as a preservative, allowing leftovers to be stored in a hot climate without refrigeration. If you can't find cassareep, substitute molasses and tamarind concentrate blended with ground cloves and cinnamon. Made by J & B Seaforths and Royal brands in 284 ml (10-ounce) brown glass bottles and Chico, BG, and Pomeroon brands in 15-ounce jars.

cassareep

Pepperpot was first made in large clay pots called canarees. First cassava juice was boiled down to make the preservative, cassareep, and meats were thrown in after a hunt and boiled every day. This later became a plantation favorite as a way to always have a pot of stew ready to feed unannounced visitors. Only cassareep, meats, and seasonings go into pepperpot—but no fresh garlic or onions as they will sour the stew. Permitted seasonings include hot peppers, cinnamon, cloves, bay leaves, powdered onion or garlic, thyme, oregano, coriander, salt, and black pepper. Pepperpot is made at home and served in Creole restaurants and many claim to serve the same dish every day, kept alive for over 20 years!

RUNDOWN SAUCE

This thick, beige-colored sauce is based on coconut milk and is used to make classic Jamaican "rundowns." Salted mackerel, shad, or cod, or fresh fish, shrimp, chicken, or vegetables are cooked in the sauce until the liquid boils out of the coconut milk, creating a thick custard-like sauce. The coconut milk sauce is seasoned with onion, garlic, white pepper, salt, Scotch bonnet peppers, scallion, thyme, and pimento (allspice). Rundowns are traditionally served with boiled green bananas and simple flour dumplings or baked slices of breadfruit. Just about anything can be cooked in the sauce—try crab or lobster or heat and pour over stir-fried vegetables, rice and beans, rice vermicelli, and baked potatoes. Some believe the name is derived from "rendang," a similar cooking process found in Indonesia and introduced in the Dutch colonies. Look for Walkerswood in 16-ounce bottles.

CHUTNEY & AMCHAR

Tangy condiments, or "palate ticklers" eaten in small amounts with meals or as dips for fried snacks and breads. First made by East Indians in Trinidad, island chutneys are based on hot, sour, and spicy ingredients including green mangoes, unripe papaya, hot peppers, tamarind, ginger, raisins, curry powder, allspice, vinegar, and sugar cooked into a jam-like consistency. Mango chutney dip is a chunky type with large pieces of tender green mango floating in a mixture of ground garlic, hot peppers, allspice, salt, sugar, turmeric, and curry powder. Good as an accompaniment to curries, stews, and rice, and as a tangy dip for fritters and fried breads. Made by Chief brand in 355 g (12.5-ounce) jars. Kucheela, also called kutchela, is an exotic brownish-green chutney made from sun-dried green mango and a blend of East Indian spices and West Indian hot peppers. This hot and tangy relish is good with fried snacks, curries, grilled meats, roasted chicken, and fried seafood. Offered by Chief and Matouk's brand in 12- and 13.5-ounce jars. Another type, called pommecythere kutchela is made from ground hot peppers, golden apples, vinegar, salt, and spices from Trinidad sold in small jars. Tamarind chutney is a tart, sticky mixture of strained tamarind pulp pureed with hot peppers and spices. Great as a tart dip for fried snacks, fritters, and breads, with jerk, barbecued meat, roasted pork or chicken, and fried fish or shrimp. Blend with yogurt as a cooling side dish or salad dressing. Made by Catak and Karibbean Flavors brands in 15.5-ounce jars. Shandon beni chutney is a coarse ground mixture of green mango, hot peppers, and shado beni (recao), with vinegar, lime juice, garlic, and a little oil. Best with hot and spicy curries, stews, and fried seafood. Made by Chatak and Chief brands in 13.5-ounce jars.

Amchar, also spelled amchur, are East Indian pickled fruit and vegetables preserved in spice mixtures and oil, made in the Caribbean. The most common is green mango amchar, made from chunks of the sour fruit in an oily paste of spices, salt, and mustard oil. This has a complex, pungent, and hot taste and goes well with grilled meats, rice dishes, and roti breads. Look for Chief brand in 12-ounce jars. The same brand also has Chalta amchur, a mix of pickled vegetables in 12.7-ounce jars. All Caribbean brand has hot vegetable pickle, a blend of carille (bitter gourd) and peppers in 12.7-ounce jars.

ESCOVEITCH SAUCE

A marinade for pickling fried fish or other seafood, based on Spanish escabeche. It is a combination of vinegar, olive oil, and spices mixed with water, onion rings, a pinch of salt and sugar, julienne strips of chochos (chayote) and carrots, minced hot peppers, and a few allspice berries. Small whole fish such as sprats or fillets are lightly dusted in flour and fried in oil until crispy. The heated vinegar marinade is poured over the fish and left to pickle overnight. A popular breakfast food in the Caribbean, escoveitched fish is also served as an appetizer or part of a meal. The vinegar sauce can also be made into salad dressing, blended with olive oil, mustard, and honey. The dressing is also good tossed with cubes of fried chicken (or shrimp), served on a bed of lettuce, and garnished with sliced bell peppers and onions. Look for Walkerswood brand escoveitch sauce in 16-ounce bottles. You can also make your own, using any clear vinegar including rice vinegar and thinly sliced onions, a bit of oil and other seasonings.

HOT CHOW

A spiced-up Caribbean version of piccalilli relish. A cooked combination of tropical fruits and vegetables, most include papaya, carrots, onions, mangoes, and hot peppers blended with sugar, vinegar, and spices. Delicious as a spread on sandwiches and hot dogs, or mixed into potato, tuna, and egg salads for color and kick. Also good served with grilled and barbecued meats, chicken, or fish. Look for Matouk's brand in 9-ounce jars. The same brand also has tropical relish, chunky orange spicy-sweet-hot mix of coarsely ground papaya, cucumber, onion, red sweet peppers, hot peppers, carrots, spices, sugar, and vinegar. Use as above, blend with sour cream as a dip, or plain as a dipping sauce for empanadas, tostones, yuca fries, and plantain chips. Comes in 8.8-ounce bottles. Matouk's also has a chunky red salsa in mild or hot, made from chopped tomatoes, onions, sweet red peppers, hot peppers, and cucumber blended with a tomato puree, garlic salt, and vinegar. Use as a dip with chips, fried snacks, and fritters and like a tropical ketchup on eggs, meats, beans and rice, or sausages. This is found in 13.5-ounce jars.

LIME PEPPER SAUCE

Also called lime sauce, this is a table condiment made from sliced limes and hot peppers in a salt brine. It has a sour, hot, and tangy taste, is spooned into soups and stews and eaten with curries and rice, jerk, and fried fish as a sort of pickle. Chatak and Chief brands have this in 12-ounce jars. There is also another type, which is an orange puree of lime pulp, lime juice, salt, and red and yellow peppers, delicious as a dip for fried foods and with grilled or roasted meats and seafood. CEP brand has this in 14-ounce jars.

lime pepper sauce

solomon gundy

SOLOMON GUNDY

Spicy fish pâté made from smoked herring ground with a little oil, vinegar, scallions, salt, spices, and hot peppers into a dark brown paste. It has a salty, smoky intense flavor. Gundy can also be made from flaked, pickled mackerel or shad. This Jamaican specialty is used as a spread on crackers and bread and in cooking. Toss a few tablespoons with pasta, olive oil, chopped tomatoes, and garlic, or add to cream sauces. Walkerswood brand has smoked red herring gundy in 5.7-ounce jars and Jamaican Country Style brand has herring gundy in 4-ounce jars.

Hot Sauces

Discover what is often called the "pirates' gold" of the Caribbean: hot sauce! While impossible to list each and every hot sauce available, the following are the more popular and widely distributed brands and some of their fiery offerings. Try a few until you find one you like at the Scoville unit of heat (a scale ranking chilies) you can handle. Some hot sauces will make your taste buds jump for joy, others will make you cry.

CARIBBEAN GOURMET

This brand offers 5.5-ounce bottles of Scotch bonnet hot sauce with vinegar and mustard—use only a few drops, as it is potent—and island marinade, a maroon-black puree of tomato paste, vinegar, onions, and garlic with thyme, scallions, and celery salt. Use this for marinating meats and as a cooking sauce.

KARIBBEAN FLAVORS

This company from Trinidad offers a hot, tart, tamarind hot sauce in 5.5-ounce bottles, made with red and yellow hot peppers, tamarind, onion, garlic, and spices. Good with fritters and fried snacks, in meat marinades and served with grilled meat, chicken, and seafood.

MATOUK'S

This reputable West Indian company has 10- to 32-ounce bottles of several types of hot sauce: salsa picante, a fruity and tangy-hot blend of pureed papaya, pickled Scotch bonnets, and vinegar thickened with cornstarch; hot pepper sauce with mustard, vinegar, onion, and garlic; mustard yellow calypso sauce made from aged pickled Scotch bonnets, vinegar, mustard, sugar, onion, garlic, and celery seed (this is slightly sweet, smooth, and hot) and lastly, red-orange flambeau sauce, a hot, tangy mustard and spice-laced sauce, that will add pizzazz to grilled and barbecued meats.

OCHO RIOS

A brand of high-quality hot sauces and seasonings made in Jamaica. Look for spicy ketchup, golden Scotch bonnet–mustard sauce, new hot heavenly sauce (a vivid red-orange, extremely hot sauce), thin, tangy red pepper sauce like tabasco, and passion fruit sauce with Scotch bonnet peppers. This last one is a creamy yellow color, made from a puree of passion fruit pulp, hot peppers, garlic, onion, vinegar, and spices. Use as a dip, drizzle over grilled meats and seafood, in cooking, and with raw oysters.

PICKAPEPPER

The dark reddish-orange hot sauce has a sweet, sour, and spicy hot taste. Pickapepper was developed by Mr. Norman Nash, a Jamaican, in 1920, and it is still bottled in the Don Figuero mountains of Mandeville where Nash began making it. The sauce is a blend of secret spices, tomatoes, onion, cane vinegar, mango, raisins, tamarind, and hot peppers, aged in oak barrels for a year. The well-known, award-winning sauce is available in 3- to 16-ounce bottles. This company also makes a type of sauce very similar to Worcestershire.

TURBAN

This West Indian brand offers a greenish-colored pepper sauce made from a puree of hot peppers, pumpkin, papaya, mustard, onion, garlic, and vinegar in 10-ounce bottles and a red, hot and spicy pepper sauce made with fruit pulp, hot peppers, mustard, and vinegar with a fruity-hot tangy taste.

OTHERS

Marie Sharp's brand from Belize has a very hot habanero pepper sauce in 5-ounce bottles. Eaton's has West Indian hot mustard sauce in 4.8-ounce bottles and crushed Jamaican peppers in brine, seeds included. Walkerswood offers its famous hot Jonkanoo pepper sauce, a brick red carnival of spices and hot peppers in 5-ounce bottles. Baron brand makes West Indian hot sauce labeled "piquant de Antilles." This thick, hot, and lusty sauce comes in 14- and 28-ounce bottles, made from Scotch bonnet peppers, vinegar, salt, mustard, onion, and garlic.

Jerk Sauce

Jerk is a Jamaican method of seasoning and cooking meats and seafood. Whatever is being jerked is marinated in a sauce or dry rub with a hot pepper base. Every vendor has his secret marinade and claims to have the best jerk in all of Jamaica.

The term jerk comes from the old English word "jirk," meaning dried beef, which evolved into jerk, meaning barbecued meat. Basic jerk sauce ingredients include hot peppers, allspice, garlic, a few sprigs of crumbled thyme, soy sauce, cinnamon, cloves, nutmeg, malt vinegar, and rum. Other additions might be molasses, onions, fresh herbs, and fruit pulps. The crucial ingredient in authentic jerk is pimento. All parts of the tree contribute flavor—the wood is used for smoking the meat, the young green branches for grill stands (patas), and the berries, better known as allspice, are crushed and added to the sauce. To taste pimento-smoked jerk you will have to go to Jamaica, but you can fire up your grill or oven to make delicious jerk at home using imported marinades. Jerk dip can be whipped up by blending yogurt with a few teaspoons of jerk sauce—serve with plantain or yuca chips while the jerk grills. Marinate meats at least a few hours before grilling or oven roasting and baste with the sauce as the meat cooks. Jerk is usually served with hardough bread, festival fritters, roasted breadfruit, and fried plantains, washed down with Red Stripe beer.

jerk sauce

Some jerk sauce brands to look for are Walkerswood Jamaican Jerk Bar-B-Que sauce in 16-ounce jars, a lively blend of banana pulp, sugar, scallions, spices, garlic, and hot peppers, and One Stop jerk sauce with mango, banana pulps, and tomato in the blend. Jamaican Country Style brand has a dark reddish spicy hot seasoning paste in 10-ounce jars and Karibbean Flavors has a similar seasoning in 9-ounce jars. Eaton's brand offers Jamaican rum barbecue sauce in 18.5-ounce bottles, a dark red blend of tomato paste, sugar, soy sauce, molasses, spices, and rum. Dry rub jerk seasonings are offered by Grace, Island, Boston Jerk, and Ocho Rios in shaker jars. Use as a dry rub or blend into a paste with water and smear onto meats before grilling.

H e r b s & S p i c e s

Many of the same spices and herbs discussed in part 1, Latin Basics, are also used in the Caribbean kitchen. Following are a few essential ones, as well as some Indian spices popular in West Indian cuisine. You will also find curry powder, garam masala (a slightly sweet brown spice blend sprinkled over curries for added flavor and aroma), annatto seeds and powder, and dried chilies. Most spices and seasoning mixtures are offered by Angel, Carib, Chief, Grace, and Ocho Rios brands in small packets and 4- to 5-ounce shaker jars.

ALLSPICE

Pimento—not to be confused with roasted red peppers. This is the sun-dried reddish-brown berry of a tree native to Jamaica. The dried berries resemble large, smooth peppercorns and taste like cinnamon, anise, nutmeg, clove, black pepper, and juniper berry all rolled into one. Some markets sell whole dried berries as allspice and the ground powder as pimento. Crush the berries to release the irregular little seeds. Allspice is used in both savory and sweet dishes and acts as a preservative, particularly in pickling. Allspice adds bite to pickled eggs, onions, beets, and fish, and seasons soups, stews, sauces, marinades, fish dishes, sausages, pies, cakes, and cookies.

CINNAMON LEAF

Cassia leaf, also known as Indian bay leaf, these are dried leaves of the same tropical laurel that produces cassia bark (a type of cinnamon). They resemble large bay leaves and are used both in cooking and medicinally. They are fried in a little oil to release the pungent, woodsy aroma and are added to meat stews, vegetable dishes, porridges, and rice dishes. Steeped as tea, the leaves relieve diarrhea and flatulence.

COLOMBO

A creole curry powder mainly used in the French Antilles and Guadeloupe. It is similar to South Indian curry powders, but is coarser and slightly tangy. Madras or other Indian curry powders can also be substituted. Colombo is made from a blend of finely ground cassava or plantain flour, ground cumin, coriander seeds, turmeric, anise, mustard seeds, cloves, green mango powder, salt, and black pepper. The powder

is usually sizzled in a little oil or butter with minced chilies or hot sauce to start a recipe. Note that dishes based on this are also called colombo. Chicken, meats, seafood, and vegetables are all spiced with the powder, usually with coconut milk and chopped tomatoes added to create a thick curry sauce, always served with rice.

CORIANDER SEEDS

Small, dried, round seeds of the aromatic herb cilantro. The seeds have a sweet smell and clean, lemony pepper flavor. They are sold whole or powdered and are an important component in curry powders and seasoning mixes. It is best to dry roast whole seeds and grind or crush them just before using for full fla-vor and aroma. Coriander enhances cur-ries, chutneys, pickles, and many meat, vegetable, and seafood dishes, gently complementing other flavors.

GINGER ROOT

Jamaican ginger is considered by many to be the best in the world. Island cui-sine makes much use of fresh ginger, sold in knobby "hands." It has smooth, beige skin and a creamy pale interior that is slightly fibrous, but easy to slice. Select ginger with smooth skins as old, wrinkled ones can be tough. Ginger adds a clean, aromatic, and spicy bite to curries, stews, sauces, chutneys, marinades, and baked goods such as cakes and cookies and coconut candies. Ginger wine is a type of home brew and ginger beer, a non-alcoholic carbonated drink, is made commercially. Ginger also flavors rum and is steeped as tea with a bay leaf and honey. To use ginger, carefully peel off the skin and slice, grate or chop. To store fresh ginger longer, cover slices with rice vine-gar or dry sherry and store in an airtight jar, refrigerated. Powdered ginger can be substituted, but the flavor is less pungent.

THYME

There are many species of thyme, but the one most commonly found and used in Caribbean cuisine is French thyme, sold in small bundles of stiff twigs with long, narrow leaves. Thyme has a warm, sharp fla-vor and in Caribbean cooking is usually paired with scallions for use in soups, stews, sauces, marinades, and stuffings. It also goes well with beans, eggs, and vegetables and broiled meats and steamed fish. To use, strip off the leaves, discarding the woody stems, or add whole, and remove the herb before serving. In the Caribbean you may also find Spanish thyme with larger leaves. It is extremely pungent and should be used sparingly to avoid overpowering other flavors.

East Indian Spices

Many Caribbean markets mix it up with a selection of East and West Indian spices and other goods all in one area, with special spices sold in bulk from wooden bins, as well as in small packets or shaker jars. The island names are different from the usual Hindi ones. Packaged spices are offered by Chief brand in 3-ounce jars or packets. Sands brand has chili powder and curry powder in spice jars.

GEBRAH

Jeera or cumin. These little, ridged seeds add earthy fragrance and a warm, peppery bite to many West Indian curries, dals, soups, breads, chutneys, chokas (roasted, mashed, and seasoned vegetables eaten for breakfast with breads), and meat or vegetable dishes. Dry roasted cumin seeds are sprinkled over salads and blended into yogurt raitas (salads) and frothed drinks. Pan jeera is a refreshing drink made from tamarind juice and water mixed with salt, sugar, and cumin powder. Most curries begin by sizzling cumin seeds in hot oil before the other ingredients are added. Cumin is also a key ingredient in colombo, curry powder, and garam masala.

MANGRICE

Nigella seeds. Often mistakenly called black cumin (another spice alltogether, known as kala jeera) and onion seeds, this is known as kalonji in India. These are tiny, black seeds of a small flowering herb with an aromatic, faintly bitter, earthy, carrot-like taste. They are roasted and ground just before using, or are sizzled in oil to start a dish. They infuse an oniony flavor in breads, yogurt raitas, salads, vegetable dishes, lentils, and chutneys. Try sizzled nigella seeds sprinkled over steamed greens, mashed yuca, or potatoes.

mangrice seeds

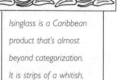

Isinglass is a Caribbean product that's almost beyond categorization. It is strips of a whitish, very pure form of gelatin obtained from the air bladders of deep-dwelling fish such as sturgeon. Isinglass is used mainly as a clarifying agent in jellies, desserts, and health drinks (it has almost no taste). It is boiled with cleaned Irish moss and linseeds, strained, and whirled with condensed milk and a banana as a refreshing drink. Crushed gum arabic is also sometimes added.

MATHEE

Methi or fenugreek seeds. These hard, squarish, angular seeds are actually a type of tiny legume collected from the small pods of the fenugreek plant. The fresh leaves are also cooked as a leafy green with a tangy arugula taste or are dried and crumbled over meat curries. Fenugreek seeds smell like curry and have a slightly bitter, burnt sugar flavor that is tempered by frying the seeds in oil for a few seconds or by dry roasting. The seeds can also be crushed or ground after roasting. Fenugreek is added to hot and sour soups, dals, vegetable and bean dishes, pickles, fish or seafood curries, and some sweets.

NEEM LEAF

Vapu. Neem leaves look like elongated, serrated bay leaves and are bitter tasting with a pungent aroma. They're added to vegetable stews, some curries and dals, and are fried with eggplant.

neem leaves

Puerto Rican Fare

In Puerto Rican neighborhoods, you'll find transplanted island traditions such as cafetines where you can grab a beer and meat-stuffed empanadilla and sidewalk stands selling cuchifitos (fried pork bits) and frituras (fritters). If you feel like dining out, warm up with piñonos, sweet plantains stuffed with spicy ground beef; crab-stuffed yuca fritters; and arapitas, the Puerto Rican take on tostones, made from grated green plantain pressed together and fried. Move on to whole fried yellow-tail snapper and pickled kingfish. Even closer to a Puerto Rican's heart is asopao, a soupy rice dish flavored with sautéed onions, garlic, peppers, tomatoes, and spices with chicken or seafood. More comfort fare includes rice and pigeon peas served with roast pork; stewed tripe; and chicken-fried steak with rice and beans or French fries.

In shops selling Puerto Rican fare, you'll find strings of bananas dangling out front, as well as of mangoes, watermelons, and green plantains set up on milk crates. Enjoy a raspado (snow cone) flavored with coconut, china (sweet orange), or melao (molasses) syrup while you ogle the candy display. The sweet parade of hits include marrayo (brown sugar, sesame seed, and coconut caramels), paper twists of turrón de coco (coconut nougat), little red lollipops embedded with sesame seeds called pilons and gofios, paper cones of powdered corn and brown sugar. At the meat counter you can get bistec de bola al pastor (marinated minute steaks), chuletas (pork chops), salt pork for adding to beans, homemade sofrito seasoning base, and blocks of queso de pais (country cheese). A freezer chest is packed with corn fritters, stuffed potato balls, and alcapurrias, plantain fritters stuffed with jueyes (land crab). Shelves hold large tins of galletas rica (crackers), bags of cornmeal and masa for tamales, pulverized coffee and ajonjoli horchata (ground sesame seeds and sugar for making a creamy beverage), flasks of chili-spiked vinegar and boxes of rice pudding and coconut temleque (custard). There are also bags of soft buttery rolls and packets of pacheco chicharrónes—fried pork cracklings just like the ones sold from street vendor's carts called panchecos. Naturally there are the

puerto rican chili vinegar

root vegetables collectively known as viandas, recao, powdered adobo spice rubs, sazón seasoning, habichuelas (beans), and pigeon peas.

A Taste of Cuba

The largest Cuban community in America is in South Florida, where its heart and soul pulsates in Miami's Little Havana, better known as Calle Ocho. Each year in March, Cuban culture and food is celebrated in a weeklong Carnaval Miami, culminating on the last day with one of the world's largest block parties and parade led by a Latino celebrity crowned king of Calle Ocho. It's like a Mardi Gras with a throbbing Cuban jazz beat. Although Miami is undoubtedly the epicenter for Cuban goods, there are Cuban markets all over the country.

In a typical mom-and-pop Cuban market, there are crates of green plantains and cantaloupes; you'll find musty bins filled with root vegetables such as shaggy malanga and stubby taro, sour oranges, habenero chilies, chunks of calabaza pumpkin, and hairy coconuts. The deli counter offers blocks of queso blanco, bocadilla (sandwich meat), and soft salchichón sausages. There are yellow bags of Bustelo coffee, cans of black beans, and slabs of quince paste on the shelves. In the freezer case look for frozen tostones and tubs of Goya sofrito and recaito seasoning pastes. In fact, the whole panoply of Hispanic island staples are here—but nothing, of course, is actually imported from Cuba.

For a taste of Cuban cuisine, try the restaurants and cafés in the Cuban neighborhood near you. Dishes to sample are sopa de ajiaco (beef and potato soup laced with garlic), bistec palomilla (breaded fried steak with a squeeze of lime), and lechon (roasted pork) with morros (black beans and rice mixed together). Try the pan con minuta, a fried fish sandwich or bistec de pollo, a chicken steak sandwich, washed down with guarapo (sugarcane juice) or a pineapple-mamey juice. Other specialties are Cuban tamales stuffed with pork served with crispy, chopped pork belly chicharrónes; fresh out of the fryer malanga and plantain chips, and whole spit-roasted chickens for take-out.

Wind up with coconut ice cream, key lime pie, or tres leches, cake soaked in sweetened condensed milk and evaporated milk topped with whipped cream. If you want strong coffee, order a large cup of dark roasted café Cubano, called a colada, which comes with tiny plastic cups for sharing, the coffee knocked back in one swift gulp. A single shot of black espresso is called a cafecito; with a shot of milk it's a coradito. Café con leche is a large cup with a shot of coffee and the rest filled with steaming hot milk. These are all usually taken very sweet—coffee and sugar are after all the essence of Cuba.

Stocking Up

Island staples include hardough bread, bammy or cassava bread, cassava flour, cornmeal, chow mein noodles, hot sauce, jerk sauce, coconut milk, browning or molasses, cassareep, ginger, thyme, and allspice. You'd also want fresh or canned callaloo leaves, hot peppers, root vegetables, plantains, tropical fruit, and fresh or salted fish.

16

The Afro-Caribbean Market

The influence of African cuisine is clearly manifested in the food of the Caribbean. African flavors are spicy, hot, bitter, and pungent with much use of dried, smoked fish with bland starches to soak up the rich mingling of flavors. Texture is important, too, and many ground seeds, leaves, and vegetables such as okra are used to create a thick, unctuous quality. Afro-Caribbean products, many imported from West Africa, are stocked in most Caribbean markets.

Afro-Caribbean staples include plantains, okra, taro, cocoyam (a small taro, also called eddoe), black-eyed peas, pigeon peas, groundnuts (peanuts), leafy greens, hot peppers, salt fish, palm oil, and cornmeal. Cornmeal is a basic part of African cuisine and fine yellow or white cornmeal, known as mealie, is used to make breads, fritters, steamed cakes, coo coo (a polenta-like mush with sliced okra), and puddings. Much more ancient grains such as millet and rice are still staples, along with corn. Other important ingredients are listed below. Many are known by different names in the various regions and dialects of Africa, and I have tried to provide the most commonly used names.

Starches & Grains

Starchy pounded pastes and steamed grains are the main event of West African meals and their Caribbean counterparts. Large portions of fu fu, pounded yams, rice, couscous, or a form of millet are supplemented with spicy sauces, vegetables, soups, and stews.

ABACHA TAPIOCA

Pale yellowish slivers of dried cassava that looks like stiff, translucent straw. To use, soak until softened and add to soups for texture. It is also mixed with a sauce made from oil bean seeds (ugba), palm oil, and ground crayfish. Sold by weight in plastic bags.

ATTIEKÉ

Couscous de manioc. A crumbly mix of very fine and coarse, irregular crumbs made from ground, fermented cassava. Resembles rough, toasted cassava meal. Steam and serve with spicy vegetable stews or a spicy sauce over chopped greens. Attieké is the traditional accompaniment to kedjenou, chicken stewed in its juices in a canari (a terra-cotta pot set in the ashes of an open fire). To microwave, add some water, mix, and let sit 5 minutes, then zap about 4 minutes. Sold in plain 1-pound bags with the store's sticker and the Marguerite brand in 500 g (17.5-ounce) bags from Côte d'Ivoire (Ivory Coast).

FU FU

Also spelled foo foo and called iyan if made from pounded yam. Fu fu can be made from simmered yams (real ones, not orange sweet potatoes) or plantains, or a combination of both, drained and pounded in a large bowl. A little hot water is added as the paste is pounded into a smooth dough, which is then hand-patted into rounded balls. This is fu fu at its most basic. Modern cooks use a food processor, but the most popular method for making fu fu is to use instant fu fu flours made from dried and ground yams, plantains, cocoyams, cassava, corn, rice, and even potatoes. The rice flour is used to make omo tuwo, a thick, white paste with a bland taste that is molded into smooth round balls. Fu fu balls float like islands in soups and stews. They're eaten with one's fingers, and you can make one big one for a communal pot or small ones to serve in individual bowls.

fu fu flour

To use any instant fu fu, mix about ½ cup of flour with ¾ cup cold water and stir into a creamy paste in a saucepan. Place over medium heat and stir with a wooden spoon, add a little boiling water, stirring vigorously, pulling dough from the center of the pan against the inside. When firm and smooth, knead and roll the dough into balls, and serve with soups and stews. The texture is like Southern-style spoonbread. Fu Fu can also be made from cassava starch, mixed into a paste, and heated with a little palm oil. Fermented, roasted cassava meal, called gari or grits, is used to make a type of fu fu, biscuits, dumplings, and gari foto, a sauté of the meal with vegetables, palm oil, and seasonings. The best brand of pounded yam flour is Ola-Ola in 5-pound bags. There is also Pride of Africa Nigerian-style pounded yam flour in 2- and 4-pound bags, Tropiway cocoyam and plantain fu fu in pink and brown 24-ounce boxes, and Sands yam or cassava fu fu in 16-ounce cans with snap-on lids. Mimi Foods and Lere brands offer yam fu fu in 2-pound bags. Mimi Foods also has cornflour fu fu, called pap, ogi, akamu, or koko, in 11-ounce bags. Elubo brand has yam fu fu in 32-ounce bags, and Twin Star brand from Canada has instant potato fu fu in 9-pound bags.

KENKEY

The African original, also called kanki, is made from a fermented white cornmeal, water, and salt mixture and is wrapped in banana leaves or tin foil and steamed like tamales. The steamed cakes have a slightly sour tang to them and are eaten with a piece of sardine or prepared salt fish with sheto, a spicy hot sauce described on page 223. Locally made kenkey are found in the fridge case, tightly rolled up in foil with about 6 to a bag. Some stores sell them individually. The fermented cornmeal is also cooked into a thick paste, to make banku, served as a starch.

To make banku or kenkey cakes, look for quick kenkey mix called dokono. Mix it with water and bring to a boil, stirring constantly to keep the mixture lump-free. Cook for about 5 minutes, mold and wrap in foil for steaming, or just roll the paste into balls to eat with stew. Caribbean versions of kenkey may be savory or sweet, made from a mixture of cornmeal, flour, grated green bananas, and sweet poatoes. Sweet types add grated coconut, brown sugar, raisins, melted butter, vanilla, and spices. The mixtures are wrapped and tied in banana leaf parcels and steamed. Names for these steamed cakes are boyo, duckoono, tie-a-leaf, and blue drawers, as the leaf stains the pudding a faint bluish color.

MILLET

Millet is a nutty and slightly bitter grain. Several varieties are grown and used to make tutwo, a coarse type of fu fu. Both pearl millet and finger millet are used to make flatbreads, porridges, boiled and steamed dishes, beverages, and couscous, called tiere. Bassi salte is a spicy chicken, vegetable, and bean stew served over steamed millet couscous. Tiere sow is millet couscous served with sweetened buttermilk. Funkaso are millet pancakes, served with a halved avocado stuffed with a smoked fish mixture. A grain known as fonio is another type of millet that you may find. Common names for it are fonyo, foni, hungry millet, and acha. It is one of the most nutritious ancient grains and has a delicious nutty taste. Fonio is sold sieved, crushed, washed and cleaned, free of hulls or dirt, and takes less than 15 minutes to steam. It is also made into couscous and is ground and mixed with other flours for bread. All types of millet are usually sold in plain bags with the store's sticker as the label.

millet

MOI MOI

Nigerian sponge pudding made from soaked, skinned, and ground black-eyed peas, pureed with onions, hot peppers, tomatoes, vegetable oil, spices, salt, and water. The batter is whisked to incorporate air and

moi moi

small amounts are tightly wrapped in banana leaves or foil and boiled about one hour, or until the pudding is firm. Akkras are fritters made from the same puree, but dropped by the spoonful into hot palm oil and deep-fried. Moi moi is served as a side dish with corn pudding, rice, and other dishes, or on its own with hot sauce. A canned version is made by the OLU OLU Company in 225 g (8-ounce) cans.

RICE TUWO

Also called tuo. This is a sort of rice fu fu and is pre-cooked rice meal, resembling fine grits. To use, boil 1 cup, lower heat, and stir in ½ cup of the rice meal. Cook about 2 minutes, stirring until smooth. Mold into balls and serve with soup, vegetable stews, or cooked greens. Look for Mimi Foods in 2-pound bags.

SANKHAL

Finely crushed millet used to make porridges and a type of drink similar to tiere sow. Mix with water, boil 30 to 40 minutes, add salt and sugar, and blend in yogurt or buttermilk for a filling and refreshing drink. Made by FWS Kumba brand from Senegal in 500 g (17.5-ounce) bags.

THIACRI

Also called tiakri. These are lentil-sized, light brown pellets rolled from a millet flour paste. They're considered a special occasion food in Senegal and a must for breaking religious fasts. Thiacri has a wheatena-like flavor and is steamed, cooled, sweetened, and served with vanilla-flavored buttermilk. The pellets can also be steamed and served with a spicy sauce and meats, chicken, or fish. Made by FWS Kunmba brand in 17.5-ounce bags.

YAMS

There are two types of yams you will encounter in Afro-Caribbean markets. One is the Ghana yam with rough, grayish-brown skin and creamy, off-white flesh. When cooked it tastes like watered-down potato. The other is yellow yam from Jamaica with similar skin but slightly slippery, pale yellow flesh. This type is also called 12 months yam, cut and come again, or yellow Guinea yam. Both kinds are

I also enjoy checking out a culture's packaged junk food. In Afro-Caribbean markets, you'll find little packets of plantain and cassava chips, some flavored with paprika and spices. There are also water crackers, coconut cookies, Nago Foods' small packets of kekele ipekere plátanos (fried plantain strips), and chin-chin pollo, chicken-flavored fried dough tidbits. Koro-Koro are thin, crunchy cornstick twists made from a deep-fried sweet cornmeal dough, good as a snack or dropped in soups and stews like croutons.

fairly large, from 6 to10 inches long and 3 to 4 inches wide. Yellow yams are softer and cook faster. Yams are boiled and pounded into pastes, thinly sliced and fried to make chips, diced and added to chicken soup with hot peppers, or cut in chunks and cooked with green beans, or red peppers and greens. Cubed yam is also added to pepper soup with fresh or smoked fish, lime juice, chopped onion, a little tomato paste, palm oil, and hot peppers. This is West African chicken soup for the body and soul. Choose yams with no signs of mold or soft spots and store in a cool, well-ventilated place up to 2 weeks.

Fish

FROZEN FISH

The freezer case holds kobi fish (tilapia), plump butterfish, snow crab legs, croaker, Mahi, jack cravel (google-eye jack), goatfish (red mullet), and large Nigerian snails. The snail meat is removed from the shell and resembles big black earplugs. They are cleaned with alum (a sulfate-based astringent) to remove the slime and are added to soups and stews. Brands of frozen fish include Carnival, Blue Boy, Pacific Isles, and Sarangani Bay.

SMOKED FISH

The pungent aroma of smoked, dried fish permeates Afro-Caribbean markets. Many types are salted before being smoked and dried, and need to be soaked several hours before adding to sauces, soups, and stews. The fish can be ground, flaked, or added in pieces. You'll also find unsalted stockfish—whole or in chunks and pungent pieces of dried, smoked fish called guedge. Other smoked fish finds include whole boni bonga fish (golden sprats), azu azu steaks, fillets of herring, mackerel, bangus (de-boned milkfish), and round catfish. This is a type of African catfish bent around the stick used to smoke it, forming a sort of black square-sided loop. Dry, smoked fish is added to spicy stews and sauces. To use, soak and remove bones and flake, or brown deboned pieces in oil and add to simmering stews or cook with black-eyed peas, yams, or rice. Flaked, smoked fish is also mixed with mashed hard-boiled eggs, mayonnaise, diced roasted red pepper, and lime juice, and stuffed into halved avocados. A smoked mollusk is called yete, from Senegal, used in dishes like thiebou dienn (spicy rice and fish stew). Most smoked fish is sold on Styrofoam trays, wrapped in plastic. Pacific Isles has smoked and salted herring with about 6 small ones to the 8-ounce package. OAU brand has bags of boni bonga.

CRAYFISH

Dried whole or ground crayfish give an authentic, pungent flavor to many African dishes. Whole ones can be ground in a blender or food processor. Almost any sauce or soup is enhanced with a teaspoon or two of ground crayfish. Crayfish are sold in small packets carrying the name of the retailer.

OPORO

Oporo are red-tinted smoked shrimp with shells and tails intact. The shrimp are coated in palm oil, giving them a red-orange color, then smoked and sun-dried. They add a pungent, rich flavor to soups and stews and are ground to thicken and flavor sauces. To use, soak about 20 minutes, drain, and grind. You can easily make your own starting with fresh shrimp; see page 274.

Seasonings,
Spices & Seeds

AGBOBO

Apon, bobo, or ogbono. Large, halved, waxy seeds with patchy, ridged shells and creamy interiors, shaped like a large split Lima bean. Also sold ground into a soft, tawny colored, crumbly powder. The seeds are found in small plastic packets and must be ground to use in a mortar or blender. The ground seeds have a slightly sweet carob aroma and are used as a thickener in sauces, soups, and stews, lending a slippery, okra-like texture and subtle flavor. A popular West African stew is beef with

ground agbobo

agbobo, tomato, and greens. Pieces of beef are sautéed in palm oil with chopped onion, tomatoes, ground agbobo seeds, and flaked smoked fish and simmered about 30 minutes. It is served with fu fu dumpling balls. Sands brand has ground seeds in 2-ounce boxes and OAU has the split seeds in small bags. Store in the fridge to keep them fresh.

AKANWA KAUN

Potash. Gray lumps of potassium-rich, salty clay from Nigeria. A little bit is added to tough cuts of boiled meat or cows' feet as it acts as a tenderizer. The substance is also mixed with palm oil to make sauce, added to boiling vegetables to keep them bright green and to tenderize ukua seeds from a type of gigantic breadfruit. Sold in small packets of several lumps.

ALLIGATOR PEPPER SEEDS

Brittle, fig-shaped pods filled with small, dark brown, spicy seeds. The flavor is like a mix of black pepper and Sichuan pepper with a sharp, anise–juniper berry bite. They are not used in cooking, but are traditionally chewed with kola nuts. Very similar is the melegueta pepper, also called grains of paradise. The tiny seeds of a dried fruit pod are used as a spice in West African cooking (much like we use black pepper), crushed in marinades, or added whole in soups, pickling brines, and stocks. Both forms are sold in small packets. Alligator pepper is so pungent that even one seed can overpower a dish.

CASSAVA LEAVES

The leafy greens from cassava (yuca) are ground and frozen in plastic bags. The green puree is cooked with other vegetables, especially Lima beans and okra, to create a smooth sauce served over rice. They taste like slightly tangy spinach with a sour touch. Ground cassava leaves are also sold in glass jars, ready to add to soups, curries, and meat stews. Pacific Isles brand has 8-ounce packets of frozen cassava leaves and Sands brand sells 1-pound jars of ground cassava leaves in brine.

DAWA DAWA

Daddawa, iru, or ogili. Extremely pungent-smelling, fermented, black seeds of the locust bean tree. Also sold in hard, round cakes, balls, and boullion cubes of fermented paste. Dawa dawa adds a rich, almost meat-smoked flavor to foods. A little piece of the paste is added to dafa duka, a rice dish very similar to jollof rice (West African arroz con pollo, but richer and spicier and with other meats added as well). The whole dawa dawa beans or hard cakes should be ground or crushed. They'll fill your kitchen with a funky aroma, but add wonderful flavor to your cooking. Add to black-eyed pea dishes, chicken, beef and okra stew, beef stew, or smoked fish dishes. The beans and cakes are sold in small packets bearing the retailer's sticker.

dawa dawa

EGUSI SEEDS

Small teardrop-shaped seeds from a little round squash called African watermelon. The seeds are toasted and sprinkled with salt and chili powder as a snack. They are mainly used ground into a slightly oily paste for thickening soups and stews, adding nutty flavor and a creamy texture.

egusi seeds

The seeds are sold both whole and ground. Finely chopped spinach or other greens are delicious cooked in a sauce made from ground egusi seeds pureed with a little water, chopped tomatoes, garlic, ginger, hot peppers, and salt, served over rice or boiled yams. You can substitute tahini (sesame seed paste) or ground pumpkin seeds. Store whole or ground egusi in the refrigerator. Look for OAU brand for both types in 4-ounce packets and Sands brand ground seeds in 8-ounce cans.

JUTE LEAVES

The leaves of a woody annual also known as moulukia or corchorus. Sold ground and frozen in plastic bags. With a taste and texture similar to cassava leaves, they are interchangeable. Jute leaves are also called West African sorrel and krin-krin and are used to make miyar turgunnuwa sou. Rosan and Saluyot brands have frozen ground jute leaves in 8-ounce bags.

KOLA NUTS

kola nuts

There are several types of kola nuts, all about the size of a large, unshelled Brazil nut. Some are creamy white or pale green with a brown streak down the center, others are pinkish or brownish-orange and called red kola nuts. The white variety is considered the best. When chewed, the taste is bitter, but food eaten afterward is sweet. Containing twice the caffeine of coffee beans, they are also known as Soudan coffee. The nuts are chewed when fresh, and dried ones are ground and used to make energy drinks. (They were featured in the original formula for Coca-Cola and gave the soft drink its name.) A guest is always welcomed with the offering of a kola nut. Most Afro-Caribbean and West African markets have kola nuts in little boxes or baskets near the register.

KUKRAKAU

Also called obi seed. Brown oval seeds that are either roasted over coals or baked. The seeds are then pounded and the oily paste used to thicken stews, adding a nutty, rich flavor. Sold in small packets.

NCHAWU LEAVES

Also known as oha leaves, these are the dried leaves of a climbing vine. Unlike many African leafy greens, this one is not bitter. It is added to soups and porridges flavored with meat or fish and is sold in plastic bags with the retailer's sticker. Check that there are no bugs.

Palaver sauce is a rich dish made with copious amounts of palm oil. The spicy, oily, and creamy combination is served with fu fu or over rice. The name palaver is derived from the Portuguese word "palavra," meaning "speech," and in colonial times, negotiations between Africans and Europeans were called a palaver. Today it means a discussion. Many villages have a palaver tree where the community gathers to resolve issues and perhaps toss an ingredient into a communal pot of bubbling palaver sauce to share together after the meeting.

PALM OIL

Manja, epo, or zomi. This brick-red oil is a staple in West African cooking. Afro-Caribbean dishes get their sheen from this rich, tasty oil, and just a little adds that authentic touch. The thick oil is almost solid in the bottle and should be spooned out and heated in a small pan to the smoking point before proceeding with a recipe. Fritters and chips are deep-fried in palm oil, soups and stews are flavored and colored with it, and it is used to sauté yams, vegetables, meats, and seafood. Jollof rice is tinted red with palm oil, tomato paste, and chili powder, simmered with chunks of chicken, beef, fish or shellfish, and chopped vegetables. African brands of palm oil include OAU in 16- and 32-ounce jars and Sands in 1-pound jars. Also Mula, Villageoise, and Zomi brands in various-sized bottles. There is also Ola-Ola brand cholesterol-free palm oil called caratino in 17- and 35-ounce bottles made from Malaysian palm kernels. It is not as thick or flavorful as regular palm oil.

PALMNUT CREAM

Palm butter. A rich orange-red paste made from oil palm kernels. It looks like slightly oily, dark, pumpkin pie puree. The paste is used as a base for soups and stews. To use, dilute 1 part cream with 1½ parts water or broth and boil 10 minutes. It imparts richness, body, flavor, and color to seafood, vegetable, bean, and meat dishes and is also mixed into cooked rice—a dish made famous in the African folksong "chicken is nice" (with palm oil and rice). Add boiled palmnut cream to sautéed onions, chopped tomatoes, okra, and eggplant and simmer, adding fish, shrimp, or crab in the last five minutes of cooking. Boiled palm butter can also be poured over mashed root vegetables. Look for Ruker cream of palm in 15-ounce cans, Ghana Fresh brand and Ghanacan in 28-ounce cans, and Trofai brand in 14-ounce cans.

palmnut cream

PRAKESE POD

A large, winged pod with a carob aroma. It has two softish wings with sweet, edible pulp and seeds, and two wider, slightly ridged wood-like wings. Very dry ones rattle with the little seeds. The pulp of the two soft wings is added in small amounts (about ½-inch pieces) to pepper soups and stews. It is sweet like honey locust pod pulp and contains small amounts of tannins, coumarins, and saponins. The saponins help emulsify the oil in the soup, so adding a little of the pod has a considerable effect on the dish's texture. It also adds a hint of sweetness. Sold by the pod in plastic bags.

SHEA BUTTER

Galam butter or karité. Solid vegetable fat extracted from the nuts of a tree native to the grasslands of West Africa. The butter of unroasted nuts is pale yellow and roasting the nuts produces a grayish-brown butter. Refined shea butter is commercially used in margarine and chocolate. It smells like cocoa butter and slightly sour buttermilk and has a mild flavor. Shea butter is used for cooking and can be stored without refrigeration. It is sold in small chunks or round balls in plastic packets. In parts of Africa, where the butter is a staple, it is sold in large loaves and the pieces sliced off. You can use the type sold in African markets for cooking as well as a hand lotion—just rub a lump around in your hands. Look for Sunny brand pure shea butter in 2.5-ounce packets.

SHETO

Sheto sauce (also spelled shito) is a dark red-black chili paste often served with kenkey. It is made from ground hot peppers, dried shrimp, salted herring, tomato paste, onions, ginger, spices, salt, and oil. Sheto sauce has a layer of red oil on top and should be stirred before using. It is also good with rice, seafood, chicken, eggs, sausages, or on burgers. Look for Adam Gourmet brand in small plastic tubs and Ruker brand sheto sauce from Ghana in cans.

sheto sauce

SUYA PEPPER

Nigerian pepper blend. This dark red powder is made from ground, dried cayenne peppers, peanuts, and ginger, with powdered onion, garlic, and paprika. It is used as a dry rub on meats before grilling or roasting. A popular northern Nigerian dish is cubes of beef, lamb, or chicken marinated in the pepper mixture, skewered, brushed with oil, and grilled, served with sliced onions and tomatoes. Suya pepper is also sprinkled over foods as a seasoning or fried in a little oil with other spices to start a stew or sauté. It is easy to make your own, using powdered garlic, ginger, onion salt, and chili powder mixed with finely ground or chopped peanuts. Suya pepper is sold in small packets with the retailer's name on a sticker.

TIGER NUTS

Atawe. Also called chufa, nut grass, and earth almonds. A type of dried tuber, tiger nuts resemble little wrinkled peanuts with light brown, ridged skins. They taste like a cross between coconut and almond and are eaten plain as a snack or are roasted to bring out the flavor. The nuts are sold by weight in small plastic bags.

UDA EWATEA SEED

The gnarled clusters of dried seed pods, these resemble a bizarre, stiff black flower with little hands of black bananas. Each seed pod contains tiny, black seeds. Several pods are broken off a cluster and added to pepperpot soup to add a pungent, allspice flavor. The pods are not eaten, but discarded like a bay leaf. They are also soaked and pounded or ground dry in a spice grinder or blender and added to yam soup. Sold in small packets of whole or broken clusters.

UGBA

Oil bean seed. Large, waxy chocolate brown seeds about the size and shape of an ear. Whole seeds have to be boiled many hours until soft and cut into small slivers. Preboiled slivers are also available. They are boiled with stockfish until tender and mixed with palm oil, ground crayfish, or smoked shrimp and shredded, cooked abacha tapioca, to make a popular dish enjoyed when drinking beer. Cooked ugba is also added to soups, stews, and salads. It has a sort of mushroomy taste with a hint of bitterness if lightly fermented. Both the whole seeds and slivers are sold in small packets.

UKAZI LEAF

Also called afang. Better known as bitter leaf, this African green is sold cut in fine strips and looks like green tea leaves. The fresh leaves are used like spinach in Nigerian cooking and are rubbed with salt and washed to remove some of the bitterness before adding to soups and stews. The dried type is prewashed and is ready to use. The leaves are cooked with yams, red peppers, and okra, and added to curried rice with tomatoes. They are also added to palaver sauce made with palm oil and ground egusi seeds with offal, fish, salt pork, beef, or chicken and vegetables. Dried ukazi leaf is sold in bags with the retailer's name on a sticker. You may also find utazi leaves, a lighter green type of bitter leaf used sparingly in pepperpot soup and meat stews.

UKUA SEEDS

Also called panapin. These are the small seeds of an African type of breadfruit the size of a beachball. They look like buff-colored coffee beans. Each tree produces thousands of seeds that ferment in the fruit after falling to the ground. (The trees themselves are gigantic and the fruits are heavy enough to do damage to roofs or to passers by below.) To use, the seeds have to be boiled with akanwa kuan (if this is not used the seeds will never soften). A small amount of the seeds will cook in 45 minutes; larger amounts require an hour or more. The color changes to green if left overnight after cooking—they are fine to eat despite the color. The cooked seeds are used like beans, mixed with corn, onions, fish, or rice. They can also be boiled and eaten plain with a little salt and have a starchy, nutty taste. The seeds are also fried in the shell, the shell peeled off and sold as roasted ukua seeds mixed with dark brown, hard kernels of the oil palm fruit. This is munched as a snack and has a nutty flavor. Be careful of the oil palm kernels as you could break a tooth—when cracked open the kernel resembles a tiny coconut encased in the hard outer shell. Both the raw and fried seeds are sold in small packets and may be labeled "bert nut."

USU

Toto yam. Dry, crumbly chunks of a type of dried tree bark. It looks like a dried piece of sponge. Usu is crumbled and added to pepperpot, goat head, and ground egusi soups as a thickener. It doesn't have much flavor. Sold in small packets with one piece.

UZIZA

Little seeds that resemble tiny peppercorns with a bit of fine stalk. They have a spicy hot flavor and are crushed or ground and added to soups with meats, vegetables, stockfish, pieces of burnt goat skin, and yams, lending a special spiciness. Sold in small packets.

Stocking Up

Afro-Caribbean essentials include fu fu flour, Ghana or yellow yams, rice, agbobo and egusi seeds, and dawa dawa for seasoning soups and stews. You'll also want some fresh or dried bitter greens, smoked shrimp or ground crayfish, palm oil, smoked fish, and hot peppers. The adventurous might want to add millet couscous, kenkey cakes, uda ewatea or ukua seeds, and ugba.

Conclusion

I hope you have become much more familiar with the contents of Latin, South American, and Caribbean grocery stores with the help of this guide—and by visiting some markets. I also hope that the next time you see the displays of root vegetables, green plantains, hot peppers, and calabaza pumpkin in your local supermarket you will be tempted to try them. If you love the full bloom of spices in your mouth and exciting bursts of tropical flavors that Latin food offers, but have only indulged in a restaurant or on an island vacation, now is the time to get into your kitchen and cook! Head for your nearest Latin market with this guide and begin putting together your own pantry of basics fine-tuned to your individual palate.

While no two Latin or Caribbean markets are the same, each one will be a treasure trove of finds—some familiar such as black beans, tortillas, and avocados; others new discoveries as in blistering Peruvian ají sauces, exotic fruit pulps, and smoked fish pâté—and that is the thrill of exploring these markets. Your best bet is to find the Latin market nearest you and make repeated forays, building confidence as you become accustomed to the sights, smells, and sounds—and ultimately the ingredients. You will also get to know the owner and meet other customers who will assist you and even share recipes. If you are planning a trip to Mexico or South America or a cruise to the Caribbean, bring this book with you for help in what you will be eating and seeing in those sprawling markets in Barbados or Puerto Vallarta.

While I could not cover each and every one of the thousands of products in the many Latin and Caribbean markets I researched for this book, I hope many of your questions have been answered. I also hope I have whet your appetite to explore the vibrant, complex, and delicious cuisines of Latin America and the Caribbean—and encouraged you to shop with confidence!

· Appendix 1 ·

Basic Cooking Equipment

Latin and Caribbean cuisine does not require a lot of special cooking equipment, and you probably have the items you'll need. Listed below are some traditional Latin kitchen aids that you might find helpful. You might also want to invest in an electric rice cooker.

Bean Masher

A club-like wooden masher for mashing cooked beans into a rough puree. Mexican cooks sauté the mashed mixture until it begins to dry at the edges, then tilt the pan from side to side rolling the beans into a loose roll, which is tipped like an omelette onto a serving plate to make refried beans. A potato masher can also be used.

bean masher

Cazuela

An earthenware casserole with a handle used on the stovetop or in the oven for cooking or baking foods. Tamales in a pot are made in them, using a mixture of seasoned cornmeal, topped with grated cheese and hot sauce. Pollo a la cazuela is a chicken casserole made by browning pieces of chicken and simmering them in broth with vegetables in the cazuela. They are sold in various sizes.

Comal

Mexican griddle. The traditional comal is a thin, round plate of unglazed earthenware used to cook tortillas over a wood fire. Light metal ones with wire handles are used on the stovetop. They heat and cook the tortillas quickly, which keeps them from drying out. You can also use an iron griddle, non-stick frying pan or stovetop griddle. If you use the earthenware type it has to be cured before using or the dough will stick. To do this, wash it, rub with lime juice and salt, and brush with a paste made from slaked lime (calcium oxide) and a little water, heat the plate, and scrape off the dried paste. It is now ready to use.

Dutch Oven

Also called a Dutchie in the Caribbean, this is a cast iron or heavy aluminum pot with a tight-fitting lid used for slow-cooked dishes. Dutch ovens are used on the stovetop or over a wood fire. Any sturdy pot with a tight cover can be used.

Flan Mold

These are found in some Latin and most Mexican stores. It consists of three parts: a water bath, the mold, and a lid. To use, fill the large pan with hot water about halfway up its sides. Grease the mold and inner side of the lid with butter and fill it with flan or custard, set it inside the water bath, cover, set on the lowest shelf of the oven, and bake. Flan is baked for about 1½ hours at 350 degrees. When done, an inserted knife blade will come out clean. Unmold and serve flan at room temperature.

Kreng-kreng

A basket or mesh wire container with a handle used to smoke meat or fish over an open fire in the Caribbean. They look a little like thin old-fashioned popcorn poppers.

Mallet

A wooden, rubber, or metal hammer-like tool with an enlarged head used for pounding and flattening meats for breading and frying. The metal type have short, stubby spikes and are used for tenderizing tough cuts.

Mano & Metate

Often called an Aztec blender, this is the traditional Mexican grinding stone (metate) and cylindrical stone (mano), used to grind dried corn,

spices, chilies, nuts, seeds, and cocoa beans by hand. The metate is a sloping slab of volcanic stone set on three stubby legs. The mano is rolled like a rolling pin over the ingredients, crushing them.

mano & metate

Molinillo & Oletta

A molinillo is a carved wooden chocolate beater used in Mexico and Central America consisting of a series of balls and rings on a stick. It is twirled between one's palms to blend and froth hot chocolate. The oletta is a large metal pitcher from which the hot chocolate is served.

molinillo

Mortar & Pestle

In the Caribbean, mortars and pestles are carved from wood. Mexican ones, called molcajetes and tejolotes, are hewn from porous volcanic rock. The molcajete is a thick bowl supported by three squat legs, about 6 to 7 inches in diameter. The tejolote is about 3 inches long and 2 inches wide, tapering to 1 inch at the end held in one's hand. The best quality are made from heavy black basalt with fine pores. The more commonly found type is made from a grayish-black volcanic stone and tends to be somewhat more coarsely pitted. The black kind just needs to be scrubbed and given a preliminary grinding. To cure the gray type, several grindings are necessary. Grind a handful of raw rice until pulverized, wash, and continue until the rice is a white powder with no gray flecks of stone. The rice also helps fill cracks and rough spots. The molcajete should hold water; if not it is no good. Dried spices, grains and nuts, or seeds are pulverized by pounding with the tejolote in the molcajete. Guacamole and other sauces are also mashed in them. You may also find small ceramic mortars and pestles used mainly for crushing small amounts of spices. Very large wooden ones are used for pounding yams, plantains, and sweet potatoes for fu fu.

Olla

Earthenware pots used for slowly simmering beans. Also good for boiling ground coffee with water, brown sugar, and cinnamon, and straining to make café de olla. Hot chocolate and atoles based on masa flour are also made in ollas.

Plantain Chip Slicer

This is a wooden board inset with a sharp metal blade. After being cut, the slices of plantain fall through a space in the board. The upper and lower parts are held together with a long screw. To use, hold it upright and push a peeled plantain down the back of the slicer, over the blade. Most are made in China and have the words "maderas y morteros" stamped on them—meaning "wood mortar" (perhaps something

plantain chip slicer

was mistranslated as this is definitely a slicer, not a mortar). It is just as easy to use a sharp knife.

Spice Grinder

Electric spice or coffee grinders (used only for spices) are an alternative to blenders and mortars and pestles but you can only grind a small amount at a time. They're also good for finely grinding roasted nuts.

Tortilla Press

This consists of two 6-inch round, cast metal or plastic discs, hinged together with a handle. It is used to flatten balls of masa dough into thin, flat tortillas. The dough is placed over the bottom disc and the press closed by pushing down hard on the handle. It helps to cover the press and dough with a plastic baggie to keep the tortilla from sticking. The press is used only for corn tortillas. Flour tortillas are rolled out on a floured board with a rolling pin. Keep either type warm in a basket, wrapped in a clean cloth.

tortilla press

Tostone Smasher

Also called a chatinera or tostonera. This consists of two pieces of wood or plastic that hinge over to enclose and flatten slices of plantain for tostones. Two cheese boards, a can of beans, or your fist work just as well. There is also the tostonera para rellenar for making stuffed tostones. This is two hinged pieces of wood with an indent on the bottom half and round knob on the upper inside half used for shaping and making a space for filling with a stuffing.

tostone smasher

· Appendix 2 ·

Cooking Techniques

There are very few special techniques used in Latin and Caribbean cooking. Such familiar methods as boiling, broiling, baking, barbecuing, steaming, stewing, pan-frying and roasting are all employed. Jamaican jerk is discussed on pages 209–210. Argentine barbecue known as asado is covered on pages 152–153. Roasting and peeling chilies is on page 31. The method of "cooking" seafood in citrus juice is explained on page 129, and the process of pickling fried fish in a vinegar marinade called escabeche or escoveitch is described on pages 206–207. Both were developed as a way of preserving seafood before refrigeration. A few other methods follow.

Deep Frying

This method produces a moist interior and crisp crust. Deep fried foods should be drained and served hot. For best results, use pure, clean oil (not recycled from frying something else). It should be several inches deep and very hot. To test if it is hot enough, drop a small bit of uncooked food in the oil. If the oil is at the correct temperature, it will immediately sizzle and bubble. Frying in small batches allows for even cooking and keeps the oil temperature constant. Crowding causes the temperature to drop and produces the dreaded greasy result. Remove fried foods with a slotted spoon and drain on paper towels.

Dry Toasting

Whole spices are often dry toasted in a hot skillet before being ground. This brings out the aroma and flavor and makes them brittle and easier to crush. Nuts or spices need to be constantly stirred while toasting to prevent scorching. Sesame seeds, peanuts, and coconut shavings are also dry toasted before grinding. Cloves of garlic and herbs are sometimes toasted before grinding for sauces, adding a smoky flavor. To toast garlic, place unpeeled cloves in a frying pan and cook on both sides until soft. Then peel the charred skins off. Herbs are toasted just until they give off a fragrant aroma, best done while shaking the pan so they don't burn.

Roasting Tomatoes

Tomatoes are prepared asados, meaning roasted, either on a hot comal or broiler. The skins become brown and wrinkled and the flesh soft if roasted on a griddle. Under the broiler, the skin becomes blistered and charred. They take about 20 minutes to cook and regardless of how they're roasted, they should be turned several times. The tomatoes are then pureed or mashed in sauces and salsas, adding rich flavor. Tomatillos can also be broiled, but should be husked and washed to remove the stickiness. They'll be done in about 6 to 7 minutes.

Shredding Meat

Meats are traditionally shredded for picadillo (although ground meat is becoming more popular), tacos, burritos, ropa vieja (old clothes), and other dishes. Start by cutting the meat into large pieces, cover with water, add seasonings, and simmer several hours until very tender. Allow meat to cool in broth, drain, and shred with your fingers or two forks.

· Appendix 3 ·

Recipes

Salsas and Starters
ROASTED TOMATILLO SALSA

Roasting the husk tomatoes adds a mellow, smoky flavor to this green salsa, good with chips, fajitas, tacos, grilled meats, and seafood—or just about any Latin entrée. If you can't find fresh tomatillos, you can used canned, but don't try roasting them.

- 1 ½ pounds tomatillos, husked and washed
- 4 fresh serrano chilies, stemmed
- 2 cloves garlic, unpeeled
- 1 medium onion, chopped
- ½ cup cilantro leaves
- 2 teaspoons salt
- 1 teaspoon sugar

Preheat the broiler. In a broiler pan, roast garlic, chilies, and tomatillos, turning once, until the tomatillos are soft and blistered, about 6 to 7 minutes.

Peel garlic and puree all ingredients in a blender. The salsa can be made 2 days ahead of the main dish and refrigerated, covered.

Makes about 2½ cups

ECUADORIAN PEANUT SALSA

In Ecuador this sauce is spooned over boiled potatoes or yuca. It's also good served with grilled or roasted shrimp, fish, or chicken. Try it tossed with cooked rice noodles. My friend Diana de la Torriente provided me with this delicious recipe.

¼ cup vegetable oil

2 teaspoons ground annatto (achiote) or sweet paprika

1 medium onion, coarsely chopped

¼ teaspoon ground cumin

½ teaspoon ground pepper

⅔ cup roasted, unsalted peanuts, coarsely chopped

½ cup milk

¼ cup cilantro leaves, finely chopped

salt

Pour oil into a small saucepan. Add the annatto and bring to a simmer. Transfer to a bowl and let stand until the annatto has settled to the bottom. Carefully pour off the oil into a skillet, leaving the annatto behind. The oil will be orange tinted. Add the onion and cook over medium heat until soft and light brown. Add the cumin and pepper and stir for 30 seconds. Add the peanuts, milk, and cilantro and bring to a boil. Transfer mixture to a blender and pulse only a few seconds so the sauce remains chunky. Season with salt and serve warm. It can be made 2 days ahead, refrigerated. Reheat before serving.

Makes 1½ cups

HAVANA CODFISH FRITTERS

In old Havana these fritters were sprinkled with lime juice and served with cocktails. They are good with orange-mango mayo or a pepper-lime dip made from minced hot peppers (or hot sauce), garlic, and cilantro mixed with lime juice. Allow 24 hours soaking time for the salt cod.

- 1 5-ounce piece of salt cod, submerged in water in a covered container and refrigerated for 24 hours, changing the water several times to remove the salt
- 1½ large potatoes, peeled and diced in large cubes
- 1 egg
- 1 tablespoon olive oil
- freshly ground black pepper to taste
- vegetable oil for frying

Cover cod and potatoes with water in a saucepan. Bring to a boil, lower heat, and simmer until potatoes are tender, about 35 minutes. Drain and allow to cool. Shred cod with your fingers and discard any skin or bones. Mash the potatoes and mix in the cod, egg, oil, and pepper.

Pour oil into a heavy saucepan to a depth of 2 to 3 inches. When hot, drop batter one soup spoonful at a time into the oil, without crowding the pan. If fritters bob to the surface, submerge them with tongs or a slotted spoon. Remove from oil when golden brown all over. Drain on paper towels and serve.

Makes about 1 dozen to serve 4

VENEZUELAN EGGPLANT CAVIAR

This creamy dip is served on a bed of lettuce, garnished with olives, as an appetizer with crackers, bread, or arepas, or as a salad drizzled in a little olive oil.

- 1 large eggplant, weighing about 2 pounds, or two 1-pound eggplants
- 1 medium onion, finely chopped
- 1 red bell pepper, roasted, peeled, seeded, and chopped
- 2 medium tomatoes, chopped
- 2 tablespoons fresh cilantro, chopped
- salt and pepper to taste
- 4 tablespoons olive oil
- 1 tablespoon lemon or lime juice

Preheat oven to 375 degrees and bake eggplant on the middle rack for about 45 minutes, or until soft. Cool, peel, and coarsely chop. Add onion, red pepper, tomatoes, cilantro, salt, and pepper; and mix. Whisk together oil and lemon juice and stir into the eggplant mixture.

Makes 4 to 6 servings

CHILEAN TOMATO AND SWEET ONION SALAD
(ENSALADA CHILENA)

This salad is served with everything in Chile. To remove some of the sharpness of onions, Chilean cooks soak the slices in salted or sugared water.

1 medium Vidalia or other sweet onion, halved and thinly sliced
1 tablespoon sugar
6 large, ripe tomatoes, sliced about ½-inch thick
    salt
3 tablespoons olive oil
1 jalapeño chili, seeded and minced
3 tablespoons chopped cilantro leaves, chopped

Place onion slices in a bowl with the sugar and cover with cold water. Soak 10 minutes, drain, rinse, and pat dry with paper towels. Layer the tomato and onion slices on a plate or in a bowl, season with salt to taste, and drizzle with olive oil. Garnish with jalapeño and cilantro.

Makes 4 to 6 servings

BRAZILIAN CHAYOTE, ORANGE, AND SHRIMP SALAD

Mild and crisp-textured chayote mixes well with more assertive citrus while shrimp and crispy fried onions add contrasting notes. Serve with rice, grilled fish or chicken, soups, or stews.

  4 chayote, peeled, cored, and grated
  4 oranges, skin and bitter pith removed and
       segments removed from the membranes
  1 large red onion, halved and thinly sliced
  ½ pound peeled, deveined, and boiled shrimp, sliced in half lengthwise
  ½ cup fresh mint leaves, chopped
  4 tablespoons olive oil
       juice of one lime
       salt and pepper to taste
       crispy fried onions, optional

Combine all the ingredients, except crispy onion, in a non-metallic bowl. Toss and mix well and garnish with crispy onions, if desired. To make these, finely slice a medium onion, pat dry with paper towels and drop into 1 to 2 inches of hot oil. Fry until dark brown and crisp. Drain on paper towels.

Makes 4 to 6 servings

MEXICAN CACTUS SALAD

This unusual but delicious salad was concocted by my friend Roberto Requeña who teaches cooking as a living and to friends. It goes well with tacos, fajitas, rice and beans, and scrambled eggs and makes a light lunch with some warm tortillas.

- 1 14-ounce jar of nopalitos (cactus strips in brine)
- 1 medium onion, halved and thinly sliced
- 3 cloves garlic, minced
- 1 6-ounce can of tuna fish in oil

Rinse the cactus in a colander, drain, and place in a bowl, discarding any onion or chilies the cactus is pickled with. Add sliced onion, garlic, and tuna with the oil. Mix well and marinate overnight, refrigerated and covered, to allow flavors to mingle.

Serves 4 to 6

CUBAN BLACK BEAN SOUP

This is a meal in a bowl and is thick enough to serve on a plate accompanied with steamed rice or crusty bread and a salad. Garnish with a dollop of sour cream and chopped cilantro. If you are in a hurry, substitute a 16-ounce can of black beans, rinsed and drained, for the soaked beans. A splash of rum adds that island touch. Serve with a lemon or lime wedge.

I pound black beans, soaked overnight

4 tablespoons olive oil

I medium onion, chopped

I green bell pepper, finely chopped

I red bell pepper, finely chopped

I celery stalk, finely chopped

I small hot red chili, minced, or I teaspoon red pepper flakes

4 cloves garlic, minced

4 strips of bacon, finely chopped

3 ounces of lean ham, diced

2 tablespoons tomato paste

2 teaspoons ground cumin

I bay leaf

   salt and pepper

I tablespoon rum

Drain the beans and set aside. In a large, heavy saucepan, sauté the onion, bell peppers, celery, and garlic in oil over low heat, about 15 minutes. Add beans and enough water or chicken stock to cover. Gradually stir in the remaining ingredients except the salt and rum. Bring to a boil, lower heat, and cover. Simmer for 2 hours, checking and stirring from time to time. Season with salt. Allow to cool. Puree half the bean mix in a blender. Pour the puree back into the pot of beans and reheat. Add rum, stir well, and serve.

Makes 6 servings

MEXICAN LIME AND TORTILLA SOUP

This is a popular soup from the Yucatan, where it is made with the juice of a small, local, bitter lime and chicken livers and gizzards. This version uses shredded chicken breast and is served garnished with fried tortilla strips, crumbled cheese, and avocado and radish slices.

Soup

    4 cloves garlic, roasted and peeled

    1 canned chipotle chili or 2 roasted and seeded serrano chilies

    2 tablespoons corn oil

    2 medium onions, finely chopped

    3 medium tomatoes, chopped, or 1 14-ounce can of tomatoes

    6 cups chicken stock

      juice of 2 limes plus the remaining rinds

    1 teaspoon dried oregano

    1 bay leaf

    1 chicken breast, poached and shredded

      salt and pepper

    6 stale corn tortillas

      oil for frying

Garnishes (served in separate bowls for guests to help themselves)

      sliced red onions

      avocado slices

      radish slices

      grated or crumbled cheese

      chopped cilantro

Puree the garlic and chili, set aside. In a large saucepan, heat the oil. Sauté the onion until soft, 2 to 3 minutes. Add tomatoes and garlic-chili puree and stir 2 to 3 minutes. Add stock, lime juice, lime rinds, oregano, and bay leaf. Bring to a boil, reduce heat, and simmer 10 minutes. Add shredded chicken and season with salt and pepper. Remove lime rinds. Set soup aside, covered.

Cut tortillas into matchstick strips. Heat an inch of oil in a skillet and fry the strips in batches until golden and crisp, draining on paper towels. Add tortilla strips to individual bowls when serving. Pass the bowls of garnishes.

Makes 4 to 6 servings

CALLALOO SOUP

This is the most famous soup of the Caribbean, also sometimes called pepper-pot. There are numerous variations, but all include a soft, leafy green such as callaloo (taro leaf) or spinach. The soup is a fairly thick, velvety green puree and is often served as a sauce over rice. Small cubes of silken tofu are not traditional, but can be added for texture. This version uses crab and spinach, as callaloo leaves may not be readily available.

1	large onion, finely chopped
3	cloves garlic, chopped
1	pound fresh spinach, washed and chopped
12–15	small fresh okra, or 1 package frozen whole or cut okra
2	cans unsweetened coconut milk
2	teaspoons thyme, fresh or dried
2	teaspoons fresh parsley, minced, or 1 teaspoon dried flakes
1	teaspoon garam masala (optional) (available in Indian and some Caribbean specialty markets) or 1 teaspoon curry powder
	hot sauce to taste
	salt and pepper
2	6-ounce cans of crab meat or the meat picked from two fresh, boiled crabs

In a large, heavy saucepan over medium heat, sauté the onion and garlic in oil until the onion softens, 2 to 3 minutes. Add all the remaining ingredients except the crab. Bring to a boil, reduce heat to low, and simmer uncovered 30 minutes. Puree soup in batches in a blender on very low speed for less than a minute. It should be a somewhat coarse puree. Return soup to saucepan, add crab, and simmer a few minutes to heat through.

Makes 4 servings

CREAMY CARIBBEAN PEANUT SOUP

This soup is based on a traditional West African peanut soup made with coarsely chopped peanuts. This version is creamier, good as a starter or spooned over rice or mashed yams. The dried shrimp garnish adds an almost bacon-like flavor and crunch.

- 2 tablespoons small dried shrimp (available in Latin and Asian markets)
- 2 tablespoons pure and natural smooth or crunchy peanut butter (sold at health food stores and freshly ground in many supermarkets)
- 4 1/2 cups chicken stock
- 1 tablespoon tomato paste
- 1 medium onion, chopped
- 2 slices fresh ginger
- 1/4 teaspoon thyme, fresh or dried
- 1 bay leaf
  salt and hot pepper sauce to taste
- 10 small okra, trimmed
- 1/2 cup diced calabaza pumpkin

Sauté dried shrimp in a little oil until crispy. Remove from pan and set aside. Beat the peanut butter with one cup of stock and the tomato paste in a bowl. Pour mixture into a saucepan and add the rest of the stock and onion, ginger, thyme, bay leaf, salt, and hot pepper sauce. Bring to a boil, reduce heat to low, and simmer about 30 minutes, covered. Add the pumpkin and okra and simmer 6 to 7 minutes or until pumpkin is tender. Serve in bowls and garnish with the fried shrimp.

Makes 6 servings

Side Dishes
COCONUT RICE

This is a favorite throughout the Caribbean and coastal parts of Central and South America. In Colombia, raisins and a little sugar are added, making a slightly sweet foil for rich meat dishes. In the islands coconut rice is cooked with pigeon peas.

2 cups long-grain or basmati rice (if using basmati soak 20 minutes)
5 cups coconut milk (3 13.5-ounce cans)
1 stick cinnamon
  pinch of salt

Wash rice in several changes of cold water until it runs clear to rinse off excess starch. Put rice into a saucepan and add the coconut milk, cinnamon, and salt. Bring to a boil, stir once, reduce heat to very low, and cook the rice, covered, until tender and dry, about 25 minutes. Fluff with a fork and serve.

Makes 6 servings

BRAZILIAN POLENTA

This recipe comes from my friend Pedro Maia. The addition of fresh corn and Parmesan cheese adds a twist on plain polenta. Serve as a bed for grilled or roasted meats, sautéed eggplant, beans, or stews; or top with tomato sauce.

6½ cups water

1 teaspoon salt

2 cups polenta

1 cup cooked fresh or frozen corn kernels

5 tablespoons butter, cut into pieces

½ cup freshly grated Parmesan cheese

In a large saucepan, bring the water to a boil. Add salt and reduce heat to low. Slowly add the polenta, stirring constantly with a wooden spoon. Cook, stirring, for 20 minutes. Add corn and cook another 5 minutes or until mixture is smooth and thick. Remove from heat, and stir in the butter and cheese. Serve immediately.

Makes 4 to 6 servings

MASHED YUCA WITH GARLIC-CHIVE BUTTER AND HEART OF PALM

Delicious as a side with grilled meats or seafood, roasted chicken or snapper, and vegetables.

Butter

> 4 cloves garlic, unpeeled
>
> 1 stick unsalted butter at room temperature
>
> ½ cup freshly snipped chives

Yuca

> 4 pounds fresh yuca or 3 pounds of frozen chunks
>
> 1¾ to 2¼ cups hot milk
>
> 4 tablespoons garlic-chive butter
>
> 4–5 stalks of canned heart of palm, drained and sliced into rounds
>
> 1 tablespoon lime juice
>
> salt and pepper

Roast garlic in a dry, medium-hot skillet until charred and soft. Peel and mash. Beat mashed garlic into soft butter with chives. (This can be made several days ahead, wrapped in plastic and refrigerated until needed.) Trim ends from fresh yuca and peel, removing all waxy brown skin and the pinkish layer underneath. Cut yuca into 3-inch slices.

Place prepared or frozen yuca in salted water to cover by 2 inches. Boil until tender and starting to fall apart, 50 minutes to an hour. Drain and transfer to a cutting board. Carefully halve hot yuca pieces lengthwise and remove woody cores. Return yuca to pot with 1⅓ cups hot milk, butter, lime juice, and salt and pepper. Mash, adding additional milk if mixture is too dry. Gently fold in sliced heart of palm. Serve immediately, as yuca hardens as it cools.

Makes 4 to 6 servings

Seafood

PERUVIAN-STYLE CEVICHE

This recipe is from my friend Eva Lewitus in Lima, Peru. She serves it on a platter of lettuce leaves accompanied by thick slices of boiled yuca and sweet potato, corn on the cob, and toasted cancha (popcorn). This makes a good appetizer with drinks.

- 1 pound very fresh white fish (sea bass, snapper, sole, or grouper)
  salt and milk
- 4 medium red onions, halved and thinly sliced
- 2 cloves garlic, minced
- 2 celery stalks, finely sliced
- 1 chili, preferably Peruvian yellow ají or red serrano, seeded and finely sliced
  salt and pepper
- ¾ cup freshly squeezed lemon or key lime juice
- 1 teaspoon cilantro leaves, chopped
- 1 teaspoon fresh parsley, chopped

Cut the fish into small, bite-sized pieces and wash three times in a bowl of very salty water, rinsing between baths. Drain and soak fish a few minutes in a bowl of milk. Drain.

In a large, non-metallic bowl, mix together the onions, garlic, celery, and chili. Season with salt and pepper. Mix in the lemon juice. Add the fish and mix well. If the fish is very fresh, it will "cook" in about 15 minutes, turning opaque white. If not extremely fresh, allow to marinate, refrigerated, about 2 hours. Sprinkle with cilantro and parsley before serving.

Makes 4 to 6 servings

BRAZILIAN SHRIMP IN COCONUT MILK

Called moqueca in Brazil, this is a type of seafood stew made with any firm-fleshed fish, including shrimp or crab—feel free to to use any combination of fish and shellfish. The seafood is poached in a rich coconut milk broth flavored with palm oil, lime juice, and tomatoes. It is usually served with rice and farofa (skillet-toasted cassava flour).

2 pounds medium shrimp, peeled and deveined, shells reserved

3 cups water

3 tablespoons palm oil (dendê) or butter

1 small onion, chopped

2 large tomatoes, chopped

1 13.5-ounce can unsweetened coconut milk

2 tablespoons freshly squeezed lime juice

¼ cup cilantro leaves, chopped

   hot sauce, salt, and pepper to taste

In a medium saucepan, combine shrimp, shells, and water. Boil until liquid is reduced to ¾ of a cup, about 10 minutes. Strain and set stock aside, discarding shells.

Heat oil or butter in a large, heavy saucepan over medium-high heat. Add onion and sauté until slightly softened, about 2 to 3 minutes. Add tomatoes and sauté 1 minute. Add stock, coconut milk, and lime juice. Bring to a boil, lower heat, and add shrimp. Simmer just until shrimp turn pink, about 2 minutes. Season with hot sauce, salt, and pepper.

Makes 4 to 6 servings

ISLAND-ROASTED SNAPPER IN
PINEAPPLE-PASSION FRUIT SAUCE

This dish can be made with either yellowtail snapper, which has a delicate, flaky texture, or slightly firmer red snapper. Serve with rice or mashed yuca and a salad.

Sauce

  ½ cup passion fruit juice (available frozen in Latin markets)
  ½ cup unsweetened pineapple juice
  3 tablespoons sugar
  1 teaspoon finely grated fresh ginger
  2 cloves garlic, chopped
  1 jalapeño, seeded and chopped
  2 tablespoons red bell pepper, minced
  1 tablespoon rice vinegar
    salt and pepper to taste

Fish

  1 snapper, about 3 pounds, cleaned and scaled
    juice of one lime
  1 teaspoon salt

In a small saucepan, combine fruit juices with sugar and bring to a boil. Reduce heat to medium and simmer until the juice is reduced by half and slightly thickened, about 15 minutes. Add ginger, garlic, and jalapeño and remove from heat. Let cool slightly and transfer to a blender. Blend until smooth, about 30 seconds. Pour sauce into a bowl and stir in red pepper and vinegar. Season with salt and pepper and set aside. (Can be made 3 days in advance and refrigerated, covered. Reheat before serving.)

Preheat oven to 450 degrees. Make several slits along each side of the snapper, about 3 inches apart. Rub fish inside and out with the lime juice and sprinkle with salt. Place in an oiled baking dish and bake until the fish easily flakes, about 30 to 35 minutes. Remove from oven, transfer to a serving dish, and drizzle with the fruit sauce.

Makes 4 servings

Chicken Dishes
ARROZ CON POLLO

This rice and chicken classic has Spanish roots and is often called paella without the fancy pan or seafood. This is a perfect one-pot meal as the chicken, rice, and vegetables simmer together. Good with crusty bread, black bean soup, and a full-flavored red wine.

  1 tablespoon olive oil
  4 chicken drumsticks
  4 chicken thighs
    salt and pepper for seasoning
  1 medium onion, chopped
  1 teaspoon red pepper flakes
  2 cloves garlic, minced
  1 red bell pepper, chopped
  1 10-ounce package frozen peas
1 ¾ cups fresh or canned tomatoes, chopped
  1 tablespoon tomato paste
  2 cups chicken stock
 ⅛ teaspoon saffron, crumbled
  1 cup raw, uncooked, white rice
  2 tablespoons fresh parsley, chopped

In a large, deep saucepan or Dutch oven, heat oil over medium-high heat. Season the chicken drumsticks and thighs with salt and pepper and add to pan. Sauté chicken, turning until well browned on both sides, 7 to 8 minutes. Remove from pan and set aside. Pour off all but 2 tablespoons of fat from pan.

Reduce heat to medium-low. Add onion, red pepper flakes, and garlic to pan and sauté, stirring from time to time, until the onion softens, about 2 minutes. Add bell pepper and peas and sauté another 3 minutes. Add the tomatoes, tomato paste, stock, and saffron and bring to a simmer. Stir in the rice and add chicken in an even layer. Simmer, covered, over medium-low heat until the chicken and rice are tender, about 20 to 25 minutes. Serve garnished with the parsley.

Makes 4 servings

AJÍ DE GALLINA

This is a classic Peruvian dish of shredded hen (or chicken) in a creamy, chili-laced sauce. This is my friend Eva's version. Boiled and shredded chicken is added to a ground nut sauce and served over boiled potatoes or steamed rice, garnished with sliced hard-boiled eggs and black olives. Peruvian ají (chili) pastes are available by mail order; see appendix 4.

    1 3-pound chicken
       salt
    2 slices stale French bread, sliced ¾-inch thick
    1 cup cream or half-and-half
    2 tablespoons olive oil
    2 medium onions, finely chopped
    2 cloves garlic, minced
    2 tablespoons sweet red panca chili paste
    2 New Mexico chilies, seeded and minced
 1 ½ teaspoons ground cumin
    1 cup walnuts, finely ground
    3 large tomatoes, chopped
       salt and pepper
  ¼ cup grated Parmesan cheese
    2 hard-boiled eggs, sliced
  12 soft black olives

Place the chicken in a large pot, cover with salted water, and bring to a boil over high heat. Reduce heat to medium-low, cover, and simmer until juices from chicken run clear, about 40 to 45 minutes. Drain chicken, reserving 1 cup of broth. When cool enough to handle, shred the meat, discarding bones and skin. Set aside.

Tear bread into bits and place in a small bowl. Add cream and set aside to soak for about 20 minutes.

Heat oil over medium-high heat, add onions and garlic, and sauté, stirring, about 2 minutes. Add panca paste, minced chili, cumin, walnuts, tomatoes, and soaked bread and cream. Season with salt and pepper and simmer, stirring often, about 5 minutes. Add shredded chicken and reserved broth. Simmer, stirring occasionally, until mixture is thick and creamy, about 10 minutes. Add Parmesan cheese, stir, and simmer for a few more minutes. Serve over potatoes or rice, garnished with hard-boiled egg slices and olives.

Makes 4 to 6 servings

PASTEL DE CHOCLO

This is a Chilean chicken pie with a corn topping, and is a sort of South American take on shepherd's pie. This recipe comes from Sabores Chilenos in Miami. It can be made in one casserole or four smaller ovenproof dishes. As it can be made ahead of time, this is a great party dish. Serve with Chilean tomato and sweet onion salad (see recipe on page 238) and crusty bread.

1 3-pound chicken, cut into pieces

4 medium onions—1 quartered, 3 chopped

2 bay leaves

salt and pepper

5 cups fresh corn kernels (cut from about 8 ears)

1 cup milk

4 tablespoons vegetable oil, separated

¼ teaspoon ground cumin

pinch of cinnamon

2 teaspoons sweet paprika

¼ cup raisins

2 hard-boiled eggs, coarsely chopped

12 small pimento-stuffed green olives

2 teaspoons sugar

Place chicken, quartered onion, and bay leaves in a large pot. Season with salt and pepper, add water to cover, and simmer 20 to 25 minutes. Remove chicken pieces, and when cool enough to handle, remove skin, pull meat from bones, and tear into large shreds. Discard cooking liquid and bay leaves, reserving onion pieces. Transfer onion to a blender, add corn kernels and milk, and puree until smooth (you may have to do this in 2 batches). Heat 2 tablespoons of the oil in a skillet over medium-high heat, add corn puree, and cook, stirring, until thick, about 5 minutes. Season with salt and pepper.

Preheat oven to 350 degrees. Heat the remaining 2 tablespoons oil in a skillet over medium-high heat and add chopped onion with 1 cup water. Cook until liquid evaporates and onions are soft, about 6 to 7 minutes. Add chicken shreds, cumin, cinnamon, paprika, raisins, hard-boiled egg, and olives. Season with salt and pepper and sauté, stirring, 2 to 3 minutes.

Spread chicken mixture in the bottom of a 2-quart casserole or in four smaller ovenproof dishes. Spread corn mixture on top, sprinkle with sugar, and bake for 30 minutes. Preheat broiler. Remove from oven and brown under broiler several minutes or until the sugar is lightly carmelized. Serve hot.

Makes 4 servings

GINGER-TAMARIND CHICKEN

This is a delicious combination of two favorite Jamaican flavorings—ginger and tangy tamarind. A Jamaican woman in Chicago gave me the recipe, although hers called for 10 pounds of chicken! Serve the mahogany-tinted, richly flavored chicken with rice and peas, hardough bread, and fried plantains, or a salad.

  3 pounds of chicken pieces
     juice of 1 lemon or lime
  1/4 cup vegetable oil
  4 cloves garlic, minced
  2 medium onions, halved and sliced
  1 tablespoon fresh ginger, grated
  2 1/2 cups tamarind nectar (sold in soda-type cans in Latin and
         Caribbean markets) or 4 tablespoons tamarind concentrate
         mixed in 2 1/2 cups water with 4 tablespoons sugar, or frozen
         pulp, defrosted
     salt and pepper

Rub chicken pieces with lemon or lime juice. Heat oil in a large, heavy skillet or Dutch oven over medium heat, and lightly brown chicken on both sides in batches. Set aside in a large bowl. When all the chicken is removed from the pan, reduce heat slightly and add garlic and onions. Sauté until soft and light brown, about 5 minutes, stirring often. Add the ginger. Pour in tamarind juice and season with salt and pepper. Return chicken to pan, bring to a boil, reduce heat to medium-low, cover, and simmer until chicken is tender, about 1 hour. Remove from liquid and serve.

Makes 4 to 6 servings

Meat Dishes

BANANAS STUFFED WITH CURRIED BEEF

This could also be made using 2 semi-ripe plantains, but allow a longer baking time. Curry-kissed ground beef is packed into slit banana skins and baked. The dish isn't particularly pretty, but it tastes great. Serve with rice and beans and a simple sauce made by mixing salt and pepper into freshly squeezed lime juice or green mango chutney for island flare.

2 tablespoons vegetable oil

1 pound ground chuck beef

1 medium onion, finely chopped

2 cloves garlic, minced

2 tablespoons curry powder

1/2 teaspoon ground cumin

1 tablespoon tomato paste, dissolved in 3 tablespoons water

1 teaspoon lemon juice

salt and pepper

6 semi-ripe, unpeeled bananas

1 red bell pepper, minced

Preheat oven to 400 degrees. Heat oil in a skillet. Add beef and brown over high heat, breaking it up with a wooden spoon, until cooked through. Reduce heat slightly and add onion, garlic, curry powder, and cumin. Sauté, stirring often, until fragrant, about 4 minutes. Stir in tomato paste and lemon juice. Season to taste with salt and pepper.

Using a small knife, make one slit down the length of each banana, through the peel. Pull the peel slightly away from the flesh and stuff each banana with a portion of the beef mixture. Arrange bananas in a roasting pan, cover with foil, and bake about 25 minutes, or until bananas are tender and heated through. Garnish meat mixture with minced red pepper and serve.

Makes 6 servings

ISLA BONITA PORK TENDERLOIN

Island spices give this dish its beautiful flavor, as if caressed by a Caribbean breeze. Good with pineapple salsa, mashed yuca, black beans, and cole slaw.

  ¼ teaspoon ground allspice

  ½ teaspoon ground ginger

  ½ teaspoon ground cinnamon

  ½ teaspoon grated nutmeg

  ½ teaspoon dry mustard

  4 pork tenderloins, 4–6 ounces each, trimmed of fat

In a small bowl, combine spices and dry mustard and stir to blend well. Pat pork pieces dry with a paper towel and rub on both sides with spice mixture. Place in a shallow dish, cover, and refrigerate 30 minutes.

Grill or broil about 25 minutes, turning several times. Cut meat into ½-inch medallions and arrange on 4 plates, garnished with a wedge of fresh pineapple, if desired. (To make pineapple salsa, combine 2 cups diced fresh pineapple or canned crushed pineapple with some chopped cilantro, a squeeze of lime juice, and a pinch each of ground cumin and white pepper.)

Makes 4 servings

SKIRT STEAK FAJITAS

In the old days, along the border of Mexico and Texas, every cut of beef was used to feed ranch hands and cattle drivers, including tough skirt steak. The steak was cut into little belts, or fajitas, marinated and grilled, and wrapped in soft flour tortillas. You don't have to be a ranch hand to enjoy these. Serve with rice and beans, salad, and cold Corona beer.

  ½ cup lime juice

  ⅓ cup tequila (optional)

  ¼ cup vegetable oil

  4 cloves garlic, minced

  1 teaspoon ground cumin

  1 teaspoon dried oregano

   salt and pepper

  1 pound skirt steak, trimmed of fat and cut into thin strips

  2 medium onions, halved and sliced

  2 red or green bell peppers, cut into strips

  2 tablespoons olive oil

 12 flour tortillas, warmed

   salsa, sour cream, and chopped cilantro for garnishing

In a large bowl, stir together lime juice, oil, tequila, garlic, cumin, and oregano. Season to taste with salt and pepper. Add meat, turning to coat well, and allow to marinate several hours or overnight, refrigerated and covered.

Drain and discard marinade and set meat aside. Heat a non-stick skillet over high heat. Add onions and red pepper strips and cook until beginning to char, 3 to 4 minutes. Remove to a serving plate. Heat olive oil in skillet over high heat, add steak, and sauté, turning frequently, until done to desired taste. Remove and pile onto serving plate with onions and peppers. Serve with tortillas, tomato salsa, sour cream, and chopped cilantro.

Makes 4 servings

Desserts

STARFRUIT SORBET

This is a refreshing, light, icy way to end a hot and spicy Latin meal. The alcohol in the rum adds a smoothness to the sorbet.

    1 cup sugar
    ¾ cup water
    2½ pounds starfruit
    1 tablespoon white rum
      squeeze of lime juice

In a heavy, non-reactive saucepan, combine the sugar with ⅔ cup water and boil 5 minutes. Cool. Peel off any brown points of the starfruit and roughly chop them. Puree starfruit with remaining water in a blender, pulsing on and off until smooth. Strain mixture through a sieve set over a bowl, pressing down with a rubber scraper or spoon to extract all the juice. Add starfruit juice, rum, and lime juice to cooled syrup, and partially freeze. Beat the slush in an electric mixer on high until frothy and refreeze until firm.

Makes 4 to 6 servings

JAMAICAN GINGERBREAD

What makes this gingerbread special is the use of fresh ginger. Delicious served warm with vanilla ice cream.

  1/2 cup molasses
   1 cup sugar
  1/2 cup butter (1 stick)
  1/2 cup hot water
   2 cups all-purpose flour
   2 teaspoons baking powder
  1/2 teaspoon salt
   1 teaspoon grated nutmeg
   2 teaspoons finely grated fresh ginger
   1 egg, beaten

Preheat oven to 300 degrees. Grease a 9-inch loaf pan. Gently heat the molasses, sugar, and butter in a medium-sized saucepan over low heat, stirring until butter is melted and sugar dissolved. Stir in hot water and set pan aside.

In a medium bowl, sift together flour, baking powder, salt, and nutmeg. Stir in the ginger and egg. Pour molasses mixture into the flour mixture and mix well. Pour batter into the greased pan. Bake 1 hour or until a toothpick inserted in the center comes out clean. Cool slightly and cut into slices.

· Appendix 4 ·

Mail-Order Sources

AFRO-CARIBBEAN CENTER, LTD.
Adam or Denise Volpendesta
207–209 South Water Market
Chicago, IL 60608
TEL: 800-993-9801 or 312-666-9800
*Afro-Caribbean and West African foods, spices, fu fu,
sauces, and Ghana yams*

OLD WORLD MARKET
5129 N. Broadway
Chicago, IL 60640
TEL: 773-989-4440
Afro-Caribbean and Jamaican foods

PEDRO MAIA
9863 Erica Court
Boca Raton, FL 33496
TEL: 561-883-8603
E-MAIL: tmaia@bellsouth.net
*Brazilian baby eggplant (jiló).
Will ship anywhere.*

PACIFICA INTERNATIONAL
Patricio Osses
TEL: 718-672-7001
Chilean fish importer based in New York. Will ship anywhere.
Chilean congrio, merluza, reineta, robalo, picoroco, and piures.

LA GUADALUPANA
Alex Castro, will Fed-Ex anywhere
4637 S. Archer Avenue
Chicago, IL 60632
TEL: 773-843-1722
masa dough for tamales (plain, strawberry, or pineapple)

AMAZONAS IMPORTS—
CENTRAL AND SOUTH AMERICAN FOODS
Willy Guillermo Veliz, importer and distributor
10817 Sherman Way
Sun Valley, CA 91352
TEL: 818-982-1377/3898
Peruvian chili pastes, sauces, chuño, beans, and
Central American products

SALSAS ETC!
126 Great Mall Drive
Milpitas, CA 95035
TEL: 800-407-2572
salsas, Peruvian panca, rocoto, ají amarillo pastes, and more

PRODUCTS PERUVANOS
15070 Edwards St.
Huntington Beach, CA 92647
TEL: 714-271-2930
black mint

LA ESPAÑOLA MEATS, INC.
25020 Doble Ave.
Harbor City, CA 90710
TEL: 310-539-0455
Mexican and Spanish chorizo, sausages, serrano-style hams,
salt cod, cheeses, Spanish rice, and sweets

RAYMOND-HADLEY PERUVIAN FOODS
89 Tompkins St.
Spencer, NY 14883

Tel: 800-252-5220 or 607-589-4415
E-mail: info@raymondhadley.com
Web:www.raymondhadley.com

PERUVIAN INGREDIENTS
243 Sixth St.
Hollister, CA 95023
Tel: 831-673-6444
Web: www.happycookers.com

FRIEDA'S.COM
Web: www.Friedas.com
exotic tropical fruits and Latin vegetables (banana leaves, cactus pears,
nopal cactus, calabaza pumpkin, tamarind, yuca and other root vegetables,
burro and manzano bananas, cape gooseberries, pineapple guava,
and much more)

GOING BANANAS
Don and Katie Chafin
24401 S.W. 197 Avenue
Homestead, FL 33031-1174
Tel: 305-247-0397
Fax: 305-247-7877
E-mail: goingbananas@bellsouth.net
tropical plant nursery (banana corms, baby banana plants, baby lychee,
and longan trees)

MESTIZOS, INC.
14655 Northwest Freeway
Suite 127-H
Houston, TX 77040
Web: www.mestizos.com
E-mail: orders@mestizos
wide range of Latin American and Spanish products

UNLIMITED LATIN FLAVORS, INC.
6816 NW 77 Ct.
Miami, FL 33166
877-477-2323 (9–7 P.M. EST)
Web: www.latingrocer.com
Latin foods

Index

· Notes ·

· Notes ·

· Notes ·

About the Author

Linda Bladholm is the author of two previous books in the successful Take it With You™ series, *The Asian Grocery Store Demystified* and *The Indian Grocery Store Demystified* (Renaissance Books). She also wrote *Kanzawa, the Heart of Japan* (Noto Printing Co.) and *Singapore Memento* (FEP International). A regular contributor to the *Miami Herald*, Bladholm is also a designer, illustrator, and photographer whose work has appeared in *Singapore and Asia Pacific Magazine* and *Big O Magazine*. She has designed books for Noto Publishing and designed and illustrated for FEP/McGraw-Hill, Gunze Company, and World Books International. For ten years, she lived in and traveled throughout Asia as a teacher, photographer, and representative of the Japan National Tourist Office. A graduate of the University of San Francisco, Bladholm now resides with her husband in Miami Beach, Florida.